Charles Wordsworth, Robert Winter Kennion

Before the table

An inquiry, historical and theological into the true meaning of the consecration

rubric in the communion service

Charles Wordsworth, Robert Winter Kennion

Before the table

An inquiry, historical and theological into the true meaning of the consecration rubric in the communion service

ISBN/EAN: 9783337223977

Hergestellt in Europa, USA, Kanada, Australien, Japan

Cover: Foto ©Lupo / pixelio.de

Weitere Bücher finden Sie auf **www.hansebooks.com**

"BEFORE THE TABLE:"

*AN INQUIRY, HISTORICAL AND THEOLOGICAL,
INTO THE TRUE MEANING OF THE CONSECRATION
RUBRIC IN THE COMMUNION SERVICE
OF THE CHURCH OF ENGLAND.*

WITH

APPENDIX AND SUPPLEMENT

CONTAINING

PAPERS BY THE RIGHT REV. THE BISHOP OF ST. ANDREWS,
AND THE REV. R. W. KENNION, M.A.

BY

J. S. HOWSON, D.D.,

DEAN OF CHESTER.

London:
MACMILLAN AND CO.
1875.

PREFACE.

From various friends, to whom warm acknowledgments have been privately made, I have received much assistance in the preparation of this essay. Notwithstanding this help, however, I cannot expect that in a volume written in fragments of time, amid many and serious hindrances, and without easy access to books of reference, I can, even with the exercise of the utmost care, have avoided some mistakes. That which I earnestly claim is, that these pages may be judged, not by collateral errors, which do not affect the general question, but by conclusions resting on the main points of the case.

In an inquiry of this kind, it always happens either that the case breaks down as the investigation becomes closer, or that the conviction becomes stronger and stronger from point to point. My experience in the matter before us has been of the second kind; and I am persuaded that, with a larger command of information and of time, this argument could have been considerably strengthened. In reading what has been written by some who have been led to an opinion contrary to mine, I have been much struck by their imperfect treatment of the subject, and by their omission of many things which, as it seems to me, imperatively demand notice. I impute no blame for such omission. We need only imagine that the habit has been formed of looking only on one side of the question, that there is an eagerly-cherished desire to prove a point, and that the writer is surrounded by the pressure of *a party* eager for success; and the phenomenon is explained. Still, such a state of things is not conducive to the elucidation of truth; and I will take leave to illustrate what I mean in two or three particulars.

The books or pamphlets to which I refer are published without the slightest intimation of the existence of other publications, containing formidable arguments which have not been answered. I will here mention more particularly the pamphlets and articles of Mr. Droop,[1] Canon Elliott,[2] and Canon Simmons.[3] I must indeed confess that I myself, in the following pages, have referred very slightly to these writers, and that I have not even yet read carefully and thoroughly what they have laid before the public. But I venture to think that it has been good policy on my own part to write independently; while certainly it will, in the long run, be found bad policy on the part of others to keep out of view those reasonings which demand a reply.

---

[1] See p. 145, *Note*. To this pamphlet by Mr. Droop is now to be added another, of nearly equal importance, on the *Edwardian Vestments*.
[2] See Appendix G.
[3] *Ibid.* See also p. 55, *Note*.

A second instance is connected with the famous name of Bishop Cosin. Again and again, in the Lower Houses of both Convocations, and in various speeches and publications, the charge which was brought against him, as regards his alleged practice of consecrating in the Eastward Position, has been reiterated; but perfect silence has been maintained, except when such silence has been forcibly interrupted, respecting that prelate's disavowal of the charge.[1] In the case of a living man it is acknowledged by all persons to be culpable to repeat an accusation which has been refuted. How far, in the case of the dead, this rule of charity and justice ought to prevail, I will not inquire. Concerning Bishop Cosin I will, to what is contained in the following pages, only add this, that since they were written, I have had an opportunity of examining the MS. notes (intermingled with those of Sancroft) in the Prayer-Book which is one of the great treasures of the Diocesan Library at Durham,[2] and that I am persuaded that if his life and opinions were fully set before us, certain results would appear not acceptable to some of those who confidently quote his authority.

Another case in point is the oblivion to which a very important and explicit passage in L'Estrange's "Alliance of Divine Offices" has been, carelessly or carefully, consigned. This writer, as one of the Laudian school of divines, is of peculiar weight. His

---

[1] See pp. 81—83.

[2] These MS. notes have been published, but not completely, in the *Correspondence* referred to below, pp. 15 and 21, *Notes.*

work has been thought worthy of a place in the "Library of Anglo-Catholic Theology;" and the first edition having been published in 1659, and the second in 1690, it bridges over, in a most significant manner, the period with which we have chiefly to do. Now in this book, among the comments on the Eucharistic Service, we find these words from the "MS. Collections of a Learned Man" quoted with approval:—"*As for the Priest standing at the North side of the Table, this seemeth to avoid the fashion of the Priest's standing with his face towards the East, as is the Popish practice.*"[1] I must confess that I have myself forgotten to quote this passage in its proper place, though it was often in my thoughts.[2] Perhaps the persuasive effect of it will be equally secured by its being placed before the reader's attention here.

Another very remarkable instance is the neglect of all reference, on the part of authors who have written on the general subject with both eager interest and considerable learning, to that rubric of the Nonjurors, which shows that the word "before" was used by them as synonymous with "on the north side,"

---

[1] P. 245 of the fourth ed. (1846. *Lib. of Anglo-Catholic Theology*). The same paragraph contains remarks, which ought not to be overlooked, having reference to the placing of the Lord's Table. The 82nd Canon is compared with Queen Elizabeth's Injunction; and these words are added — "Nothing can be more express and demonstrative that the Table placed where the Altar stood was but seposed, set out of the way, during only the time of non-communication, and that at the time of the Communion it was to be removed."

[2] I had fallen into a similar omission, which I cannot account for, in respect of certain equivalent and most explicit words in the Catechism of 1674. This omission I have endeavoured to remedy at the end of Appendix D.

in reference to the Lord's Table, even when it was placed altarwise. If L'Estrange gives us the general view of divines of his school for the period of 1662, this other evidence carries us, on the same lines, to the early part of the following century. But I need not here dwell on this point further.[1]

The strangest omission of all, as it seems to me, is the deliberate leaving on one side, in a document which recently emanated from the Lower House of the Convocation of Canterbury, of one particular, as if it were of no moment, whereas it is a subject of vital importance in this whole controversy. I refer to the recent report on the Eastward Position, where the question of the placing of the Lord's Table itself is avowedly made of no account; though it is quite evident that the placing of the Table (whether viewed legally or historically) must be a very important element in determining the true meaning of the rule for the position of the Consecrating Priest.[2]

This leads me to make a brief allusion to what took place a short time previously, in the Lower House of the Convocation of York. There a resolution was passed to this effect: that whatever position is assumed by the minister during the Consecration Prayer, no doctrinal meaning is to be assigned to it: and, further, that the Church of England has connected no doctrinal meaning therewith.[3] I doubt whether this second statement in the resolution is historically correct; but, leaving that part of the subject, I can-

---

[1] See pp. 91—93.   [2] See pp. 20, 25, 73.
[3] See p. 53.

not see anything but disaster as likely to result from granting an optional use in this matter, under the shelter of the former proposition.[1] If to those who demand a certain thing on the ground that it is full of meaning, this thing is granted on the ground that it means nothing, we are brought into a very strange position. To those who feel seriously on the subject, the gift, clogged by such an interpretation, seems almost an insult; while of others, who have no such serious feeling, it would surely be a breach of charity to suppose that they are willing to endanger the safety of the Church for the sake of that which is not a matter of principle, but merely of preference.

It is too late now to insist that there shall be no doctrinal significance in a ceremonial act, which was introduced among us on the special ground that it had a doctrinal significance. It would be very difficult now to exorcise that which has been so thoroughly *possessed*.[2] Those who have taken so much pains to secure a recognized place in the Church of England for this new ceremonial act have not been remiss in telling us its emphatic doctrinal significance. Dr. Pusey said, in a letter to the *Times* (March 24th, 1874), that "the position of the Celebrant is not a matter of mere dry law, but an expression of our faith," and, more

---

[1] Mr. Gladstone urges (*Contemporary Review* for July 1875, p. 212), that, in the matter of Ritual, "all existing latitude of law or well-established practice should as a rule be respected." But if a new practice, contrary to law, is introduced, and then, by the adhesion of a strong party, becomes "well-established," and is therefore to be sanctioned, is not this a method which might gradually revolutionize all our Ritual?

[2] This image is suggested by Mr. Gladstone's own strong language, p. 201.

explicitly, at a meeting of the English Church Union in the same year, that "the standing before the altar means the primitive doctrine of the Eucharistic Sacrifice;" and Archdeacon Denison had said previously, "In two or three years the Ritual has done as much as, or more than, the teaching has done in five-and-twenty." With such statements[1] before us (and they might easily be multiplied), I find it impossible to share Mr. Gladstone's hope that this ceremonial act can, in the eyes of the English people, be denuded of doctrinal intention.

My misgiving, too, is increased, when I read what has been written by Mr. Skinner since the well-known essay in the "Contemporary Review" was published. "It seems to me," he says, "that the position from which my own argument sets out, is just that 'basis of doctrinal significance' which Mr. Gladstone deprecates as 'the noxious element' in the discussion: just that 'consideration of devotional significance' which conflicts with his 'first condition of sanity,' and which, he says, ought to be 'expelled from the controversy as a demon from one possessed.'" Mr. Skinner proceeds to say that a Parish Priest is bound to defend "Catholic Ritual" by pleading "the significance which has been traditionally assigned to it," rather than "the insignificance with which some may think it would be wiser to be content, in order to ward off or postpone attacks;" he thinks "that 'to cease altogether from importing devotional significance' into

---

[1] I quote them from an important speech by Archdeacon Prest, made in Convocation at York last February.

devotional acts is a course incompatible with devotion;" he urges that "a Ritual that means nothing has no place at all in the Church of Christ;" he submits that "the plea for Eucharistic Ritual is precisely the plea for Eucharistic Doctrine;" and for himself he declares that he should feel himself no more able to yield the Ritual which has always expressed the Faith, than the Faith, which has always been expressed by the Ritual of the Catholic Church of Christ;"[1] and he quotes Hooker, who says that exterior acts of worship are "memorials wherein they which cannot be drawn unto hearken to what we teach, may, only by looking upon what we do, in a manner read whatsoever we believe."[2]

It has been urged by the Bishop of Lincoln that inasmuch as each of the two positions of the Celebrant has its own special significance,—"the one representing the divine grace and gift to man, the other expressing man's plea for mercy and acceptance with God,—the one looking manward from God, the other looking Godward from man,—the one position exhibiting the benefits of communion with Christ, the other commemorating and pleading the merits of His one Sacrifice for Sin," it might be well that the Church, by permitting and authorizing both positions, should set before her people this double aspect and meaning of that Sacrament; and he adds that it

---

[1] *The Church Crisis of* 1875, *reprinted from the Literary Churchman, with a Preface touching Mr. Gladstone's doctrine of "Significance,"* pp. i. v. 4, 8, 11.

[2] Keble's Edition, vol. ii. p. 406.

might be right and safe to permit that third position, which is "perhaps the most ancient of all," in which the Celebrant looked westward towards the people from the East side of the Holy Table : and then a comparison suggests that we should derive benefit from this variety ; " We should have a fuller view of the manifold significance of the Holy Eucharist, from these three positions, just as we have a clearer view of the Gospel from having four Gospels, than if we had only one Gospel."[1]

Whatever is written by the Bishop of Lincoln must be read with the respect due to his learning and with a desire to imitate his charity. But may not a double answer be offered to this argument? While granting that two different aspects of the Eucharist are presented to us by the two supposed positions of the Priest during the Prayer of Consecration, the further question arises, whether *sanction* for both these aspects of that Sacrament is to be found in the Prayer Book and the Bible. If one aspect is made conspicuous and emphatic in both, while the other is not to be discovered in either, then to allow choice in the Priest's position during Consecration is to disturb "the proportion of the Faith." But again, assuming both the

---

[1] *Plea for Toleration by Law in certain Ritual Matters*, reprinted with *Senates and Synods, their Respective Functions and Use*. Pp. 21, 22. I must here hazard a criticism on what is found upon an earlier page. It is there said that an alternative mode of placing the Holy Table is allowed in the Church of England—viz., either in the Chancel, in which case it stands North and South, or in the Body of the Church, when it stands East and West. It seems to me that in either case the lengthwise or breadthwise position of the Table is quite an open question. See p. 50, *Note*.

Eastward and Southward positions to be equally authorized, they will *not* be equally used *by the same persons;* but on the contrary, they will supply the opportunity for a strongly marked contrast between two different sections of the Church. The *same persons* study the four Evangelists with a reverent regard to each. Thus the parallel seems to break down. In order to maintain the parallel, we ought to compare the state of things which would ensue from optional orientation at the Eucharist, with the study of the Synoptists in order to throw discredit on St. John, or the study of St. John in order to throw discredit on the Synoptists; and nothing could be further than such a thought from the mind of the Bishop whom I have quoted.

I will add only one remark in concluding. It is said that this, after all, is a trivial matter, and that much harm is done by treating "the infinitely little" as if it were important. To this I must simply reply that, after the exercise of careful thought, I have been brought to the conclusion that this is a very serious matter indeed. I honestly believe that the granting of an optional use of the Eastward Position would strain to the utmost the Church of England's power of cohesion, and that it would place a most powerful instrument in the hand of those who desire to transform the character of our public worship.[1] This being

---

[1] *Potentially*, as it seems to me, there is more in the Eastward Position than in the use of Vestments. The latter (as in the case of the Cope on high festivals in Cathedrals) might be viewed as merely part of the outward enrichment of worship. The former might work a gradual change in the whole conception of our services.

the case, I cannot possibly abstain from offering the following argument to the notice of my fellow-churchmen; and, taking the lowest view of the subject, I am re-assured by the reflection that no harm can be done to those who come after us by such an investigation of the true sense of a disputed rubric. One indirect advantage which may perhaps be expected to result from "the present distress," is that it may lead some of us to a more exact knowledge of the history and meaning of our precious Book of Common Prayer.

Ellergreen, Kendal,
  Oct. 16, 1875.

CONTENTS.

I.

INTRODUCTION.

Distress caused by the present controversy—Its apparent triviality and real importance—Manner of approaching the subject—A party identified with the Church—"Table" assumed to be synonymous with "Altar."—Heb. x. 13 . . . . *Pages* 1—9

II.

CHANCELS AS IN TIMES PAST.

Bearing of the Ornaments Rubric on our subject—Direction concerning Chancels—Question concerning its meaning, originally and afterwards—Opinion of Wren, L'Estrange, Cosin, and others—The general question not affected by this point . . . . *Pages* 10—17

III.

RULE FOR THE PLACING OF THE HOLY TABLE.

Fourth rubric before the Communion Service—Its important bearing on the subject before us—Defeated attempt to alter it—Eighty-second Canon—Danger of enforcing this rubric and this canon—A possible compromise suggested . . . . *Pages* 18—26

IV.

THE TROUBLES OF 1640.

The Canons of 1640—"Declaration concerning some rites and ceremonies"—Its strong protest against Romanism—Illustration from the Diocese of Chester—Brian Walton—Letter from the Vice-Dean to Bishop Bridgeman . . . . *Pages* 27—35

b

V.

HISTORY OF THE PLACING OF THE HOLY TABLE.

Recollection in 1662 of 1640—Eastward placing of the Table improbable—The evidence from books—The case of kneeling and the Surplice in 1662 not really similar to the case of Vestments and the Eastward Position now—Catechism of 1674—Evidence from Parliamentary debates—From the continuance of chancels in their old condition—Recorded defeat of the attempt to change . . . . *Pages* 36—45

VI.

THE "NORTH SIDE" OF THE TABLE.

Imaginary analogy with Jewish Altars—The late Archdeacon Freeman—"End" and "Side"—Mr. Beresford Hope's argument from length as opposed to breadth—Extreme importance of the change from the front to the north side—Indirectly it involves doctrine—Benefit of the change in promoting congregational worship . . . . *Pages* 46—55

VII.

THE PRIEST STANDING "BEFORE THE TABLE."

Intermediate rubrics in the Communion Service—True meaning of the words "Before the Table"—Discussion in Convocation at York—Testimony of the Welsh Prayer Book . . . . *Pages* 56—62

VIII.

THE BREAD BROKEN "BEFORE THE PEOPLE."

This act the main point of the Rubric—Possible meaning of *coram populo*—Its true historical meaning—How understood by the Puritans—The act suggested by them—Evidence of the Savoy Liturgy—Religious meaning of this act—Testimony from devotional writers—The Welsh Prayer Book . . . . *Pages* 63—73

IX.

USAGE BEFORE 1662.

Custom from 1552 onwards—Evidence from Bishop Jewel—Wren's approval of Jewel—Bishop Wren's defence of himself—Archbishop Laud's chapel—His answer to his accusers—Bishop Cosin's answer to his own accusers—Defence of these three prelates against the charge of dishonesty . . . . *Pages* 74—85

X.

HISTORY OF THE USAGE SINCE 1662.

Settlement of 1662—Contentment of the Puritans with the position of the consecrating priest—This view confirmed by the events of 1689—No choice admitted by this rubric under the Act of Uniformity—Consecration still in the Southward position, when the Table was placed altarwise—Liturgy of the Nonjurors—View of Wheatly, Mant, and Blunt—The Eastward position a novelty . . . . *Pages* 86—96

XI.

CRITICISM OF THE PURCHAS JUDGMENT.

Mr. Morton Shaw's verbal arrangement of the Consecration Rubric—Correct grammatical analysis of the sentence—The late Professor Selwyn—The Parenthetic view not necessary—Speech of Lord Cairns—The Purchas Judgment substantially correct and just . . . . . *Pages* 97—103

XII.

THE DOCTRINE OF THE NEW TESTAMENT.

Exaggerated language concerning the Eastward Position—Determination to obtain a victory, if possible—The first three Evangelists and St. Paul—St. John VI.—The natural interpretation of words on this subject used in the New Testament—No trace there of a sacrificial Christian priesthood—The Holy Communion as an act of worship . . . *Pages* 104—112

XIII.

TEACHING OF OUR COMMUNION SERVICE.

Final exclusion of the word "Altar" from the Prayer Book—True meaning of the word "Priest" in the Prayer Book—Teaching of the rubrics in the Communion Service—Teaching of the prayers and thanksgivings in that service—Doctrine of the Consecration Prayer. . . . *Pages* 113—120

XIV.

TEACHING OF OUR OTHER FORMULARIES.

Language of the Ordination Service—Doctrine of the Church Catechism—The Articles—The Homilies . . . . *Pages* 121—127

XV.

PERMISSIVE ORIENTATION.

The School of Jacobean and Caroline Divines—Freedom to hold an opinion does not imply freedom to express it by a ceremony—Liberty in this respect would disturb the balance of doctrinal expression in the Church—This mode of introducing doctrinal change not fair—Option, in this respect, contrary to the principles of the Prayer Book—And full of peril for the future—Would foment religious discord—Further results to be feared . . . . *Pages* 128—140

XVI.

CONCLUSION.

Bearing of this subject on the question of the Reunion of Christendom—Its connection with other parts of the Romeward movement of the day—The Confessional—Party combinations—Changes in our religious phraseology, our devotional manuals, and the arrangements of our churches—Appeal to Moderate High Churchmen—The lesson of Whitsuntide—Duty of maintaining the right proportion of the Faith . . . . . *Pages* 141—158

APPENDIX . . . . *Pages* 159—186

SUPPLEMENT . . . . *Pages* 187—196

ERRATA.

P. 16, l. 20, *for* "conditions" *read* "condition."
P. ,, l. 22, *for* "furnish" *read* "furnishes."
P. 24, note 1, l. 1, *for* "this" *read* "this volume."
P. 34, note 3, *for* "Scotis" *read* "Scotist."
P. 35, l. 14, *dele* the second comma.
P. 50, l. 1, *for* "term" *read* "terms."
P. ,, l. 21, *for* "verbally" *read* "verbatim."
P. 54, note 2, l. 2, *dele* "while."
P. 60, note 1, l. 2, the inverted commas should be commas.
P. 72, l. 21, *for* "have" *read* "has."
P. 73, l. 8, *for* "depends" *read* "to a considerable degree depends."
P. 80, l. 6, *for* "if the Table was" *read* "the Table being."
P. 83, l. 16, *for* "heard" *read* "have heard."
P. 92, l. 23, *dele* semicolon.
P. ,, note 2, *for* "third" *read* "first."
P. 109, l. 16, *for* "θάνατον" *read* "τὸν θάνατον."
P. 130, l. 21, *dele* inverted commas.
P. 131, l. 7,   ,,   ,,
P. 172, l. 1, *for* "Bishops'" *read* "Bishop's.'
P. 184, l. 18, *for* "recents" *read* "recent."
P. 186, l. 17, *for* "questions" *read* "question."
P. ,, l. 19, *for* "those" *read* "these."

"BEFORE THE TABLE,"

ETC., ETC.

I.

INTRODUCTION.

Distress caused by the present controversy—Its apparent triviality and real importance—Manner of approaching the subject—A party identified with the Church—"Table" assumed to be synonymous with "Altar."—Heb. x. 13.

BEGINNING to write these pages on the morning after Christmas Day, I feel very deeply both the loving severity and the solemn truth of the Saviour's words: "Think ye that I came to send peace upon earth? I came not to send peace, but a sword." As the history of the Church of Christ passes through its various stages, contention is inevitable. Yet this contention, if rightly conducted, is for peace in the end. The "wisdom that cometh from above" is "first pure, then peaceable;" and those who seek to follow this Divine order may still hope for some share in that which has been well called "the most musical of all the Beatitudes"[1]—*Beati pacifici, quoniam filii Dei vocabuntur*. Mere compromise for the present

[1] Rev. H. N. Oxenham in the preface to his translation of Dr. Döllinger's *Lectures on the Reunion of the Churches*, p. xxxiii.

is, at all events, a very clumsy and weak expedient for securing peace in the future.

There is another sad reflection which comes into my mind as I enter upon my task. Our harshest struggles at this moment are connected with the very ordinance which represents our unity.[1] It seems strange that the course of most of our modern controversy in the Church of England has been determined by the two Sacraments. A mathematical theologian might say (and the comparison would be very just) that it has revolved in the curve of an ellipse, of which these two ordinances are the *foci*. Those who remember the agitation that set in upon us soon after the publication of the earlier "Tracts for the Times," will easily call to mind the angry debate which was connected with Holy Baptism. Now that Sacrament of initiation seems to have been left almost unnaturally in the shade, and the battle rages round the Sacrament of communion.

There is much also to humiliate us, and to make us ashamed, in the form which this contest is for the moment assuming. Nothing more grave appears, at first sight, to be at issue than the vestment and the position of the officiating priest during the Administration of the Lord's Supper; and these might well be said to be trivialities unworthy of a Christian's serious thought and earnest zeal. The battle, however, must be fought out; for these outward things are the flags which represent great principles contradictory of one another.

The uneasy feeling which has been for some time

---

[1] See Matt. xxvi. 27, and 1 Cor. x. 17.

eddying round the Holy Eucharist has for this obvious reason concentrated itself with extreme violence on these two points, because we are here brought in contact with the great question whether a proper sacrificial priesthood is or is not a part of the religious system established by Christ on earth; and it is incumbent on every one who has strong convictions on such a subject to make his convictions known. It is not much that any one man can do; but each man who has thought calmly and carefully on what is before us can do something. In a case like this some division of labour is almost inevitable among those who are in general agreement with one another; and, leaving to others more competent to deal with that matter, the "Eucharistic Vestments," I have turned my thoughts, using as much time as I could command, and to the best of my ability, to the question of the "Eastward Position."[1] Observing, too, that the fifth chapter in Mr. Beresford Hope's recent work on Public Worship in the Church of England, and the Rev. Morton Shaw's pamphlet on the position of the "Celebrant" at the Holy Communion, are viewed by many persons as able and careful expositions on one side of the question, I have kept these two essays more particularly in view, without limiting myself to their contents, or making my own essay a formal reply to theirs.[2]

[1] Though these two questions are constantly, and very naturally, grouped together, it ought to be carefully remembered that they must be settled on different grounds. In their relation to the Rubrics they do not depend upon one another. If they were re-argued before the Courts, it is conceivable that the Vestments might be declared legally binding and the Position again declared illegal.

[2] While the writing of these pages was in progress, two of my friends— I am sure they will allow me to call them so—the Rev. Canon Trevor and

In dealing with a subject like this, which confessedly has its difficulties (otherwise highly competent men could not have written so confidently and so well on both sides) much depends on the manner in which the subject is approached. These two writers, and others in a more excessive degree, appear to me to have entered on their work by giving to the whole matter a colouring which interferes with their own candour, and therefore diminishes the force of all their reasoning. I will illustrate what I mean by two instances before proceeding to my argument on the special subject that is before me.

It is assumed that the true expression of the Church of England is given by a certain party, which is represented by such men as Laud in 1640, by Sancroft in 1660, and by Wren at both periods. Those who are in harmony with the sentiments of this party are viewed as having the proper spirit of our Church, while those who hold the opposite sentiments, though sometimes spoken of with condescending kindness, are treated as really hostile to that spirit.[1] Now the settlement of 1662 does not represent the victory of this party, but rather its

the Rev. Malcolm MacColl, published their thoughts on the subject, the former in a pamphlet entitled *The Disputed Rubrics*, the latter in the first of his letters on *Lawlessness, Sacerdotalism, and Ritualism*. In various parts of this pamphlet I have carefully kept in view their remarks on the topic before us.

[1] Thus "the revisers of 1662" are constantly spoken of by Mr. Morton Shaw and Mr. Beresford Hope, as if they were the sole depositaries of the true doctrine and settled policy of the Church of England. That with which we, however, are concerned is not what the Bishops, or some of them, or any particular party, wished to introduce into the Prayer-Book, but what was ultimately agreed on by Convocation and Parliament.

defeat.[1] Setting on one side Laud's mode of procedure, which does not seem very worthy of admiration or imitation,[2] he was really foiled. He helped to convulse the country, and he is perhaps the author, more than any other one man, of English Nonconformity. In 1662 our Book of Common Prayer came into its present (which for us, hitherto, is its ultimate) form, before indeed Nonconformity existed as a great external fact, but while the remembrance of those troubles was very fresh in the minds of the men who did retire from the Church of England on the celebrated St. Bartholomew's Day. There is no doubt that revisers of the school of Wren

[1] In justification of this remark, it is enough to adduce two facts, the evidence of which is clearly supplied by the photozincographed *Facsimile of the Black Letter Prayer-Book, with manuscript additions and alterations made in the year 1661*, recently published by authority. Attempts were made, but in vain, to procure the placing of the Lord's Table " at the communion time," by rubric, " in the upper end of the chancel, or of the body of the church where there is no chancel," and to alter, in the title of the prayer which follows the offertory sentences, " Christ's Church militant here on earth,' into " the Catholic Church of Christ." Had these changes been effected, a great part of the argument of this pamphlet would have been impossible, and Prayers for the Dead might plausibly have been claimed to be a recognized part of our public supplications. Not that the placing of the Lord's Table against the east wall implies eastward consecration, or that Wren and Cosin, in desiring the former, advocated the latter. But much of the argument against eastward consecration depends on the rule for placing the Table otherwise. So as regards the above-mentioned part of the Communion Service, the change of its title would not have sanctioned prayers for the dead, unless such prayers were introduced into it; but the removal of the words " militant here on earth " would have removed a protest against such prayers.

[2] Mr. Beresford Hope (p. 189), writing with natural sympathy of Laud's endeavour to secure everywhere the placing of the Holy Table altarwise at the communion time, says : " However persons may differ as to the nature and manner of the proceeding, there is no doubt of the fact." I should have thought that few persons now would differ as to Laud's manner of proceeding, however sorry they may be that what he endeavoured in 1640 was not done in 1660.

and Sancroft would have obtained much more, if they had been able, from the Convocation and Parliament of their day. It seems to me a very curious kind of reasoning to say that because these men wished to obtain certain things and failed, therefore our rubrics are to be understood as denoting what they wished they might denote.

But I will here, as in duty bound, refer to another name, which comes before us at every turn of this controversy. The long and energetic life of Cosin bridges over the whole period with which we have chiefly to do. He represents Laud's principles, alike in 1640, when the famous Archbishop was living, and in 1660, when the harvest was growing of which, during that archiepiscopate, the seed had been sown. To concentrate the whole matter in one point, no one who reads Cosin's notes on the Prayer-book can doubt that he would gladly have replaced the word "altar" in that book if it had been possible.[1] But in

---

[1] A learned friend, to whom I have shown this, doubts whether I am right, at least as regards the latter part of Cosin's life, when his views had been modified. Still I think my statement is justified by that prelate's notes, at various dates, on liturgical questions. A good illustration will be found in his donation of "ornaments" to his chapels in Durham Castle and at Auckland, where the terms "Altare" and "Mensa Dominica" are used interchangeably. See the second volume of his *Correspondence, &c.*, as published by the Surtees Society (1870), p. 169.

In the use, however, of this phraseology, there does not appear to have been perfect agreement among the members of this school. In answer to the charges made against him, Bishop Wren admitted that he had ordered the "communion table" to be placed altarwise at the east end of the church, and not removed; but in his defence, which was written deliberately, and not given out in the midst of danger on the spur of the moment, the following words occur: "He saith that he was ever so far from having any thought or intention of resembling the Popish manner of altars, that he believeth that he never did by any words of his own so much as name the word *altar*, in any of his Articles or Directions; much less did he ever term the Table an Altar."—*Parentalia*, p. 75.

1662 no power could bring back this word into our Book of Common Prayer. This introduces my second illustration of the great importance of the mode in which we approach the subject under our present consideration.[1]

This second illustration is found in the habit which some writers have of using the word "Altar" as if it were synonymous with "Table." I do not allude to a mere conversational habit, acquired before existing controversies forced upon us the duty of being exact. Nor should I think it necessary to be very critical in judging the language, on such a subject, of Architects, Antiquarians, and Poets. But when Theologians, writing theologically, use as synonymous two words which are vitally distinct, it seems to me that, whether consciously or unconsciously, they give an unfair twist to the subject which they are handling. Mr. Beresford Hope faces the matter boldly, and argues that these two words ought to be treated as meaning the same thing. With this deliberate argument I shall endeavour to deal on a later page. What I am objecting to now is the tacit assumption of that which ought to be proved. Thus, Mr. Morton Shaw speaks of consecrating in front of the "altar," of moving the "altar" into the body of the church, or allowing it to remain against the east wall; of the "altar" as symbolising our united approach to the Divine Mercy-

---

[1] The free use of the word "Puritan" as a term expressive of contempt and dislike is also to be marked as unfavourable to fairness of argument. Several instances of this could be quoted from the volumes before us. Canon Trevor (p. 87) goes so far as to use the word "devotion" as the antithesis to "Puritanism." Such language cannot be expected to be persuasive with those who see a great deal of devotion in Baxter's *Saints' Rest*, or Rutherford's *Letters*, and very little in the *Book of Sports*.

seat.¹ This kind of language, while not justified in the least degree by our Prayer-book, prepares the mind of the unreflecting reader to accept, without proof, the doctrine of a strictly sacrificial priesthood. And as with the word "altar," so with other language used in the same manner, and so as to produce the same result. Thus, while I am writing these pages and reading the controversial letters which each week produces, I find it urged that the Eastward Position is most natural in the Consecration Prayer, because it is the most natural position for the priest *when he makes an offering,*—in utter forgetfulness, apparently, that whether the priest does make an offering in the Consecration Prayer is the very point to be established. Thus again, about the same time, I have the pleasure of receiving from Canon Rawlinson² a sermon on the "Eucharistic Sacrifice." To the substance of the sermon I will refer again. I am here objecting to the manner in which the text is used. That is *taken for granted* as to the meaning of those words in the Epistle to the Hebrews, "We have an altar," which (to say the least) requires very skilful argumentation to prove consistent with the whole tone and tenor of the Epistle.³

But, without further introductory remarks, I hasten to my subject, which is the position of the officiating priest, in regard to the Lord's Table, during the

¹ See pages 8, 9, 61, 66, 137, 145, 146, 151.
² See Appendix A (The Brighton Church Congress).
³ The point I am urging here is that a literal and earthly meaning is assumed for one sentence of an inspired argument, the whole general drift of which is spiritual and heavenly. It would surely be more to the purpose to *prove* that Aquinas was wrong in saying, as Epiphanius said before him, and Waterland after him: "*Per altare significatur ipse Christus.*"

saying of this Prayer of Consecration at the Holy Communion. It will be convenient first to take the question historically, and to see what the circumstances were under which the regulations of our Prayer Book, in regard to this matter, came into existence, and then to turn to the *rationale* of the subject, and to inquire into the true religious meaning of the rubric with which we are specially concerned.

II.

CHANCELS AS IN TIMES PAST.

Bearing of the Ornaments Rubric on our subject—Direction concerning Chancels—Question concerning its meaning, originally and afterwards—Opinion of Wren, L'Estrange, Cosin, and others—The general question not affected by this point.

I BEGIN with the Ornaments Rubric. The Vestments indeed I leave on one side, except to make this one remark, that neither in the period immediately succeeding 1559, when this rubric first came into existence, nor in the period immediately succeeding 1662, when, with some very significant changes, it was reinstated, is there any satisfactory proof that "Eucharistic Vestments" were used in the Church of England; but very much the contrary. Now laws are not commonly made for the precise purpose of being broken; and the whole *onus probandi* in this matter rests on those who have disturbed, or desire to disturb, the usage of the Church of England for 300 years. This point, however, I leave. And yet I must pause, and must ask my reader to pause, on the Ornaments Rubric, even when nothing beyond the position of the "celebrant" in the Consecration Prayer is in question. There are, in fact, two stepping-stones on which it is desirable to stand, before we reach our main point in the rubric prefixed to that prayer. It is because so many persons have insisted on taking this whole space in one leap, that so many persons have set their feet in the wrong place. On the first of these steppingstones, indeed, which is the Ornaments Rubric, I lay comparatively little stress; yet I think it ought not to be altogether overleapt.

In one part of this Rubric it is directed that "*the Chancels shall remain as they have done in times past.*" Two questions here arise, first as to the meaning of this direction in 1552, when it made its earliest appearance; secondly, as to its meaning in 1662, when it was fixed as a rule which is still binding. On these points we derive no help whatever from the Reports of the Ritual Commission.[1] And yet I conceive this sentence is not without its argumentative value in reference to the subject before us.[2]

I was first led to give close attention to this particular sentence, or at least to publish some thoughts in regard to it, in connection with a curious Catechism of Church Doctrine and Church Practice, which was printed in 1674; and I will write of the matter in this connection now, though I shall have occasion to refer more particularly to this book afterwards.[3]

---

[1] No complaint is implied in this phrase. So far as I know, this subject was never separately before the attention of the Commissioners. It is important however to note that new rubrical topics have come into prominence even in the short interval that has elapsed since the sitting of the Commission.

[2] I must confess that I have less confidence in the argument of this chapter than I had when I first drew it out. Still I leave it as it stands. I have no wish that this should be merely a partizan book: and whatever the worth of my remarks may be, I shall be glad to have called attention to a neglected part of this general subject. See *note* below, p. 16.

[3] The argument concerning Chancels, arising out of the consideration of this book, was the subject of correspondence in the *Guardian* for January 6, 20, 27; February 24, and March 24 in the present year.

This sentence concerning Chancels first, as I have said, found a place among our rubrics in 1552; and, amid great variations in other rubrics, it has held its ground ever since. It appears to me that it ought to be understood now in the same general sense which was intended originally. Great changes had been made in the chancels during the two or three years immediately preceding;[1] the main particular in these changes being, I imagine, the substitution of a movable Table for communion instead of the previously fixed Altar for sacrifice.[2] This state of things receives illustration from the volume in question. I do not refer merely to the picture representing the administration of the Lord's Supper, which exactly fulfils the conditions of the fourth of the rubrics prefixed to our Communion Office, as well as those of the eighty-second canon, the Holy Table standing free in the chancel, and the Priest standing on its north side; but to two other pictures, the subjects of which are Matrimony and the Churching of Women.[3] In the former the Lord's Table appears to be placed against the east wall; in the latter it is removed from that position, the priest standing close to the east wall, the woman kneeling before him, and a boy holding the book standing by his side. I name these particulars by the way as an elucidation of the condition in which (as will be pointed out more fully afterwards) I conceive the chancels to have generally been,

---

[1] Bishop Ridley in 1550, and Bishop Hooper in 1551, took, if I am not mistaken, very definite steps for transforming the condition of the chancels in the churches of their dioceses.

[2] To this end the removing of steps would in many cases be necessary.

[3] In each of these three pictures the Commandments are conspicuously placed on the east wall. This particular, however, belongs to a later period.

in harmony with this rubric, during the period immediately succeeding the year 1662.

But this whole mode of viewing the matter may be disputed, and has been disputed. It is contended that this rubric concerning Chancels does not refer to their condition at all, but merely rules that they shall be preserved, and not pulled down; and in reply to the view here advocated, it is urged that, according to this theory, the sentence ought to stand thus—"and the chancels shall be as they were in times past." It must in candour be admitted that there is some force in this verbal criticism.[1] The phrase is perhaps not exactly what we should expect, if it related merely to the maintenance of the arrangement and condition of the chancels. But then I answer that it is not exactly what we should expect, if it related merely to their preservation from destruction. On this theory it would have been enough to say "the chancels shall remain," or "the chancels shall not be destroyed." Something, in fact, of the obscurity of the Ornaments Rubric in general seems to have crept over this clause.

Let me now submit to the reader that the following considerations are of some weight in favour of interpreting the clause as having respect to the condition as well as the retention of the chancels.

The clause first appeared at that exact moment, when "alb, vestment, and cope" were expressly forbidden, and when the "surplice only" was allowed, and when

---

[1] Stress also has been laid upon the fact that in 1552 there was, after the word "remain," a comma, which afterwards disappeared. This, however, seems to me an argument in favour of my theory. Whatever ambiguity there may have been in the rubric at the first, the removal of the comma has decided that the chancels are not simply to remain, but to remain after a certain particular fashion.

other most significant changes in the Protestant direction were made in the Prayer Book and its rubrics. It is hardly likely that just at that moment any special love for chancels, or earnest anxiety for their preservation, should have been manifested; but it is extremely probable that importance would have been attached to the condition into which they had been brought. This mode, too, of interpreting the rubric derives some justification from a Latin Prayer Book published in the reign of Queen Elizabeth, where the words are—"Chorus etiam manebit *eadem forma, qua superiorum temporum fuit.*"[1] I turn now to the remarks of Bishop Wren, recently made known to us by the present Bishop of Chester in a most interesting volume. Wren asks, in reference to this rubric, "Who knows *how* the chancels were in those times past, so many having since been demolished, and many disused?" from which language I think it is evident that he regarded the words as having reference rather to the condition of the chancels than to their mere retention.[2] From Wren, who wrote shortly before the revision of 1662, let us now pass to L'Estrange, the second edition of whose book was published in 1680. Commenting on these words, he quotes Queen Elizabeth's order, "that the steps which be as yet remaining in any our cathedral, collegiate, or parish churches, be not stirred nor altered, but be suffered to continue; and if in any chancel the steps be transposed, that they be not erected again, but that the

---

[1] *Liturgies set forth in the Reign of Queen Elizabeth* (Parker Soc.) p. 327. I do not quote this Latin Prayer Book as an authoritative translation, but as showing the popular understanding at that time of the phrase under consideration.

[2] *Fragmentary Illustrations of the History of the Book of the Common Prayer*, p. 55.

place be decently paved." The reference here is clearly not to retention but to condition. L'Estrange adds :—" By which words evident it is authority had no design to end the dispute by closing with either party, but by stating things in their present posture."[1] My last quotation shall be from Mr. Beresford Hope's work, where he says, in one place, that the phrase in question "obviously refers to *the furniture* of the chancel."[2] In another place he brings forward, to the same effect, the authority of Bishop Cosin, who considers that the rubric refers to the open screen separating the chancel from the nave, and to the row of chairs or stools on either side within.[3] I am not concerned with the conclusion drawn alike by Bishop Cosin and Mr. Beresford Hope, which I venture to controvert, but with their *mode* of interpretation, in which I am disposed to agree.

The only question which remains relates to the particular period, which we ought at this day to view as indicated by the expression "times past." In 1552, when the words were first used, they certainly cannot have pointed to the *condition* of the chancels in the reign of Henry VIII. It is equally evident that in 1559, when they were again used (and this is, perhaps, the

---

[1] *Alliance of Divine Offices* (Lib. of Anglo-Catholic Theology), pp. 103, 104. I cannot help here noting what seems to me worthy of blame in the *Hierurgia Anglicana*, edited in 1868 by members of the Ecclesiological Society. There (p. 67) the second half only, relating to the *retention* of steps, is quoted from the Queen's order, the fact being thus withheld that she equally forbade the *replacing* of steps.

[2] *Worship in the Church of England*, p. 67. See also p. 129.

[3] So far as I know, the only proposal to change this phrase in our Rubrics was made by Bishop Cosin, who suggested the following words : "And the chancels shall be divided from the body of the Church, and remain as they have done in times past." *Correspondence*, published by the Surtees Society, Part II. p. 44.

best point from which to look backwards, for then they formed part of an "Ornaments Rubric" very similar to that which our Prayer Book contains now), the words cannot have referred (in this sense) to the reign of Queen Mary. It seems to me obvious, on the other hand, by parity of reasoning, that it would be equally unfair to suppose that, when used in 1662, they referred to the times of the Commonwealth immediately preceding, when the chancels were treated with a disregard which none of us now would wish to see repeated. On the whole I venture to contend, from the nature of the case, that these words, as finally adopted in 1662, are an echo of 1552. This interpretation, too, is in harmony with the fourth rubric before the Communion Office and with the canon of 1603, both of which (as we shall see) contemplate the Lord's Table as movable, and as liable to be moved "at the communion time." All lines of thought in reference to this subject appear to me to converge to this result, that the conditions of the chancels in the times immediately preceding 1552 furnish to us a theoretical standard and guide.

I am aware that this argument concerning chancels, derived from the words of the Ornaments Rubric, taken in connection with the history of changes in the Church of England, and with a consideration of the probabilities of the case, will be closely criticised; and I have no wish to press it except as subsidiary.[1]

---

[1] At first sight it might appear that this whole argument could easily be turned against me. In 1549 there was an "altar" at the east end of the chancel, and the consecrator stood "in the midst of it." Looking back from 1552, it might be said that these were the arrangements "in times past," which were now directed to be retained. On this view however the rubrics of 1552 would be made to contradict themselves. The

But believing it to have some force, and not having observed that it has been made use of before, I have thought it right to set it forth; and I have two remarks to make in regard to it. First, the argument at this point is, to use Archdeacon Paley's expression,[1] *cumulative:* the force of what follows does not depend upon what is here laid down: if all that I have said concerning chancels is fanciful, the weight of what may be urged on other grounds, to which I now proceed, is unimpaired. And, secondly, this reasoning on the phrase in which chancels are mentioned derives some confirmation, as we shall see, from the condition in which some chancels are known actually to have remained in the Church of England to a comparatively late period. But now let us turn to the fourth rubric at the beginning of the Communion Office, which rubric is the second of our stepping-stones as we approach our main subject, and a stepping-stone on which for a short time our feet ought to be very firmly set.

strong objection to my argument is that "times past" would more naturally refer to long usage than to the years between 1549 and 1552. If this objection is decisive, then I admit that we are forced to restrict the phrase before us to the mere *retention* of the chancels.

[1] See "the exposition of the argument" in the *Horæ Paulinæ:* "I have advanced nothing which I did not think probable; but the degree of probability by which different instances are supported is undoubtedly very different. If the reader, therefore, meets with a number which contains an instance that appears to him unsatisfactory, or founded in mistake, he will dismiss that number from the argument, but without prejudice to any other."

III.

RULE FOR THE PLACING OF THE HOLY TABLE.

Fourth rubric before the Communion Service—Its important bearing on the subject before us—Defeated attempt to alter it—Eighty-second Canon—Danger of enforcing this rubric and this canon—A possible compromise suggested.

The fourth rubric prefixed to "the Order of the Administration of the Lord's Supper," consists of two parts, the first having respect to the placing of the Lord's Table at the Communion time, the second to the Priest's position at the Table when he is engaged in this sacred service. It is the latter part to which we are ultimately tending: but the first part must occupy our attention at this point; nor can we reach our ultimate destination without travelling this way. The history of the Prayer Book forbids us to consider the Minister's position in the Communion Service till we have first considered the position of the Table.

The words of the rubric are as follows:—"*The Table having at the Communion-time a fair white linen cloth upon it shall stand in the body of the Church or in the Chancel where Morning and Evening Prayer are appointed to be said.*" Now what is the fair and natural interpretation of these words, taken simply as they stand, without any regard to collateral evidence? First, a distinction is evidently drawn between " the Communion time " and other times. No question is raised as to where the Table is to stand in the intervals between two successive administrations of the Lord's Supper. So far as any inference can be drawn from these words, we are quite free to place it, in this interval, against the east wall at the upper end of the chancel. But when the Holy Communion is to be celebrated, the Table is to be placed *either*[1] in the Body of the Church, *or* in the Chancel, but *always* "where Morning Prayer and Evening Prayer are appointed to be said." In whatever part of the church it is the custom, under authority, to celebrate those other parts of the service, there " at the Communion time," according to this rubric, the Holy Table is to be placed. It follows further, quite obviously and without any doubt, that the table itself is contemplated as being easily movable. Now accepting those arrangements which have been customary, under the sanction of our Ordinaries, during two hundred years, and having no wish to change those arrangements, we must still admit that, according to the rubric, the Holy Table ought, "at the Communion time," to have been brought out into the free part of the nave or the chancel, so as to be, thus to speak, in easy contact with the congregation. In fact this rubric has not been duly observed. A very careful and deliberate regulation, dating from 1662, has fallen into desuetude.

At this point I cannot help putting forward a question which seems to me very serious, and to which I invite the most careful attention. The whole

---

[1] It is to be observed that *preferentially* it is to be placed in the body of the church, *i.e.*, in the nave.

stress of the argument, which, comparatively new as it is, now is pressed upon us so urgently from many quarters, that "*before the Table*" in the rubric preceding the Consecration Prayer, must mean "*in front of the Table facing eastwards*," depends upon the assumption that the table is placed altarwise against the east wall during the Communion Service. The Table is there, and the word, it is contended, can mean nothing else, and the Priest may stand in this position at this time. Now I do not admit that even thus the phrase "before the Table" is necessarily so restricted in its meaning. I have also to point out that it is hardly consistent to contend for an *optional* use under a rubric understood as *imperative*. But, conceding these two points at present for argument's sake, I will ask whether it is candid to plead for a ceremonial act on the strength of an interpretation of one rubric, which interpretation depends upon the breaking of another rubric. A sense of great unfairness has often come over my mind in reading discussions on this subject, when I have observed that the fourth of the rubrics before the Communion Office is buried out of sight as much as possible, while yet a new sense of another rubric, made possible by the violation of this, is brought out into a relief as strong as possible. A plea of simple justice demands that peculiar attention should be given just now to this rule, which regulates the placing of the Table "at the Communion time."

And the case is made very much stronger by evidence which has recently come to light, that an attempt was made to alter this rubric with which we are now concerned, so as to confine the Lord's Table to a position which really would have supplied a plausible ground for that interpretation of the Consecration Rubric which is now so urgently recommended to us, and that this attempt was defeated.[1] In the facsimile of the Black Letter Prayer Book of 1636, with the marginal manuscript notes and alterations from which the copy attached to the Act of 1662 was written, we find that, instead of the words "*in the body of the church or in the chancel,*" it was proposed to substitute, "*in the most convenient place in the upper end of the chancel, or of the body of the church, where there is no chancel.*" Nothing could be more significant than the suggested change.[2] But it was not accepted. It was decided by Convocation and Parliament that the rubric was to remain as before. Hence this retention of the old form is a fact of extreme importance. The failure of an attempt to change is a very strong argument to prove a serious meaning in that which is unchanged. That we have gradually become accustomed to act in our churches as if this projected alteration of rubrics had really been accomplished we all know. It does not, however, follow that it is fair to reason from the violation of a rule, as though its intention were something totally different from that which it expresses.

[1] See above, p. 5, *note*.

[2] To this evidence of a desire, deliberately entertained, but decisively disappointed, is to be added that which is supplied by Bishop Cosin's Annotated Prayer Book, preserved at Durham. The rubric relating to this subject, which he recommended, was as follows: " The table *alwayes* standing *in the midst of the upper end of the chancell (or of the church, where a chancell is wanting)*, and being at all times covered with a carpet of silk, shall *also* have at the Communion time a faire white linen cloth upon it, with paten, chalice, and other decent furniture, meet for the high mysteries there to be celebrated."—*Correspondence*, Pt. II. p. 52.

But I proceed to further evidence. Let us turn to the Canons. It is to be presumed that the rubrics of 1662 are consistent with the canons of 1603, unless there be some declaration to the contrary. Now in the 82nd of those canons, after provision for the proper repairing and reverent covering of the Lord's Table, we find that between the placing of the Table at the time of Holy Communion and its placing at other times a sharp distinction is drawn by the phrase "*saving when the Holy Communion is to be administered*,"—"at which time," it is added, "the same shall be placed in so good sort within the church[1] or chancel, as thereby the Minister may be more conveniently heard of the Communicants in his Prayer and Ministration, and the Communicants also more conveniently, and in more number, may communicate with the said Minister." Nothing, as it seems to me, can be clearer than both the spirit and the literal meaning of this part of the canon. It could not possibly have been written under the inspiration of that feeling concerning chancels which is so constantly urged upon us now. The chancel is not viewed as being inherently more sacred than any other part of the church. The only question raised is that of congregational convenience. Wherever the Table can be most suitably placed for securing the ends of common participation in this most sacred rite, there it is to be placed at this time; and it is impossible to resist the conclusion that this position during the celebration and administration of the Sacrament,

---

[1] Again we observe that the "church" is mentioned before the "chancel." See above, p. 19, *note*. By the "church," as Mr. Beresford Hope correctly remarks, is meant the "nave."

was to be, not in contiguity with the east wall, but in some part of the church further to the west. But here is presented to us a most serious question, on which it may be wise to pause for a moment before we pass on.

This new insisting on an eastward position of the Priest during consecration, based upon a particular interpretation of the rubric which affects this point, has forced on us a reconsideration of the rubric and canon which affect the position of the Table itself. This question might otherwise have slept; and most of us would have wished that its sleep should have been unbroken. But what if this is no longer possible? What, if in consequence of a verbal advantage gained by some persons in the interpretation of one rubric by help of the violation of a different rubric, some other persons should insist on their claim to observe that other rubric literally? What if to counterbalance the claim to consecrate eastwards at a Table placed altarwise, the claim to place the Table, not altarwise at all, but free in the midst of the congregation, should be asserted and acted on? Can anyone contemplate without fear the sharp contrast which would then be presented by two sets of churches, and two types of congregations, in all parts of the land? This would make the division amongst us far more palpable than it has ever been before. The division would be shown not simply in the position of the officiating minister at the Lord's Table, but by conflicting practices in the placing of the Table itself. This would, indeed, be a triumph of "the Catholic Revival." It may be said that in every case the Ordinary might prevent this alarming result by refusing to allow the Holy

Table to be placed otherwise than according to present custom. But is it quite certain that the Ordinary could follow this course in defiance of both rubric and canon? And if it were legally possible, can we suppose that our Bishops would deferentially yield to one party, who, against a legal decision,[1] can only build their case on a doubtful interpretation, and would refuse to listen to another party which could quote authoritative documents, concerning the sense of which there cannot be any doubt?

For myself I dread extremely the establishing of such a sharp line of angry separation, running visibly through the Church of England, Sunday by Sunday, when our congregations are assembled for their most solemn act of worship. And yet I fear such a state of things may be inevitable, if those who are urging on a crisis with so much determination will not pause.[2] Let me add that for my own part I earnestly deprecate any change in that position of our Communion Tables which has long been customary. If the change

---

[1] The argument in this volume is quite independent of the Purchas Judgment, though I have made it the subject of some separate remarks. I am quite aware that this judgment is viewed by many persons as having little weight, partly because it was given in an undefended suit, partly because the judges on the occasion were few in number, and partly because of a certain utterance by the present Lord Chancellor, to which reference will be made below. Still the judgment is law; and by law the Bishops, in their administration, are bound.

[2] In the *Record* of January 18th, I read the following: "At our last Sunday Evening Communion I had the Table placed 'east' and 'west,' and therefore was not compelled for one moment before reading the Consecration Prayer to turn my back on the congregation. I do not intend that to be the position always. I should wish to have it so at times of Holy Communion, and believe the eighty-second Canon and Rubric will bear me out." And I could produce later private evidence of the manner in which such thoughts have been *forced* into the minds of those to whom they were not naturally welcome.

does take place, the responsibility of it must rest with those who will have forced a strict observance of rubric and canon upon those who would willingly have been content with an irregularity sanctioned by usage.

Yet even here some thoughts of peace and hope suggest themselves. We hear much said, in reference to this matter, of conciliation and compromise. If conciliation is to be a reality, it must be offered chiefly, not to those who have caused our difficulties, but to those who are conscious of injury. If there is to be compromise, it cannot be by means of a bargain all on one side. Now, inasmuch as some feel earnestly concerning the eastward position, which has not yet been legalised, and is not in harmony with usage—and others have an undoubted right to insist upon a position of the Holy Table which would make the eastward position impossible—might not a compromise be effected on this basis, that the right should be given up by one party, and this earnest desire of an authorised change by the other? So far as I know, there is a perfect readiness among all men to acquiesce in that position of the Lord's Table which, though not really sanctioned by law, has long been familiar to us,—provided that this position is not used for making ulterior demands. May we not hope that these ulterior demands will be given up, if only that position of the Lord's Table is secured, to which so much importance is attached? I assume, of course, that our official documents are in due time to be brought into harmony with this supposed agreement—that, on the one hand, the canon of 1603 and the fourth rubric before the Communion Office are altered, so as to sanction only the present customary place of the Lord's Table—and, on the other hand, the rubric before the Consecration Prayer made incapable of any interpretation which would sanction the Eastward Position.[1]

[1] The rubric for the placing of the Holy Table is seen in its true force when it is put in juxtaposition with the rubric of the same date for the place of Morning and Evening Prayer. This is done by Dr. Blakeney, who adds: "Viewing these two rubrics together, and remembering their *common origin*, we have no difficulty in understanding the words, 'in the body of the Church or in the Chancel where Morning and Evening Prayer be appointed to be said.' The object at which the Reviewers of 1552 aimed was the location of the Minister in such a place, whether in the body of the Church or Chancel, as he should *best be heard*. The reason of the *option* as to the position of the Table is obvious. It was to stand either in the body of the Church or in the Chancel, *wherever* prayer was appointed to be said, as the position best adapted to the edification of the hearer. This exactly harmonises with the canons 14 and 82, the former prescribing the most convenient place for hearing, and the latter directing the Table to be placed, 'as thereby the Minister may be more conveniently heard of the communicants.'"—*Book of Common Prayer in its History and Interpretation.* Third edition, p. 466.

IV.

THE TROUBLES OF 1640.

The Canons of 1640—"Declaration concerning some rites and ceremonies"—Its strong protest against Romanism—Illustration from the Diocese of Chester—Brian Walton—Letter from the Vice-Dean to Bishop Bridgeman.

THE case for the free placing of the Holy Table "at the Communion-time" is by no means yet complete. We must now enter upon the history of the period when this subject convulsed the country, and thus left us a caution, to which, if we are wise, we shall take good heed. And here I will turn at once, without any introduction, to the canons of 1640, which represent the culminating point of Laud's success. It is true that these canons have no binding authority; but they are a striking and instructive landmark of Church history. The seventh of these canons, entitled "a declaration concerning some rites and ceremonies," has been lately quoted to justify the official use of the word "altar" in the Church of England; and in studying this document, it is perhaps discernible that those who wrote it would gladly have secured this result, if they could. Yet, even so, the term "Communion Table" is used in the canon throughout as the official phrase.[1] This, however, is not the

---

[1] In reply to the undoubtedly true statement that the term "Altar" is no part of our official church vocabulary, it has been replied that neither is the term "Communion Table" a part of that vocabulary. This, however, is an error. The 82nd of the Canons of 1603, which are certainly official, is headed with the words "a decent Communion Table in every church."

question before us, though evidently it bears upon it. Our subject for the moment is the position of the Communion Table in 1640.

Now, in this canon, after an expression of strong approval of the means taken at the Reformation for rooting out of the minds of the people both "the inclination" to "the gross superstition of popery" "and the memory thereof," "especially of the idolatry committed in the Mass, for which cause all popish altars were demolished," it is added that in the royal chapels of three princes, and most cathedrals, and some parochial churches, the holy Tables had continued to stand where the Altars stood.[1] This, it is urged, "doth sufficiently acquit the manner of placing the said Tables from any illegality or just suspicion of popish superstition or innovation." "And, therefore," continue the writers of the canon, "we judge it fit and convenient that all churches and chapels do conform themselves in this particular to the example of the cathedral or mother churches, *saving only the general liberty left to the bishop by law during the time of administration of the Holy Communion.*"[2] I might here dwell on the strong Protestant language of this canon, its abhorrence of "popery," its approval of the demolition of "popish Altars," to illustrate the extreme difference which separates the opinions of the Laudian divines, even at this their point of highest success, from those sentiments concerning "the Mass"

---

[1] Even this phrase, as it stands, is absolutely contradictory to the theory that "Table" and "Altar" are synonymous. The sharpest distinction is drawn in the canon between "popish Altars" and English Communion Tables, whereas now the most active exertions are made to lead us to believe that they are exactly or nearly the same thing.

[2] See Cardwell's *Synodalia*, vol. i. pp. 404—406.

with which we have now to deal. But what I desire to lay stress on is the distinction drawn between the position of the Communion Table "*during the time of administration*" and its position at other times. It is true that the canon of 1640 is not quite consistent with the canon of 1603, that of the earlier date contemplating the free position of the Table during communion as the rule, whereas that of the latter date contemplates it as an exception.[1] Still the later document is quite enough for the argument in support of which I quote it. When we study it carefully, we perceive very clearly that it represents an endeavour, which was *not successful*, to procure *a change* of position in the Lord's Table ; and that even this endeavour was carried on *under reserve*. Thus the canon furnishes evidence, both of the custom of the period, and of public opinion on the subject.[2]

This year (1640) was a very serious time for the Church of England, precisely in connection with this very subject. The resemblance too between that period and our own, in regard to some Church questions,

---

[1] It is impossible not to remark a certain adroitness of language in this Canon of 1640, as compared with that of 1603. The impression is created that the deviation from the altarwise position of the Table during Communion was simply within the *permission* of the Ordinary, whereas it was *prescribed*.

[2] It must not be forgotten that near the close of this Canon or declaration the following words occur :—" We declare that this situation of the holy Table doth not imply that it is, or ought to be esteemed, a true and proper altar, whereon Christ is again really sacrificed : but it is only to be called an altar by us in that sense in which the primitive church called it an altar, and in no other." So far as I know, this sentence and the Coronation Service are the only documents which can be quoted to sanction the use of the word "Altar" for the Communion Table in the Church of England. The Coronation Service will be referred to below. Of this Canon it is enough to say that it has no official authority at all.

was very close. The disasters which followed certain religious movements in the former period were very great. Hence we have more reasons than one for reading very carefully this part of the history of the past. Then one of the great efforts of Laud and his party was to change that character of the Chancels which had previously been customary in the churches, and more especially to remove the Communion Tables from the places which they had occupied, so as to fix them altarwise against the eastern wall. The manner in which this was done was very arbitrary, and often attended with violent proceedings; and the indignation which it produced through the country was extreme. Evidence of this can be furnished in abundance from the recorded proceedings of the House of Lords and House of Commons, and from the general literature of the period. Two very marked cases were connected with St. Gregory's, London,[1] and with Gloucester Cathedral.[2] I will content myself with illustrations supplied by the Diocese in which I happen to live, and not, so far as I know, made use of before in discussions on this subject.

The two Bishops of Chester who immediately preceded and immediately followed the interval of the Revolution, John Bridgeman and Brian Walton, were both men of mark, and both worthy to be held in high respect. They belonged, on the whole, to the school of Laud, but neither of them was notorious as

---

[1] See Cardwell's *Documentary Annals*, Vol. ii., p. 185. In this case the royal prerogative was exerted to effect what was contrary to law. Those who, in resistance to the secular power, identify themselves with the Laudian divines, seem to forget that they are opposing the very principle on which those divines were glad to act.

[2] See a pamphlet by the Rev. Canon Ryle, entitled, *Archbishop Laud and his Times*, p. 151.

a hot partisan; and while Bridgeman, deprived by Cromwell, was living a secluded life in Shropshire, Walton found solace in Biblical studies, and in preparing his great Polyglott. Previously, after maintaining in his act for the degree of Doctor of Divinity at Cambridge, the thesis that "the Roman Pontiff is not the infallible judge in controversies of faith," we find Walton, when rector of a London parish, "accused of ordering his churchwardens to place the Communion Table under the east window, which the churchwardens declining," continues the biographer, "Dr. Walton himself, the Bishop of Rochester, and other friends then present there placed it."[1] This is a specimen of the unseemly parochial squabbles which were then prevalent over the country, in consequence of the attempt of many bishops to rearrange the chancels of parish churches, in violation of both canon and rubric.[2]

Bishop Bridgeman's life affords an instance of similar troubles, at the same time, connected with cathedrals; and this passage of diocesan history can be illustrated very fully, and in a most amusing and instructive manner, by a letter addressed to him by John Ley, who held a Parochial Cure in Cheshire, and was also at the time Vice Dean of the Cathedral.[2] A few extracts from this book, harmonising as they do with the thoughts of many persons in our own time, are quite worthy of being given and examined here in illustration of our subject.

[1] See Archdeacon Todd's *Memoirs of the Life and Writings of Bishop Walton* (1821), Vol. 1, p. 14.
[2] *A Letter (against the erection of an Altar) written June 29. 1635, to the Reverend Father John, L. Bishop of Chester* by John Ley, Pastour of Great Budworth, in Cheshire, London, 1641.

In Chester Cathedral a "new structure of stone" had been erected "at the upper end of the Old Consistorie."[1] The "Papists" "had talked of this as an altar, whereupon they exalted their hopes of a re-edification of their Babel amongst us." "It was one of them," says Ley, "from whom, being at Budworth, I had the first notice of that newes; which I told him I would not beleeve: for it seemed to mee more strange than true, that a Papist, dwelling at least fourteene miles from Chester, and comming thither seldome, should know better what was done in the Cathedrall, than I, the Sub-deane of the Church, who was there almost every weeke throughout the whole yeere. .... But at my next comming to Chester, I saw hee had but too much and too solid ground for his report ... and some said, as I was told to my face, that though your lordship, as Bishop, were the Author, I, as Sub-deane, was in some way an Actor or approver of that which was so great an eye-sore unto many good people."

It is interesting to mark some of the arguments on which Ley bases his respectful but earnest expostulation with his Bishop. Read in the light of our time they are still very fresh.

Among other things he urges "the danger of depravation and corruption of the doctrine of the Church, by changing the Christian Sacrament into a Popish Sacrifice—for," he adds, "from literall and reall Altars

---

[1] This "Old Consistorie" is the Lady Chapel, which happens at this time to contain some fine woodwork marked with Bishop Bridgeman's initials, being part, in fact, of the pulpit which he erected in the choir. It was in this "consistorie" that Marsh, in Queen Mary's reign, was examined and condemned to be burnt. See Foxe's *Book of Martyrs*, Vol. viii. p. 49 (Seeley's edition, 1861).

a litterall and reall Sacrifice is inferred: Altars and Sacrifices inferre one another." He admits that "the like inference" might be made from the word "Priest," but not, he says, "with like advantage, for the one is offered but to the eare, the other to the eye; the one is but a transient word, the other is a permanent worke; the one is properly an *Altar*, the other noteth not properly a *Priest* in the Evangelicall Church."[1] And another exception which Ley takes to " such new altars" is that they are " schismaticall novelties," inasmuch as from the year 1550, till the time then present, "altars had, by the most authentick constitutions and constant custome of our Church, stood excommunicated, and tables of wood authorised in their stead: and the Canon took it for certaine and undoubted that there be decent and convenient Tables provided in all the churches of the Realme." In this case, in fact, he adds rather quaintly, there would be "schisme upon schisme, a division from the generall, and a subdivision in our particular church; for that in the Quire there is a table of wood, and above that, in the upper end of the old Consistorie, an Altar of stone."[2]

An appeal, which in a later passage is made to the Bishop, is honourable both to him and to the writer. "To another sort of men, who, by way of gratitude for your great moderation towards them, have held it their duty to present their hearty devotions to Almighty God for your long and comfortable continuance among us, this Altar will be a rock of offence, and make them as stiffe against kneeling at the Sacrament, as any of their adversaries

[1] Pp. 9, 10.   [2] P. 15.

flexible or pliable to bow to an Altar;"[1] and then it is added, on the other hand, that "though some men's slighting both of the Lord's Table and Temple required a remedy to keep off contempt, yet there was great care to be taken in this case that the remedy of Prophanenesse might not be such as might foment Superstition."[2] And, to quote one passage more, the writer says: "Since the Papists never, or very rarely, use the word *Table*, but *Altar*, both out of too much devotion to it, and too great disaffection of us and our Church, it were convenient that we were (at least) more sparing in the use of the word *Altar*, and generally more accustomed ourselves to the name *Table*, the rather because since we have seemed in tearmes, and some other wayes, to comply with them more then in former times, they have multiplied in number and advanced in confidence."[3] The result was that the Bishop caused this structure to be taken down, and an "ironical elegy" commemorated its demolition.[4]

---

[1] We should not fail to observe here the parallel with our own times. Extreme ritual has often the effect of hindering improvements in our Church Services. High Churchmen are apt to boast that the improvements of late years are due exclusively to themselves. This, however, is a mistake, and Evangelicals have been kept back from various things which they would willingly have done, but for the suspicion and alarm caused by each new change.

[2] Pp. 16, 17, 29.

[3] P. 31. Remembering the persistent efforts recently made, and still made, to identify Anglican and Roman doctrine, I cannot resist the temptation to quote one more passage: "A man may sooner eat up an altar of stone, though it were as big as a church, than reconcile our Church and the Romish together, whatsoever the quirking Scotist "Damport" masked under the title of "Franciscus à Sancta Clara," hath devised," p. 19. This work of "Damport" (or "Davenport") has recently been republished.

[4] See Appendix B. (Elegy upon an Altar.)

These are only samples of an agitation which could be illustrated by contemporary notices from every county in England. But these have a local interest for such as live in Cheshire,[1] and they suffice for the purpose of the moment. And now that we have before us this subject of the placing of the Holy Table " at the Communion-time," in church, it is desirable to pursue the subject historically, till we reach the latter part of the seventeenth century. If it can be established that the Communion Table was not in 1662 customarily placed as we place it now for the administration of the Lord's Supper, but, according to this rubric and canon, free in the church or the chancel, then a very firm basis will have been laid for the argument which is to follow.

[1] Mr. Beresford Hope (p. 206) has occasion to refer to another Bishop of Chester, Cartwright, whose character was not so respectable as those of Bridgeman and Walton; and the incident may be mentioned here, though it anticipates a notice of one fact to which careful attention must be turned presently, viz., that, to use Mr. Beresford Hope's own words, "it is a mistake to suppose that, with the Restoration, the altarwise position became universal." I cannot agree with him in thinking that the non-observance of this position was a *disorder*, since a different position was *ordered*, and is *still ordered*, by both a rubric and a canon. But it is interesting and important to note that in 1687 Bishop Cartwright found in Liverpool the Holy Table not placed altarwise.

V.

HISTORY OF THE PLACING OF THE HOLY TABLE.

Recollection in 1662 of 1640—Eastward placing of the Table improbable—The evidence from books—The case of kneeling and the Surplice in 1662 not really similar to the case of Vestments and the Eastward Position now—Catechism of 1674—Evidence from Parliamentary debates—From the continuance of chancels in their old condition—Recorded defeat of the attempt to change.

THE year 1640 has just been prominently mentioned. The year we are aiming at is 1662. It is sometimes assumed that because very successful efforts were made about the former year to place the Communion Tables in English churches altarwise, at the upper extremities of the chancels, therefore they so stood in the latter year.[1] Could anything be more whimsical? To write as if the ecclesiastical history of England worked its way quietly and progressively from 1640 to 1662 is to write very wildly and quite at random. It is nothing less than to leave out Cromwell from the middle of the seventeenth century. The course pursued by the bishops at the earlier of these dates did not proceed continuously and prosperously, till it reached its highest point of success at the later, but, on the contrary, it was interrupted in the most violent manner, and with a strong recoil of feeling that pervaded a very large part of the community. Is it likely that the very thing which convulsed the

[1] See Appendix C. (The place of the Lord's Table between 1640 and 1662.)

Church and country in 1640 would be accepted, without hesitation or opposition, as the law of the Church and country in 1662?

Let the probabilities of the case be considered.[1] A method of church arrangement, associated with reminiscences so serious and disturbing, could not possibly be accepted without dispute. No storm so violent, except by a miracle, was ever converted into an immediate calm. Let it be remembered, too, that in 1661 those resolute and earnest-minded men were within the Church of England, who on St. Bartholomew's day in the following year withdrew from it, and became the founders of systematic Nonconformity; and to these we must add a large number of weaker men,[2] who shared their convictions without in the end following their example. Can we suppose that such persons, whether of the stronger or the

[1] As to the *facts* of the case, see what is said by two writers who advocate the Eastward Position. Mr. Scudamore says, quoting Heylin: "Certain it is that long after the Restoration in most country churches the Holy Table was still set 'at the hither end of the Chancel.' To restore it to the place in which we almost invariably see it now was mainly the work of the last century."—*Notitia Eucharistica*, p. 147. Mr. Walton says: "It would seem to be certain that at the actual time of the Restoration the Holy Table was almost universally set lengthwise. . . . . It may be held indeed that even at the date of the Revision the lengthwise arrangement was well-nigh universal. . . . . The Puritan arrangement was being practically acquiesced in; and, what is more, it prevailed very extensively for a long time afterwards. . . . . Evidence of a more positive kind might be added as to the long continuance of the Puritan arrangement,—in other words, of the literal observance of the Fourth Rubric as re-inserted in 1662."—*The Rubrical Determination of the Celebrant's Position.* Note K.

[2] By this phrase I do not by any means intend to say that these men ought to have seceded with Baxter, but that at such a time there are always many, who agreeing in general sentiment with those who secede, yet shrink from the formation of a great schism. I write this under a vivid recollection of the Scotch disruption of 1844. There is good proof that in 1662 Baxter expected a much larger secession.

weaker class, would have acquiesced in that which within a few years had been so conscientiously resisted?

But we are not left to hypothesis or conjecture in this matter. At the Savoy conference this question of the placing of the Lord's Table "at the Communion-time" was never mentioned; other matters, far less obnoxious, such as the use of the surplice and kneeling at the reception of the Communion, were made points of the most determined resistance. But no allusion was made to this. It was evidently taken for granted that as regards the placing of the Lord's Table the law of the Church, clearly expressed in canon and rubric alike, was to remain as before. Whatever new regulations for the administration of the Lord's Supper were to be introduced, they were understood to be adapted to a Communion Table placed, at the time of the sacramental service, in the body of the church or free in the chancel.

In further confirmation of this view, various kinds of evidence can be produced—from books—from Parliamentary debates—from the condition in which chancels have remained, in various parts of the country, to a date comparatively recent—and, above all, from the fact that a definite attempt was made in 1661 to cause the communion tables to be placed altarwise against the eastern walls of our churches, and that this attempt was decisively foiled and defeated under the combined action of Parliament and Convocation. That a canon and a rubric declare explicitly against such a position "at the Communion-time" is certain. It is also certain that this canon and this rubric were deliberately left unchanged. But it is certain, likewise, that the placing of the Lord's Table altarwise at the east wall did gradually become the custom of the Church of England. In some instances the change probably took place very speedily; and in some districts and dioceses more speedily than in others. Evelyn mentions a case within his own knowledge very soon after 1662.[1] Under these circumstances it is desirable to bear in mind and to point out that there is collateral evidence of the true intention of the Church, and of its recognised practice, in this matter of the placing of the Lord's Table.

As to the first class of evidence, I will again refer to that Catechism of 1674, which has been brought forward above in general illustration of the state of the chancels at the period now under our attention. In this book is a picture of a chancel with its Holy Table, at the time of the celebration of the Holy Communion. The Table stands free in the chancel, and lengthwise, east and west, with two clergymen facing one another on the north and south sides. The people are kneeling reverently at the west end and at the north and south sides. But one very curious circumstance ought here to be noticed by the way. The two officiating clergymen appear to wear gowns. It seems to me extremely probable that, inasmuch as serious scruples were felt and expressed in 1662 as to the wearing of the surplice, this point was not in every case, for some time at least, very harshly pressed. This picture cannot represent a merely Puritan communion; for, as I have said, the communicants are kneeling. We have, in fact, as it seems, here before us a very good illustration of the curious

---

[1] Swainson, *The Rubrical Question of* 1874, (Second Edition) p. 24. See p. 35.

transitional character of that time. Before any long period had passed away, all scruples regarding both kneeling and the surplice had ceased.[1]

And at this point, by the way, I could imagine that a question relating to our present difficulties might easily come into the mind of some reader. If all doubts respecting the surplice and kneeling, which were the great topics of dispute two hundred years ago, were gradually set to rest, why may not this same result be hoped for with regard to the Eastward Position and Eucharistic Vestments, concerning which debate disturbs us now? To this question I think an easy and very confident answer can be given. At that time the use of the surplice and the attitude of kneeling at the Communion were not only legal, but absolutely prescribed. The use of Vestments and the Eastward Position are not now legal. The utmost that can be said for them is that it is bad law which forbids them, and that the perseverance in these two irregularities is right, in order that good law may be procured.[2]

But, passing on from a remark made by the way, let us turn to the second of the above-mentioned kinds of evidence. It will be enough here to quote some remarkable words used by a man of note in the House of Commons during a debate on Comprehension in

---

[1] See Appendix D. (Catechism of Church Doctrine and Church Practice in 1674.)

[2] To make the parallel complete, it would be necessary to suppose that kneeling at the Communion and wearing a surplice was made *authoritatively optional*. No one, so far as I am aware, wishes the Eastward Position and the Eucharistic Vestments to be made obligatory on all. It is the power of choice which is claimed; and it is precisely in this power of choice, as I venture to think, that our danger resides.

1667–8. We find Sir Thomas Littleton, the future Speaker, addressing the House as follows: "So long as the Church was true to herself, the Nonconformists never hurt the Church; but as soon as innovation and alteration came in by the Churchmen [Clergy], and they favourites with the Crown, the Church declined. In ceremonies we have much alteration; the Communion Table set altar-manner, whereas it ought to be in the body of the Church, that the guests might come to the Table, and the Second Service might be better heard."[1] This seems very clear as to the recognised law of the placing of the Holy Table, as to the change in its position which was already in progress, and as to the discontent felt in consequence, by some of the Laity against some of the Clergy. But let us turn to the third class of evidence.

If even one chancel had remained till our times in the condition contemplated by our canons and rubrics, this would be a collateral argument of some

[1] I quote this from *Parliament and the Church of England*, an important book recently published by Professor Montagu Burrows. So far as I know he is the first who brought this passage to view. He adds in a note, "This passage seems to show that the custom of placing the Holy Table altarwise or 'altarmanner,' which had obtained largely under Laud's auspices before the Great Rebellion, was not legalized at the Restoration, and was considered illegal in 1667. An alteration of the fourth rubric before the Communion Service, in order to allow the Table to be placed altarwise, and to make the Eastward Position of the celebrant optional, had been attempted in 1661 by some party, probably by one or other House of Convocation; but it failed, and the rubric had been left exactly as before, and as we now have it. Yet we see that custom was already settling the question of the position of the Holy Table; not so the Eastward Position of the celebrant, which Sir Thomas would have been sure to mention, as also the Vestments, if they had been worn." Pp. 91, 92. On this I will only remark that I think an attempt to make the Eastward Position optional was not so clearly a part of the foiled endeavour of 1661 as was the attempt to place the Communion Table altarwise.

value in attestation of the intention of the Church. Had it been intended in 1662 that every Communion Table should be fixed altarwise at the east wall, we can very well imagine that the changes necessary to secure this result would in many cases have been made gradually and considerately; but it is difficult to believe that a single chancel would have remained unchanged during two centuries, whereas, in truth, examples of this kind, overlooked till the present controversies began, have been brought to view in various parts of the country.

The first example I will adduce is that of Hawarden, in the immediate neighbourhood of Chester, where the Lord's Table is still recollected by many persons as standing not only free in the chancel, but with a considerable space to the east of it. As a second instance, I have now before me a drawing of the church of Langley in Shropshire, where kneeling-boards and desks are fixed on the southern, eastern and northern sides of the chancel, the Table standing east and west in the midst.[1] Similar evidence of a somewhat earlier date is furnished by a manuscript in the Chapter Library at Carlisle, containing Bishop Nicolson's record of a visitation of his Diocese. Here we find the east and west position of the Table noted in three churches, Brough, Ormside, and St. Michael's, Appleby. Of Ravenstondale, the Bishop remarks, that "the Altar stands at a distance from the east window," of Burgh-by-Sands, that "the Communion Table is not placed in the east end."[2] And, to come again to

---

[1] An engraving of this chancel will be found in the volume of the Anastatic Drawing Society for 1857.

[2] See Appendix E. Bishop Nicolson's Visitation in 1703.

what is more recent, I give the following extract from a letter which has lately been placed in my hands :— "The Lord's Table in the parish church of Orford stood in the middle of the chancel, with rails and kneeling-stools all round; and, if I remember rightly, it was an oblong within a square. The parish church of Llangybi in Carnarvonshire is a historical and very ancient church: there the Communion Table stands with one end against the east wall of the church, so that one side of the Table is really the north side; and in the adjoining parish of Llanharmon the Table held the same position till within the last few years."[1] The village church of Lyddington in Rutland, is specified by another writer as one in which the Table "does not stand against the east wall, but is surrounded by an enclosure of rails, passing between it and the wall."[2] The arrangement, in this respect, which subsisted till very lately, in the church of Wiggenhall, St. Mary, in the county of Norfolk, is thus described to me by a friend: "There was a sort of pew in the chancel, which began from the chancel-arch on either side, just like cathedral stalls,[3] but continued the whole way round the east end, the Table standing in the chancel, lengthwise." I have preferred to lay stress on these instances, which have been brought indirectly before my own notice: but others are given

---

[1] This, it will be observed, is from personal recollection. I may add that since this was printed, the writer has communicated with me directly to the same effect.

[2] I take this from a private communication, dated March 1, 1875.

[3] A sketch, accompanying this description, shows a narrow entrance to the chancel, with what might be termed "return stalls" on each side, the Table standing free to the east of them, but not in contact with the east end of the church.

by Canon Swainson in his recently published pamphlet on "the Rubrical Question of 1874."[1] Nor is this list so complete as it might easily have been made:[2] but it suffices to show that there survived for a long period evidence of this kind to prove that the chancels of our churches in the period immediately succeeding 1662 were in a very different condition from that in which we commonly find them now.

There is no doubt, as we have seen above, that an attempt was made in 1662 to secure in these chancels the permanent altarwise position of the Holy Tables against the east walls, whether at the Communion time or at other times; and this very attempt furnishes the fourth kind of evidence to which allusion has been made, and the evidence perhaps which is the most conclusive of all. There is no need for quoting here again the words which have already been given from the Facsimile Black-Letter Book and Bishop Cosin's Durham Book;[3] but it is essential to repeat with the utmost emphasis the conclusion to which this testimony leads. It is sometimes said that the questions connected with the placing of the Lord's Table and the position of the priest during the administration of the Lord's Supper were purposely left by Cosin, and by men of his school, in a state of hesitancy and doubt, with the hope that better times would come, and that advantage would afterwards be taken of this uncertainty. If this were so, I cannot think that such an intention was honourable; for it would virtually have amounted to this, that one aspect

---

[1] Second edition, p. 24.

[2] See Appendix F. (Further instances of Chancels remaining in their old condition.)

[3] See above, pp. 5, 21 and notes.

of these subjects was presented at the time as satisfactory to those who were very sensitive in regard to them, while another aspect was secretly transmitted to the future, for the purpose of being substituted for the former. But I can find no trace of so insidious a design. What Cosin and those of his school desired, in regard to the placing of the Lord's Table, is perfectly clear. They made a most definite proposal, and met with a decisive defeat. The Church and State of England ruled, in 1662, that they would not sanction that arrangement of the chancels, the attempt to procure which, twenty years earlier, had convulsed the country.

All this cannot be stated too strongly; for on the rule of the Church of England in regard to the placing of the Communion Table depends, in a great measure, the right interpretation of the rubric which precedes the Consecration Prayer. We must presently enter upon an examination of that rubric itself. But before we begin to deal with it directly, it is desirable to pause still longer on what I have termed the second stepping-stone in the approach to our main subject.

VI.

THE "NORTH SIDE" OF THE TABLE.

Imaginary analogy with Jewish Altars—The late Archdeacon Freeman — "End" and "Side"—Mr. Beresford Hope's argument from length as opposed to breadth—Extreme importance of the change from the front to the north side—Indirectly it involves doctrine—Benefit of the change in promoting congregational worship.

WE are now brought to the consideration of the second part of the fourth of the rubrics which stand on the first page of our Communion Office. We have seen sufficiently the meaning of the first part, which concerns the placing of the Communion Table. Let us turn to that which relates to the Priest's position at that Holy Table on the occasions when he administers the Lord's Supper. The direction is simply that he is to "*stand at the north side of the Table.*" It has been shown that, in obedience alike to the canon and to the earlier half of this rubric, and in harmony too with historical evidence, so far as we can obtain it, we must view the Table as standing in the body of the church or in the chancel, conveniently for the hearing of the congregation, and at a distance, greater or less, from the east wall.

Now I dismiss, as utterly trivial and unworthy of notice, two theories, on which it is to be hoped no more time will be wasted. It has been suggested, by help of some curious analogies with Jewish altars, very inaccurately treated, that by the north side of the Lord's Table is meant the northern part of the west side, the Table itself being presumed to be placed altarwise. And again we have been asked to believe (on the same presumption of the "altarwise" position of the Table) that "side" cannot be synonymous with "end," and that "the north side" must now be viewed as transformed into the "west side," because the north *side* is now the north *end*. To each of these subjects I should think it mere loss of space and an utter trifling with the reader, if I were to devote more than one or two sentences.

As to the theory that "the north side" means "the northern part of the west side," it is a very significant fact that neither Mr. Beresford Hope nor Mr. Morton Shaw take any notice of this theory at all. They clearly view it as untenable, otherwise they would have availed themselves of the obvious advantage which it would have given them. It ought not, however, to be forgotten that this theory has been brought forward and refuted, that an attempt has been made, and made in vain, to justify the Eastward Position on this ground.[1] The last echo of this endeavour is to be found in some words used by Mr. MacColl. Writing of the direction to stand "at the north side of the Table" which I am surprised to find that he regards as "ambiguous," he says : "Two interpretations have been suggested. One is, that the north side means the *cornu Evangelii*, or north corner of the west side. This interpretation is not to be treated with contempt, for much may be said in favour of it."[2] He does not,

---

[1] See Appendix G. (Theory that "the north side" is the northern part of the west side.)
[2] *Lawlessness*, &c., p. 194.

however, adopt this interpretation, and it is evidently not worth while now to regard any grave argument as resting upon it. I should hardly have said even thus much on the subject, but for one honoured name, which I could not possibly forget during the writing of these pages. I am aware that the view, which I have here ventured to regard as obsolete, was held by the late Archdeacon Freeman.[1] Whether he ever discovered his mistake I do not know. Those who respected him most (and no one could be acquainted with him without respecting him) will admit that he was tenacious in his opinions, and that minute points often filled a large space in his acute and ingenious mind. But this cannot hinder his friends from remembering with affectionate regret his wide learning and exact scholarship, his playful humour, his steadfastness of character, and his earnest and gentle piety.

As regards any difficulty in understanding the north side to mean that boundary of the Table, whether it be broader or narrower, at which the Priest standing, with the Table in front, would look southwards, this difficulty does not really exist at all. The point may be settled sufficiently by the mere customary use of words. Even with the Lord's Table standing altarwise against the east wall, with its narrower boundaries on the north and south, this language is perfectly natural. I was recently conversing with a friend, whose sentiments were not quite coincident with mine, in the choir of a cathedral, on some restorative work connected with the Communion Table, and he spoke, quite instinctively, of

[1] See his *Rites and Ritual*, pp. 70-74.

its front and sides, meaning by the latter word its two narrow ends. And such language has always been used. Those who are acquainted with the controversies of Laud's time have met with complaints to this effect, that after the Table had been so placed as if it were an altar, curtains were added *on its sides.*[1] Even Euclid was quoted in connection with the quarrel between Bishop Williams and the Vicar of Grantham,[2] as Euclid has been quoted recently, to the effect that a parallelogram has four sides which are not necessarily equal.[3] But we have this matter settled for us in a most decisive manner by the rubric of the Scotch Liturgy of 1637, in which, though it is ruled that the Holy Table itself is to stand at the Communion time, "at the uppermost part of the chancel and church," yet the direction follows that "the Presbyter" is to stand "at the north *side or end* thereof," when he begins the service.[4] To this must be added what we find in Cosin's Durham book. He too desired, as we have seen, the Table to "stand alwayes in the midst at the upper end of the chancel or the church," but, even thus, that the Priest should stand at the north "*side or end*" of the Table.[5] It is quite evident from this either that these prelates

---

[1] It may suffice here to refer to a very useful little pamphlet entitled, *An Examination of the Walton-Scudamore Theory of the North Side Rubric,* p. 5.

[2] This famous quarrel has recently received new illustration in a paper read by Canon Venables at the last meeting of the Archæological Association.

[3] See the *Quarterly Review* for October 1874, p. 556, and the *Christian Observer* for July 1874, p. 528.

[4] See Dr. Bulley's *Tabular View of Varieties in the Communion and Baptismal Offices,* p. 5.

[5] I have before me a photograph of this part of Bishop Cosin's book; but the facts of the case may be seen in his *Correspondence,* as published by the Surtees Society.

viewed the term "side" and "end" as practically synonymous, or that if they had different senses, according as the Table might be placed lengthwise or breadthwise,[1] still in either case the Clergyman in the service was to direct his face to the south. No argument can be built here on any lengthwise position of the Table. And what if the Table were square? There is no rule in the Church of England which directs the Lord's Table to be made of any special form, and in any special proportions. It seems that Communion Tables were sometimes cut, under particular circumstances, in order that their shape might be changed. Canon Trevor tells us of one in his own immediate neighbourhood, which is square to this day.[2]

But Mr. Beresford Hope places this question of "end," or "side," in a light so extraordinary, that I must be allowed to devote a few lines to his argument. His theory was first put forth last summer in his " Hints towards Peace in Ceremonial Matters," and has since been repeated verbally in his work on " Worship in the Church of England."[3] The points of the argument are these, that " the usage of the Universal Church points to the celebrant standing at the *broad* side of the Lord's Table"—that on the old Basilican method, when he stood at the further side, facing the

---

[1] It is generally assumed that if the Lord's Table was in contact with the east wall, it was always placed breadthwise, if free in the chancel or nave, lengthwise. I can see no reason for taking either of these things for granted. The point of importance is whether the Priest stands with his face to the south, or his face to the east.

[2] *Disputed Rubrics*, p. 70. *Note.* The name of the place is Fraisthorp.

[3] These *Hints* were printed in April, 1874, and are embodied in the fifth chapter of the book on Worship.

people, he still "faced the *broad* side"—that, in the Church of England, when the Table was placed lengthwise, "the north side was really one of its *broad* sides, while likewise *this identical north side became the west one* as soon as the Table was turned round and put altarwise."[1] And he says again that "relatively to the 'Board'—whether 'Altar' or 'Table'—upon which the Holy Communion is celebrated, the position of the Minister himself *remains unaffected;*"[2] and, once more, "after the permanent change in position in the altar, the west side was *the actual north side turned round.*"[3] Thus the essential point of the matter is represented as one having reference not to the edification and convenience of the congregation, but to the dimensions and shape of the Table. Questions of worship are disregarded, if only the Priests stand correctly in reference to an ornament of the church. The "Lord's Board" is everything, the Lord's people, "the Royal Priesthood," is nothing. This great subject, after all, is not a matter of religious principle, but merely of geometry : everything in it turns upon the question of *breadth*. I have looked at this argument again and again (and others besides Mr. Beresford Hope have used it), and each time I look at it I am lost in wonder.

Assuming then—all questions of "end" or "side" being discarded—that the position of the officiating priest, as regulated by the initial rubric, is to be on the north of the Lord's Table, with his face directed to the south, I ask the reader to pause for a moment,

---

[1] *Worship in the Church of England*, pp. 170, 171.
[2] P. 181.
[3] P. 190.

and to consider the extreme significance of this regulation, introduced first into the Prayer Book in 1552, and maintained there ever since. It seems to me that we have in this sentence a very important landmark of ecclesiastical history and a most emphatic expression of the mind of the Reformed Church of England.

The two bare facts, that the southward position at the beginning of the Communion Service was adopted and prescribed,—and that this rule has stood since in full force and is still unaltered—are very remarkable. Whatever may be said in depreciation of the Prayer Book of 1552 (and in some quarters it is now the fashion to depreciate it), at all events the fourth of the initial rubrics has held its ground. It remained untouched in 1559 and 1662, and no proposal was made to alter it in 1689.[1] Why was the position of the officiating minister at the Lord's Table changed at all in 1552? and why was the change, once made, so tenaciously kept? no precedent can be quoted from ancient times. There is not a word in the New Testament which touches this subject: nothing can be more contrary to the spirit of the New Testament than the connecting of devotional and ministerial acts with the points of the compass. Nor was the new position suggested by any earlier liturgy. And yet it was maintained at each subsequent revision, notwithstanding the preference felt, at various times, by learned and excellent men, for a different position.

---

[1] The words proposed in 1689 were: "And the Minister shall at the North side of the Table say the Lord's Prayer with the collect following, all kneeling." *Copy of Alterations prepared, &c.*, printed in 1854.

There must in this deliberate and continued choice be an expression of the mind of the Church of England: and if we ask for the meaning of the selection of the north side [1] for the officiating minister, the answer, as it appears to me, must evidently be this, that it was intended to select for him a place, which, while convenient for congregational worship, should also be neutral in regard to theology, so that no expression should be given by a ceremony to any doctrine not contained in the words of the Prayer Book. It has been asserted lately in a document of high authority [2] that no doctrinal meaning has in the Church of England been formally assigned to the "celebrant's" position, and this assertion is undoubtedly correct. But it appears to me that, though not formally, yet virtually and inferentially, there is a doctrinal meaning in this rubric. Nothing indeed of this kind is stated in its words. But rubrics do not give the reasons for their existence. They express results and not processes; and yet, by the light of history, it may often be that through the result we can see the process.

And, connected with this rubric, another topic, just touched above, deserves consideration, as we pass on.

[1] It may be asked why the north side, and not the south, was selected. To this it would probably be enough to answer that the north would instinctively be felt to be the more natural. Archdeacon Freeman (*Principles of Divine Service*, Vol. II. Part ii. p. 464, *note*), referring to St. Luke i. 11., says: "The north or *right* side (the Presence being westward) was the side of sacrificial power;" and he adds: "The north is still the 'Gospel' side, the side for procuring peace by Jesus Christ; still the 'side' at which the earlier part of our Office is appointed to be said. . . . The consecration, from the 'Sursum Corda,' should doubtless be in the midst of the Holy Table or Altar."

[2] I allude, of course, to the recent allocution of the English Bishops, which was signed by all our Prelates except two.

Our manual of public devotion is emphatically, as its name denotes, a book of *Common* Prayer. All arrangements in it were made, so as to throw mere priestly functions into the background, and to promote the realisation of the congregational idea. This is manifestly part of the meaning of the rubric under our notice. But this has been so well stated in a recent paper by the Bishop of St. Andrews,[1] that I will make use of some of his words. He points out that this question, apart from all symbolical and doctrinal significance, has an important bearing on the comfort and religious benefit of congregations. Whatever be the case with the Clergy who are in the chancel, it is not at all the same thing to a poor man in a distant part of the church, whether the Clergyman "officiates at the Holy Table in the eastward position with his back to the congregation, or at the north end with his face sidewards." We are "pre-eminently a practical people" adds the Bishop; and he proceeds to say in reference to the rubric prefixed to the Consecration Prayer, to which we shall presently come, that "a regard for practical considerations" has in a great measure, hitherto, "determined the sense in which it was to be obeyed." I am disposed to quote at length the remarks which follow: "In addressing the people, we have felt it only reasonable to turn towards them; but in addressing Almighty God, who is present 'in the midst of us'[2]—while to turn away

[1] This paper on "The Eastward Position and the Convocation of York," was published last Easter in the *Times*.

[2] It is remarkable that Mr. Morton Shaw (in his Appendix A. p. 136, *note*), while quoting this scriptural phrase "in the midst of," objects to our understanding it as though "any mere geometrical centre" of Christian gatherings were referred to, while yet he does desire to localise our

from the people would make it more difficult for them to hear and follow the service—we have felt it no less reasonable to adopt a sideways position, whereby the strictly devotional parts of the service have been sufficiently distinguished, and this principle—which has produced in the Church of England a model of congregational worship such as no other Church, east or west, reformed or unreformed, has yet attained to—had, till of late years, been adopted and acquiesced in as the law of the Communion Table no less than of the Prayer Book." [1]

worship in what may truly be called a geometrical manner in regard to the eastern part of our churches, concerning which not a word is said in Scripture.

[1] The following remarks of Canon Simmons in the first of two excellent papers in the *Contemporary Review* (October 1866 and January 1867) are well worthy of attention :—" No doubt they did intend a change from the front ; and indeed a change from this position seems the natural complement of a book of *common prayer*. When the old prayers were first translated. . . . the priest was directed to 'begin with a loud voice the Lord's Prayer,' and to say the Prayer of Consecration ' plainly and distinctly,' instead of secretly as before. So long as the services were in Latin, it made no difference to the people whether they could hear or not. . . . When the first book came to be revised, four years later, the principle of 'Englishing' the prayers, namely, that public worship was henceforth to be *congregational*, as it was at the first, led to further change, and the priest was no longer to turn away from the people, now that they had been required either to join in with, or follow, the service." Vol. iii. p. 264.

VII.

THE PRIEST STANDING "BEFORE THE TABLE."

Intermediate rubrics in the Communion Service—True meaning of the words "Before the Table"—Discussion in Convocation at York—Testimony of the Welsh Prayer Book.

THE initial rubric, with which we have hitherto been dealing, from the very nature of the case, controls the whole of the Communion Service, and must be held to comprise within its scope the Consecration Rubric, unless reason can be shown to the contrary. We must now proceed to a direct examination of our main point; and on our way it is desirable to glance at the intermediate rubrics.[1]

It is to be observed that in no other rubric is any allusion found to any point of the compass. The introductory prayers are to be said by the priest "standing at the north side." In the rehearsing of the Commandments he is to "turn to the people." During the prayers which follow he is "to stand as before." Whatever this may mean, it is certainly not intended that he is to say these prayers in the eastward position. No rule is given for the Priest's position during the reading of the Epistle, Gospel, or Nicene Creed. After the sermon he is to "return to the Lord's Table:" but how he is to stand in refer-

---

[1] These intermediate rubrics, especially the earlier of them, will require very careful attention in any general revision of the rubrical directions of our Prayer Book. In two or three cases there is in them ground for real perplexity, and abundant opportunity for great disturbance of congregational comfort.

ence to it during the reading of the offertory sentences is not prescribed; nor is any rule given for his position while "humbly presenting the alms for the poor, and other devotions of the people," or while "placing upon the table so much bread and wine as he shall think sufficient" for the Communion.[1] In these matters much would depend, as regards convenience, on the placing of the Holy Table itself. No positional rubric is prefixed to the Prayer for the Church Militant or to the General Confession. In the Exhortation it is to be assumed that the priest "turns to the people" as he is directed to do in pronouncing the Absolution. He does not "turn to the Lord's Table" again till the service reaches the Trisagion, with or without a Proper Preface. In saying the Prayer of Humble Access he "kneels down at the Lord's Table," in the same direction, it is to be presumed, which he took when turning to it. This brings us to the Consecration Rubric, which is our present subject of inquiry.

This slight inspection of previous rubrics has cleared our ground. We have seen that up to this point there is no intimation whatever, even in the precatory parts of the service, of an eastward position or of any deviation from that southward position which the priest was directed to assume at the outset.

[1] It is frequently assumed that when the alms and other devotions are "humbly presented and placed on the Holy Table," and when the Priest, if there is a communion, "places upon the Table so much bread and wine as he shall think sufficient," these acts must be done in the middle of the Table; and hence it is sometimes inferred that from this point the precatory parts of the service must be gone through in this position. But there is no rule to this effect; and it is allowable to do both acts at the north end.

So we come to that which is the main point in all this argument, our inquiry into the true sense of that rubric preceding the Consecration Prayer, which we read thus: "*When the Priest, standing before the Table, hath so ordered the Bread and Wine, that he may with the more readiness and decency break the bread before the people, and take the cup into his hands, he shall say the Prayer of Consecration, as followeth.*" Our inquiry here is very simple. What is meant by "standing before the Table?" What was intended by these words when the rubric was written? In what sense ought we to understand them now? and what is the fairest and most candid mode of observing the rubric, if irregular usage has brought about any change as regards the placing of the Table itself?

Now, I confess I am unable to feel any difficulty as to the natural interpretation of this much-contested phrase. To stand "before the Table" is simply to stand "with the face towards the Table."[1] With the Table standing free, this condition could be satisfied on any one of its four sides. As to which of these four sides is to be chosen, this is left quite undetermined by the phrase itself. But another rubric, as we have seen, determines this point. It is settled at the outset of the service that the "north side" is to be selected.

A synonymous[2] expression would be "standing *at*

[1] If his back were turned to the Table, he might equally be said to be standing *before* it; but we are here concerned with certain acts which must be done with the face of the priest *towards* the Table.

[2] I regard, in fact, the "standing *before* the Table" in the Consecration Prayer as a mere change of *posture*, not of *position*, from the "kneeling *at* the Table" in the Prayer of Humble Access. And this is really the view of Mr. Malcolm MacColl. "The priest had been previously directed to 'turn to the people,' then to 'turn to the Lord's Table,' then to 'kneel

the Table," with this difference, indeed, that the preposition "*before*" is more natural and appropriate, and more in harmony with that openness and publicity which, as we shall see, are to characterise the whole of this solemn transaction; and, to prove that I am not straining a point, or dealing perversely with words, I will bring forward evidence, which suffices to remove any such imputation. And here let us look at this point as a merely verbal question, without any of that collateral proof which can be furnished in abundance and part of which will be the subject of the next section.

The proposal to take the word "before" in this simple, unsophisticated sense, has been treated as if it were absurd;[1] and when jokes are made on such a subject, they are indeed just so far useful in debate as to

down at the Lord's Table;' and now, 'standing before the Table,' he is directed to do certain things. Does not this imply that he had been kneeling 'before the Table?' Where is then the faintest scintilla of an indication that he is to change his place?" p. 190. The only difference between Mr. MacColl's view and mine is that he conceives the priest throughout (except when addressing the people) to be facing eastwards, I conceive him to be facing southwards, in obedience to the initial rubric. I may add that Mr. Beresford Hope points out himself (p. 180) that in the Prayer Book of 1549 "standing *afore* the midst of the Altar" is equivalent to "standing *at* God's Board." Again in Bishop Wren's notes we find the direction that in the Prayer of Humble Access the Priest is to "kneel *before* the Table." See the *Christian Observer and Advocate* for last April, p. 254. Even if this is to be taken as meaning that he is to kneel eastwards, still it follows that "kneeling *at*" is equivalent to "kneeling *before*."

[1] In his postscript Canon Trevor says (p. 104) that I am "always actuated by the best intentions," but that my view of the meaning of "before the Table," as stated at York, is "as if one should say that the cart before the horse means a cart having the horse before it." He adds in the paragraphs which follow, that the north part, whether side or end, was originally introduced and is defended to this day on "false pretences," that to get the Table back from its legalized position Laud was "guilty of a similar pretence," that in 1662 an attempt was made by an

turn the mind aside from a close examination of the question in hand. I will, however, leave behind this manner of treating the subject, and will turn to what was recently said in reference to it, with more gravity, in Convocation at York. This whole question is so completely a controversy of the day, that it is peculiarly important to observe what is passing around us in regard to it, during the present year.

In the debate which took place at York, last February, our Prolocutor laid stress on the verbal aspect of this phrase, as decisive in itself. He urged that the words "before the Table" interpret themselves in the sense of ruling that the priest must, at this time, stand on the western side of the Table, facing eastwards. His words were to this effect :—" What does *before the Table* mean ? Does it mean *behind the Table* or *under the Table* or *on the top of the Table?* or does it mean *before the Table?*" Now it is surely evident that a great historical question is not to be settled in this easy manner. We are looking, however, just now at its merely verbal aspect, and I desire to bring forward what was said on the same occasion by another speaker. I believe the true sense to have been expressed by the Dean of Manchester, in the same debate, when he proposed[1] that it should be

---

ambiguous word to legalize the Laudian "sophism," that when it failed, the defeated party reverted to an "equivocation," and that Wheatley constituted himself the advocate of a "further false pretence" and a "sophism." It would seem that all those who have touched the rubrics have been rogues, except Canon Trevor himself, whose honesty no one doubts.

[1] The proposal was made in an amendment, which was lost, to a motion, which was carried, to the effect that no present change in the Consecration Rubric is desirable. It is important to quote the exact words from the notice-paper. The Dean of Manchester, while agreeing that it is not

made lawful for the minister to stand "*before* the Table in *any* position," this choice being extended to the *northern, western,* or *eastern* sides. From the proposal to legalize this option I utterly dissent, believing it to be inconsistent with the other rubric which fastens upon the north side, and believing also, as I shall attempt below to prove, that it would be full of peril for the future. But this mode of interpreting the words "before the Table" I conceive to be entirely correct. And it is of some importance to mark this antithesis between the Dean of York and the Dean of Manchester, because with the Dean of St. Paul's they gave last year the weight of their names to a memorial claiming for all clergymen the right to assume at this Consecration Prayer the position which they conscientiously think right.[1] I will not pause here to remark that a system of rubrics constructed on the theory of giving free play to each individual conscience would set us afloat upon an ocean of disorder. I am only now calling attention to the fact that among those who signed the petition relating to these words there is difference of opinion as to the meaning of the words themselves, and that my interpretation is shielded by high authority from the charge of being ludicrous.

But here let me add, as a very important part of the verbal argument, the testimony supplied by the

---

desirable to alter any words in this rubric, recommended the addition of "a note which should declare that *any* position of the Priest standing *before* the Holy Table, may be lawfully adopted;" and this is made more explicit by the form of note suggested, wherein it should be "declared that the Priest may stand *before* the Table on the *west* side, or *east* side, or at the *north* end thereof."

[1] "Declaration" published in the *Guardian* of May 20th, 1874.

Welsh Prayer Book. This translation must give the impression of the meaning of the Rubrics at the time when it was made: and in it we find precisely the same preposition to represent *"before"* in the Consecration Rubric, as that which represents *"at"* in the rubric before the Prayer of Humble Access. This too is felt to be of the greater force, when we find that the word *"before"* in a rubric of the Marriage Service, which is often quoted in connection with this subject, is rendered by a different preposition.[1]

---

[1] "*The Psalm ended, and the man and the woman kneeling before the Lord's Table, the Priest, standing at the Table, and turning his face towards them shall say.*" Here the Welsh equivalent of "*before*" denotes "*in the front of.*" When this rubric in the Marriage Service is quoted, it is sometimes forgotten that it directs the married couple and the Priest to face each other.

VIII.

THE BREAD BROKEN "BEFORE THE PEOPLE."

This act the main point of the Rubric—Possible meaning of *coram populo*—Its true historical meaning—How understood by the Puritans—The act suggested by them—Evidence of the Savoy Liturgy—Religous meaning of this act—Testimony from devotional writers—The Welsh Prayer Book.

But now, leaving the ground of merely verbal criticism, let us attend closely to the spirit and real drift of the rubric under our attention. The words "before the Table" are in a subsidiary part of it. The language of the whole works up, so to speak, towards another point, the breaking of the bread "before the People." Whatever be meant by standing "before the Table," it is to be made subservient to the great end of breaking the bread openly in the sight of the congregation. Hence any interpretation of the former phrase, which makes that which is intended by the latter phrase to be impossible or difficult, cannot be correct. If a rubric is made to contradict itself, it has evidently not been treated with propriety and respect.

But here a great question is very confidently, and even vehemently raised. It is urged that the breaking of the bread "before the people" does not mean the breaking of it so that they may see the act—may be thus vividly reminded of what the Lord did at the Last Supper—and may by this method have their devotions quickened: but that the true meaning will be apprehended by comparing the attitude of the Priest, who is presumed at this moment to be making an offering to God, with the attitude of an eastern shepherd preceding his sheep, or of some one who is presenting a petition to a sovereign on behalf of those who stand behind him. It is sometimes stated very confidently that this must be the meaning of this phrase in the rubric, and can be its only true meaning,—sometimes more timidly suggested that this is a possible meaning,[1] and that therefore the eastward position of the "celebrant," though not compulsory, is allowable.

What we are concerned to know is not the possible meaning of this phrase, taken apart from its historical context, but its true meaning as determined by all the evidence that can be brought to bear upon it. And, first, if the meaning is merely this, that the priest, at this point of the service, is to lead the devotions by turning eastward at their head, as he may have done in saying the Litany at a faldstool, or reciting the Nicene Creed[2] at the Lord's Table, is it not obvious

---

[1] That "*coram populo*" might be used of a priest when engaged in an act of presentation with and on behalf of a congregation standing or kneeling behind him, is obviously true. But whether it is suitably so used in our service depends on what the priest is doing in reference to the congregation. If the chief meaning of the service is, not that they are making an offering to God, but that they are receiving a blessing ministered to them, then it is natural to give a different meaning to "*coram populo*." See Mr. Morton Shaw's pamphlet, pp. 31, 32.

[2] I will say once for all that there is a great difference between turning to the east during the recitation of the Creed, and turning in that direction during the Consecration Prayer. In the latter case the change of position has a distinct local reference to the Lord's Table, and to a transaction locally connected with it. The former practice, which to my mind has much to recommend it, may be viewed merely as part of the poetry of Public Worship.

that the rubric is very strangely worded? "Standing before the Table," he is so to order the elements that he may more conveniently "break the bread before the people." There is a stress laid by the very structure of the sentence upon its concluding words, which shews that its main point is to be found there. In answer to this objection I have met with only one argument, and that rests on a mere theory, besides in truth refuting itself. Mr. Morton Shaw suggests (and the Prolocutor at York brought forward this suggestion as if it were an authoritative decision) that these words might be intended to denote that the bread was to be broken publicly in the church during the service, instead of being so made ready previously in private in the vestry. And certainly the seemliness of this provision must be admitted by all. But does not this concede the very point which is disputed as to the meaning of the phrase? for thus, *publicity* instead of privacy, not *turning eastward* instead of turning in some other direction, is made to be the essential part of the meaning.

But now, to pass from verbal to historical arguments, is it conceivable that, if this were intended and understood to be the meaning of "before the people," when this rubric was proposed at the last revision, it can have been accepted without any recorded resistance? The Puritans demurred to a direction that the priest in pronouncing the Absolution should "turn to the people," alleging that it was desirable that he should turn to them always in all parts of the service.[1] Now, in this part of the ser-

---

[1] Mr. Beresford Hope's remark (p. 205) is important that, when the Bishops gave their answer, their words "*did not especially refer to the*

vice, so understood, they were likely to see something more than the mere saying of a prayer with the face turned away from the people. They knew very well the old Roman view of the subject, and they were made nervously solicitous by any apparent approximation to Romanism. They withdrew afterwards from the Church of England because they could not sanction the wearing of the surplice, or kneeling at the Holy Communion. Is it not quite certain that if they had understood that they were commanded " to break the bread before the people " in the sense of turning eastwards to do this, while the people were behind, we should have heard something of this objection also to the Act of Uniformity?[1]

But in naming the Puritans in connection with this rubric, we encounter something more than a mere argument from probability. There seems the best reason for believing that the rubric itself, if not directly due to their influence, was at least, in some degree, a concession to them. It must be carefully observed that until the last revision there was no provision for " the breaking of the bread " at the time of consecration in the Communion Service, and that this defect was noted very strongly from the Puritan side during the Savoy Conference. It may have been the custom with some, or many of the Clergy, to break the bread

Eucharist:" so also is the remark of the Bishop of St. Andrew's that if the words quoted by them from St. Augustine are closely pressed, they prove too much.

[1] Either the sense in which the rubric was accepted was the true sense or it was not. If the avowed meaning was that the minister was to turn eastwards during the Prayer of Consecration, it could not have been accepted without debate. If the avowed meaning was different from the true meaning, a fraud was practised at the time, and an injury inflicted on us.

at the time of consecration;[1] but there was no rule to this effect; though there is no doubt that others besides the Puritans were conscious of the need of some addition to the Prayer-Book, so as to make this imperative. We first encounter the subject in the following note, laid by the Puritans before the Bishops in connection with the Consecration Prayer: —" We conceive that the manner of the consecrating of the elements is not here explicite and distinct enough, and the minister's breaking of the bread is not so much as mentioned."[2] This is not very consistent, it may be observed by the way, with Mr. Morton Shaw's theory that the rule for the breaking of the bread "before the people" was merely a provision that it should not be previously broken in the vestry. But the point which I desire to urge here is that the Bishops made no reply to this objection, whereas to most of the Puritan objections their replies were very ready and very decided, and that soon afterwards, when the new Prayer Book appeared, it contained the rubric which we are now discussing. That which the objectors had so much desired was now introduced.

But the argument may be made more complete by examining the Savoy Liturgy itself, as printed in 1661, and presented by the Puritan divines to the bishops. In this book a most distinct rubric is inserted, thus: "*Then let the Minister take the Bread, and break it in the sight of the people, saying:* The body of Christ was broken for us, and offered once for all to sanctify

[1] The practice of the English Clergy, as to breaking the bread during the consecration, in the period between 1552 and 1662, is a subject well worthy of inquiry, if only sufficient materials exist for making the inquiry. See Appendix H. (The breaking of the Bread before 1662.)

[2] Cardwell's *History of Conferences*, p. 321.

us—behold the sacrificed Lamb of God, that taketh away the sins of the world;" and this is followed by equivalent words relating to the cup: "*In like manner let him take the Cup, and pour out the wine in the sight of the congregation, saying:* We are redeemed with the precious blood of Christ, as of a Lamb without blemish and without spot."[1] Can any one who reads and considers this calmly and candidly doubt that the phrase "before the people" in our book is synonymous with the phrase "in the sight of the people," which we find in the Savoy book?

But an objection of a religious kind to this view of the words is here presented to us, which objection, on being closely examined in the light of history, results in furnishing a new and very strong argument in favour of the view. It is contended that the actual sight of the breaking of the bread is not conducive to religious benefit; that devout people, at this moment of the service, would rather close their eyes than direct them to the manual acts of the minister: and then perhaps the objector will go so far as to quote the words of our twenty-fifth Article, in which we are told that "the Sacraments were not ordained of Christ to be gazed upon." Sometimes indeed this argument is pressed upon us with a sarcasm which is very unseemly, and in a manner hardly consistent with the reverence with which we ought to recollect our Lord's original institution of this Sacrament. In each one of the four accounts of the Lord's Supper, the breaking of the bread before the disciples is emphatically mentioned; and St. Paul adds that the Saviour Himself

[1] See Hall's *Reliquiæ Liturgicæ*, vol. iv. p. 70.

said, "This is my body which is *broken* for you." With such a scene in our recollection there is no excuse for employing satirical arguments in reference to those who desire their service to resemble as nearly as may be the original institution, and to be consciously, as it were, associated with those early disciples to whom the Lord was "made known in the breaking of bread."[1]

And such seems to have been the view of English Churchmen of various shades of thought, two hundred years ago, when an obvious want in our Prayer Book was supplied by this rubric. I said above that this objection, duly examined, supplies a strong argument in refutation of itself; and that this is the fact will be seen very clearly by some quotations from devotional books of the period. A considerable amount of evidence to this effect could be furnished. I will select some which is connected with three eminent names, none of which can be associated with any Puritan tendency, and all belonging to the period subsequent to 1662 and ranging over a time sufficiently long for our purpose.

The first name is that of Anthony Horneck, who wrote two devotional treatises on the Sacrament of the Lord's Supper. In his "Crucified Jesus" he says to the communicant: "See here what reflections thou art to make, when thou *seest* the Holy Bread broken

[1] I am here quite content to fall back upon the general impression produced by the narrative of the Last Supper, by the scene at Emmaus, by the account of what took place at Troas (Acts xx. 11), and by St. Paul's question (1 Cor. x. 16), "The bread, *which we break*, is it not the communion of the body of Christ?" This is really the sum of the information we possess regarding primitive observance in this part of the Eucharist; and if it is said that the information is scanty, this is no reason for neglecting it, but rather a reason for making the most of it.

before thine eyes at this Sacrament;" and in a later part of the volume he gives directions for devout acts of the mind corresponding with the acts of the priest during consecration.[1] In his "Fire of the Altar" he says: "I must now make some spiritual reflections on the breaking of the bread;" and these reflections begin as follows:—" Behold, O my soul, *thus* was thy Blessed Saviour's body broken: *thus* was His unspotted flesh torn asunder. O my sins, ye did this barbarous deed." And afterwards: "*See here, O my soul, the bread which is broke. Is it not the communion of the Body of Christ? See how many pieces are here,* which all make but one loaf."[2] We may question the wisdom or edification of instructions so minute for the communicant; but this very minuteness proves the point which is under our thoughts. And as to Horneck himself, and the time at which he lived,[3] he became Vicar of All Saints, Oxford, in 1663, was afterwards a Canon of Westminster, and was chosen preacher at the Savoy in 1671. His life was written by Bishop Kidder.[4] And now, to revert to Kidder's famous predecessor in the See of Bath and Wells, we find in Bishop Ken's own remarks on the Church Catechism such words as these: " When at Thy altar

---

[1] *Crucified Jesus* (1686), p. 168.

[2] *Fire of the Altar* (1690), p. 73.

[3] By birth he was a German, like Grabe.

[4] Kidder himself may be quoted to the same effect. He succeeded Ken in 1688. In 1684 he had published a book entitled *Convivium Cœleste*, in which this passage occurs at p. 167: " When we *see* the bread broken and the wine poured out, let us meditate at once upon the Passion of our Lord and the heinous nature of our sins that put Him to that pain. Think you *saw* your dearest Saviour hang upon the cross, that you were *eye-witnesses* of the shame and sorrow that He underwent. O think you *saw* the blood that He shed running down His body, that you *saw* the spear and the nails that pierced His hands, His feet, and side."

I *see* the bread broken, and the wine poured out, O teach me to discern Thy body there: O let *those sacred and significant actions* create in me a most lively remembrance of Thy sufferings."[1] And from Ken we turn to another prelate, whose name it is always natural to associate with his. Bishop Wilson, whose episcopate in the Isle of Man ranged from 1698 to 1755, wrote some "Instructions for the Indians,"[2] where, in answer to the supposed question on the part of the Indian, "You will now, Sir, let me know how this Sacrament is observed amongst Christians," the Missionary says, "They do it after this manner: First the minister of Christ placeth, or causeth to be placed,[3] upon a table in our churches a portion of bread and wine in the sight of the people. This bread and wine, which are to *represent* the sacrifice of Christ's Body and Blood, are sanctified, or set apart, for this holy use, by a giving thanks to God for all His favours, and especially for having sent His only Son to redeem us by His death, and by begging of Him that when

[1] "Church Catechism" in his *Prose Works*, p. 324.
[2] *Works* of Bishop Wilson in the Library of Anglo-Catholic Theology, vol. iv. p. 275.
[3] These words, "causeth to be placed," should be noticed by the way. There is a curious passage in the Treatise of Hickes, the Nonjuror, on *the Christian Priesthood* (Pref. p. liii., ed. 1707), from which it would appear that this rubric regarding the placing of the bread and wine at this time by the minister on the Holy Table was not very carefully observed in the early part of the eighteenth century. "As the disuse of this practice had taken deep root from the fifth year of King Edward VI., and helpt to obliterate the notion of the Christian sacrifice in the minds both of Priest and People; so this restored Rubrick, to the great reproach of the Clergy, was almost never since observed in Cathedral or Parochial Churches." This seems to me to show that this rubric was then regarded merely as having reference to convenience or propriety, and that the placing of the bread and wine on the Lord's Table was not generally viewed as an *oblation*. Hickes was, of course, desirous to assign a sacrificial meaning to this act.

we receive and eat and drink this bread and wine, we may be so far partakers of the sacrifice of His most blessed Body and Blood, as to share in all the benefits which He hath obtained for us by His death. At the same time he breaketh the bread into pieces, and poureth out the wine into a cup, to *represent* unto our senses, by these *outward* and *visible* signs, the death of Christ, whose body was *broken*, and blood *poured out*, upon the cross." It must be remembered that this paragraph occurs in a course of catechetical teaching; and it seems fair to use it for the sake of giving fulness and definiteness to Bishop Wilson's meaning, when he says, in a shorter manual of instruction,[1] "When God's minister breaketh the bread, and poureth out the wine, and blesseth them, let them put you in remembrance of Christ's Body broken and His Blood shed."

To the same effect Bishop Beveridge might be quoted:[2] but to St. Asaph I turn for corroborative testimony of a different kind. The Welsh translation of the rubrics in the Prayer Book of 1662 have preserved for us, unchanged, the impression of their meaning which prevailed at the time when the translation was made. And the present Bishop of that ancient see, whose accurate knowledge of his native language no one will dispute, tells us distinctly, in a note appended to his Second Charge, that the Welsh words for "before the people" denote "in the presence of the people," and *always involve the idea of sight*.[3]

[1] *Works*, vol. iv. p. 117. Library of Anglo-Catholic Theology.
[2] See Appendix I. (Bishop Beveridge on seeing the Bread broken.)
[3] *Charge delivered to the Clergy of the Diocese of St. Asaph*, Sept. and Oct. 1874. *Note* p. 38, where reference is made to the use of the same preposition in Isaiah i. 7.

When we connect all this argument with the fact that it belongs to a Table, not fixed altarwise against an eastern wall, but placed free in the chancel, or in the body of the church, so as to be in immediate contact with the congregation, we see how harmoniously all parts of this subject hang together. The true interpretation of the rubric which regulates the position of the consecrator depends on the rubric which regulates the position of the Table. The two subjects cannot, with a due regard to history, be treated separately from one another. Theoretically, however, they can be separated: and even if we are to leave the position of the Table an open question, we can find abundant historical evidence to prove that it has never been the custom or understood rule for the priest of the Church of England since 1552 to consecrate with his face to the East. To this narrower view of the subject we may now turn.

IX.

USAGE BEFORE 1662.

Custom from 1552 onwards—Evidence from Bishop Jewel—Wren's approval of Jewel—Bishop Wren's defence of himself—Archbishop Laud's chapel—His answer to his accusers—Bishop Cosin's answer to his own accusers—Defence of these three prelates against the charge of dishonesty.

HITHERTO the position of the "celebrant" has been treated chiefly in its historical connection with the placing of the Lord's Table. Let us now take the first subject separately, and turn to the simple consideration of actual usage in the Church of England. This usage must very seriously either weaken or strengthen the arguments which have been drawn out above. If it could be shown to have been the custom of the Clergy of the Church of England since 1552, when the rubric relating to the "North Side of the Table" was first introduced, to have consecrated in the eastward position, then it would be necessary to reconsider all these arguments, however perplexing the inconsistency might appear. If the contrary custom has prevailed, then we have in this matter that consistency between rule and practice which it is very difficult to refute. If there has been a general habit in one direction with occasional exceptions, then it is our duty to ascertain the number of these exceptions, the circumstances under which they have occurred, and the reasons by which they have been justified and thus to enable ourselves to estimate them at their true value.

It is obviously desirable to divide such a survey into two periods, separated from one another by the great date of 1662. The usage, indeed, with which we are more immediately concerned is that which succeeded this chronological landmark; for our true starting-point for present practice is the last revision of the Prayer Book, when the rubric in question was first introduced. Still, the opinions and controversies of the earlier period led by paths more or less direct to the results which we have inherited; and the subject would be treated very incompletely, if we were to take no note of the ecclesiastical practices which preceded the Restoration.

During this earlier period the rubric in question did not exist, but another rubric did; and the rule concerning "the North side of the Table" being in full force during the whole of this time, and no other rubric being existent which suggested any change of position at the Consecration Prayer, I am not aware of any reason for imagining the prevalence of any habit out of harmony with these facts.[1] But if historical instances can be given to show that the harmony subsisted, they are certainly of some value. I will refer chiefly to circumstances connected with the names of Bishop Wren, Archbishop Laud, and Bishop Cosin; but first I will refer to a circumstance, which seems to have been somewhat overlooked, associated with the name of another and earlier bishop.

[1] Any one examining a Prayer Book of 1552 or 1559 would assume that all the Service was said at the north side: for no other place is mentioned or hinted at. Does "orientation" at the Consecration Prayer depend on the words "before the Table?" Then it was not prescribed before 1662. And further, what authority is there now for any "orientation" in the Service previous to this prayer?

The following sentence from Bishop Jewel has been recently used in this controversy, and very naturally:[1]—"What father or doctor taught us that the priest should hold the bread over his head, and *turn his back to the people?*" This mere sentence is of some importance; but, taken in conjunction with a fact which comes to view in some Visitation Articles of the period subsequent to Jewel's death, it acquires a more emphatic meaning. The quotation is from a sermon on a text from the prophet Haggai,[2] and shows clearly the mind of Bishop Jewel on the subject. But on consulting a large number of the originals of such Visitation Articles, which are preserved in the Library of Jesus College, Cambridge,[3] I observed that a copy of Jewel's "Apology" was in some of them reckoned as one of the "ornaments" of the church. I may particularly specify the articles issued by Wren when he was Bishop of Hereford.[4] This is not the only instance of the kind; but for obvious reasons it is very apposite to our purpose. Just as the inquiry in such articles whether there be

---

[1] This passage is quoted in an excellent pamphlet by the Rev. J. Bardsley, Rector of Stepney, *Eucharistic Vestments and the Eastward Position*, p. 16.

[2] Hagg. i. 2—4. See the Edition of Bishop Jewel's *Works*, published by the Parker Society, II. pp. 990, 991.

[3] I owe the opportunity of seeing these original documents to the kindness of the Rev. Dr. Corrie, Master of Jesus College. Some of these Visitation Articles are not found in the collection published in the Appendix to the *Second Report of the Ritual Commissioners*.

[4] The requirement that Jewel's *Apology* should be among the ornaments of the Church seems to have been a great point with Wren. We find it both when he was Bishop of Hereford and also when he was Bishop of Norwich. This fact helps us to appreciate at its true worth the argument drawn from the consecration of a church in Herefordshire, on which great stress has recently been laid. See Appendix J. (Consecration of Abbey Dore Church).

in the church "a faire large comely surpless with sleeves," is of some moment in regard to the question of Vestments, so I venture to think the inquiry whether there be in it "a fairly bound copy" of this book, gives some help towards determining the view then current concerning the Eastward Position. The churches were expected to be officially supplied with a copy of a theological treatise by a Bishop who had written emphatically against that position. It is to be observed that we are concerned here not simply with Jewel's opinion, but with Wren's acceptance and approval of his writings.

But let us come to more direct evidence affecting Wren, and afterwards pass on to Laud and Cosin. It is evident that the opinion and practice of these three men are likely to present the Church of England on the side most favourable to the advocates of the Eastward Position. It will be remembered, too, that I am here treating the position of the Lord's Table itself as if it were an open question.

It is well known that Wren was accused both of placing the Lord's Table altarwise against the east wall, and of saying the Consecration Prayer with his face to the east, at a Table so placed. His answers, calmly and deliberately written,[1] to these two accusations, we find in the "Parentalia." The former he admitted; the latter he denied—or, at least, he declared that any such action was a matter of mere accident and convenience, and thus placed it altogether out of the range of principle. His words are as follows:—"He acknowledgeth that for the better taking of the bread, and for the easier reaching both

[1] See above, p. 6. Note.

of the flagon and the cup, because they stood upon the table further from the end thereof than he, being but low of stature, could reach over his book unto them, and yet still proceed on in reading of the words without stop or interruption, and without danger of spilling the bread and wine, he did in Tower Church in Ipswich, anno 1636, turn unto the west-side of the table; but it was only while he rehearsed the fore-mentioned collect, in which he was to take the bread and the wine, and at no other time. And he humbly conceiveth that although the rubric says that the minister shall stand at the north-side of the table; yet it is not so to be meant as that upon no occasion during all the communion time he shall step from it. For it is usual to go before the table to read the Epistle and Gospel, and necessary to go from the table to the pulpit to preach, and, with the Bason to receive the offerings, if any be; and with the Bread and Wine to distribute to the Communicants. Inasmuch, therefore, as he did stand at the north-side all the while before he came to that collect, wherein he was to take the bread and the wine into his hands, and as soon as that was done, thither he returned again, he humbly conceiveth it is a plain demonstration that he came to the west-side only for more conveniency of executing his office, and no way at all in any superstition, much less in any imitation of the Romish priests; for they place themselves there at all the service before, and at all after, with no less strictness than at the time of their consecrating the bread and wine."[1] If any

[1] *Parentalia*, pp. 103, 104. Three things of some importance come clearly to view incidentally from this passage. In the first place, Wren distinguishes between the "north side" and the "west side;" hence, in his view, the north side cannot be the northern part of the west side. Next,

one, after reading these words, adduces Wren in justification of making the Eastward Position so serious a matter of principle that it cannot be given up, he commits an offence against the prelate's memory. Wren treats this position simply as a matter of accident or convenience.

From Wren let us now turn to Laud; and first I will put in evidence the engraving of the chapel which was arranged by him when he was Bishop of St. David's. I cannot help thinking that some persons have mentioned this engraving in debate without having seen the thing itself. It will be found opposite page 123 of the book called "Canterburie's Doom," published in 1646;[1] and nothing, as it seems to me, could tell its story more plainly than "the cushion for the service-book," at the north end of the Lord's Table (which is placed altarwise) with "the kneeling stoole covered and stuffed" in the same place below. And it must be remembered that Prynne, who published this, was Laud's most bitter enemy, that he wished to make him as Popish as he could, and that, if the chapel had afforded evidence of the habit or intention of consecrating in the Eastward Position, the evidence would certainly have been produced.[2]

---

he uses the word "side" as synonymous with "end;" this is certain, because he admitted that he had placed the table altarwise. Thirdly, he entirely disowns any turning to the east during other precatory parts of the Communion Service; hence he did not do this, for instance, in the Prayer of Humble Access.

[1] This chapel is said to have been arranged after the model of that of Bishop Andrewes; thus it affords testimony to the practice of that prelate as well as of Laud himself.

[2] Among "this arch-prelate's manifold traitorous artifices," Prynne notes his placing of the Table altarwise against the wall as "not consonant

And now we must connect this pictorial testimony with the words which Laud used at a later period, when he was Archbishop of Canterbury, in reference to the rubric of the Scotch Liturgy before the Prayer of Consecration. That rubric, as is well known, was different from ours, and did give freedom (if the Table was placed altarwise against the east wall) to the priest to consecrate, as well as to order the elements, with his face towards the east. The words are as follows:—"*Then the Presbyter, standing up, shall say the Prayer of Consecration as followeth, but then, during the time of consecration, he shall stand at such a part of the Holy Table where he may with the more ease and decency use both his hands.*"[1] To this grave exception was taken. It was viewed, very naturally, as meaning somewhat more than it literally expressed. But what was Laud's answer? "They say this very remove of the Presbyter during the time of consecration, upon trial imports much. The Rubric professes that nothing is meant by it, but that he may use both his hands with more ease and decency about that work; and I protest in the presence of Almighty God I know no other intention herein than this."[2] If Laud thought it necessary to use an oath when he made this

---

to Queen Elizabeth's injunctions, which require the Communion Table, when the Sacrament is distributed, to be removed and "placed in such sort, &c." Is it conceivable, if Laud had been in the habit of saying the Consecration Prayer towards the East, that Prynne would not have noted this "traitorous artifice" likewise?

[1] Either in Keeling's *Liturgiæ Britannicæ* (p 214), or in Bulley's *Tabular View of Variations* (p. 53), this Scotch rubric can be seen in very instructive juxtaposition with our own.

[2] See Canon Craigie Robertson's invaluable volume, *How shall we Conform to the Liturgy of the Church of England?* (third ed., 1869) pp. 290, 291.

statement, it does not seem very respectful to his memory to quote him in defence of the theory that consecrating at the Eucharist in the Eastward Position is a matter of principle. We have seen that he did not himself, when at St. David's, consecrate in that position. It is almost an insult to him to bring forward his name and practice as giving sanction for the ceremonial act for which every possible shelter is now so eagerly sought.

The name of Cosin is, for the purposes of the present argument, still more important than that of Laud; for Cosin, like Wren, belongs to 1662 as well as to 1640, and moreover he is believed, whether correctly or not, to be the author of our present consecration-rubric. The weight of his authority is sometimes set before us, very neatly and compactly, in this way. Cosin wrote the rubric;[1] Cosin was accused of consecrating in the Eastward Position: therefore the rubric means that we are to consecrate in that position. But a case of this kind is hardly complete when it is rested on the accusation only, without the defence being heard. By a strange freak of controversy Bishop Cosin's answer is constantly kept out of view, while the charge brought forward by Smart is unceasingly repeated.[2] In Convocation at York, last February, the accusation of Cosin was made prominent; and I was glad of the opportunity of undertaking his defence.[3]

[1] I will not attempt to decide whether Bishop Cosin did write this rubric or not: but it is well worth while to observe that in the Bishop's private notes, on which Mr. Morton Shaw seems to rely for this opinion (see his pamphlet, pp. 28 and 49), great stress is laid on *breaking the bread before the people* and nothing said of *the priest standing before the table.*

[2] Mr. Beresford Hope (p. 194) makes the accusation very prominent, but passes over Cosin's denial in absolute silence.

[3] The same duty was discharged, quite independently, by Canon Swainson, in the Lower House of the Convocation of Canterbury.

The charge ran thus:—" Concerning Dr. Cosens bowing and officiating towards the East, with his back to the people, and several other postures which he used before the altar." His defence was given thus: "Denieth that he did ever officiate with face purposely towards the East; but he constantly stood at the north side or end of the Table, to read and perform all parts of the Communion Service there; saving that the bread and wine being usually placed in the middle of the Table, which is about seven foot in length, he might haply do so as others did there before him (though he remembreth not to have done so these twelve years) and step to the former part thereof, to consecrate and bless those elements, which otherwise he could not conveniently reach."[1] Can we suppose, if Cosin had been in the habit of consecrating Eastwards during those twelve years, and had made this habit a matter of vital principle, as is done by some who quote his authority, that he should have totally forgotten this? Or must we resort to the shocking conclusion that in a matter of such solemn import he told a deliberate falsehood? Or again, are we to imagine that we have here one of his early utterances, and that in a later period of his life he changed both his opinion and his practice? When Smart brought forward his accusation, Cosin was a

---

[1] *Court of High Commissioners at Durham*, published by the Surtees Society, pp. 215—218. It should be remarked that four things come incidentally, but very clearly, into view here. (1) Cosin uses "end" and "side" as equivalent terms. (2) Herein his language is consistent with that which he used afterwards in the rubric which he proposed for acceptance. See above, p. 49. (3) He distinguishes the "north" end or side in the most emphatic way from the "west" or "former" side. (4) He utterly rejects all thought of turning eastwards generally during the precatory parts of the Communion Service.

Prebendary of Durham. After 1660 he was Bishop of Durham. Did he modify his views on this subject during that interval? There is no proof that he did, so far as I am aware. On the contrary, there are two grounds of probability for supposing that it is even less reasonable to quote him at the later period than the former. First, the conversion of his son to the Church of Rome is believed to have given to his liturgical opinions a more Protestant colour;[1] and secondly, the placing of the Lord's Table permanently at the east end of the church was not officially allowed in 1662, whereas the Bishops were endeavouring to procure this placing of it when he was a Prebendary of Durham.[2]

When the argument drawn from the very words used by Wren, Laud, and Cosin, is strongly urged, it is sometimes replied (and I heard this in conversation, besides having seen it in print) that these three men were on trial, and possibly in danger of their lives, and therefore spoke with what is termed "economy." They were not bound to put weapons in the hands of their enemies; moreover, those enemies would not have been able to understand their religious convictions; thus they concealed their true reasons and alleged what was merely superficial and accidental; and in this way they sought to secure their own safety.[3] But is it not evident that, on this supposi-

[1] See Cosin's *Correspondence* (Surtees Soc.) Introd. p. xxxvii.

[2] It cannot be too carefully remembered that the troubles which took place about 1640, in consequence of the attempt of various Bishops to fix the Communion Tables permanently at the upper end of the chancels were previous to the final ratification of the rubric which, in harmony with the canon, distinguishes between their position "at the communion time" and at other times.

[3] I am utterly perplexed when I see the extraordinary laxity with which both Mr. Morton Shaw (pp. 40, 41, 44, 45) and Mr. Beresford Hope

tion, they lost an opportunity of asserting a great principle, and that they showed they were as far as possible from possessing the spirit of martyrdom? Wren, in fact, as we have seen, wrote under no such pressure. Laud distinctly swore that he knew of no reason except that which he stated.[1] Of a character so distinguished and influential as that of Cosin it is very difficult to believe that it was utterly destitute both of courage and honesty. Such an apology, made on behalf of these men for such action, when great principles were at stake, shocks our moral sense. Either the assuming the Eastward Position at the time of consecration was with these bishops not a matter of principle, but a matter merely of accident and convenience, or they prevaricated. There is no escape from this dilemma. If the latter supposition is true, I cannot understand why such deference is paid to their authority. I am astonished that men can continue to reverence the idols whom they have dishonoured; and I cannot help remembering that a century earlier, when danger did arise out of questions connected with the Holy Eucharist, three other

(pp. 194, 195) treat the question of truthfulness in these prelates. Mr. Malcolm MacColl (pp. 199—201) uses the word "economy;" and with great pain I add that both he and Mr. Morton Shaw justify this method of self-defence by referring to the example of our Blessed Lord, to Whom the hearts of men were open, and Who taught them as they were able to receive the truth. It would have been better to have justified these prelates by referring to such a parallel as that which Canon Robertson quotes from Dr. Littledale, "We who, in our own day, have known lights on the altar excused on the ground of the darkness of a chancel, need feel no surprise at their employing the only argument to which their adversaries would listen." *How Shall we Conform, &c. ?* p. 291.

[1] From the time when I first became acquainted with Archbishop Laud's *Private Devotions*, as published by F. Faber in 1839, I have been very reluctant to think that he can have been a bad man.

English bishops did not prevaricate to save their lives. If we are driven by the exigencies of controversy to view our subject in this way, then, to say the least, we see Cranmer, Latimer, and Ridley on a much higher moral eminence than Cosin, Wren, and Laud.

X.

HISTORY OF USAGE SINCE 1662.

Settlement of 1662—Contentment of the Puritans with the position of the consecrating priest—This view confirmed by the events of 1689—No choice admitted by this rubric under the Act of Uniformity—Consecration still in the Southward Position, when the Table was placed altarwise—Liturgy of the Nonjurors—View of Wheatley, Mant, and Blunt—The Eastward Position a novelty.

BEFORE proceeding to a short review of the history of usage between the Restoration and our own day, in respect of the consecrator's position at the Holy Eucharist, it is desirable that we look at two broad features of the settlement of 1662, which really cover a great deal of the ground before us. It has already been shown [1] how distinct that settlement was in regard to the placing of the Holy Table itself, a question on which this other question largely depends. Here, however, we put that topic on one side. We are separating in thought two subjects which are not separable historically, and considering simply the position of the "celebrant," leaving that of the Holy Table itself an open question.

Now we remember that those whom we term "Puritans" (though many of them would now be regarded as loyal Church of England men) were within the Church till the Act of Uniformity was put in execution. We have seen, too, that they raised

---

[1] See Sections III. and V.

no question as to the mode of placing the Communion Tables in the churches, clearly because they were satisfied with the rubric and the canon which related to this subject. Is it not quite certain that they would have raised very serious questions, unless they had been satisfied, likewise, in regard to the position of the officiating minister during the Communion Service? Is it not quite certain, in fact, that one reason for their contentment in reference to the placing of the Table was because it was a security against the assuming of the Eastward Position during the act of consecration? This subject has been touched before;[1] but it is important to recur to it at this point in order to make it clear what the common understanding must have been in 1662 regarding the "celebrant's" position.

In confirmation of this view it is natural to refer here to the attempted revision of the Prayer Book which was made in 1689. No legislation, indeed, took place in consequence of this attempt, but we know the recommendations which were made by those to whom the task was entrusted.[2] We know, too, that the contemplated revision was undertaken with the view of satisfying, and, if possible, reconciling Dissenters. Yet we find no change proposed in the rubric which prescribes the position of the minister at the very point of the service concerning which the Dissenters were most sensitive. It is quite evident that on this point they needed no reassurance. It was not the custom of the English Clergy to consecrate otherwise than at "the North side of the

---

[1] See above, pp. 38 and 66.
[2] See *Note*, p. 52

Table:" and if it is urged that by this time the Table was frequently, if not generally, placed, even during the time of communion, as the Altar used to be, at the upper end of the chancel, this only gives strength to the present part of my argument; for it is thus shown that even when the altarwise position of the Table was resumed, this change did not carry the consequence of an eastward position on the part of the consecrating priest.

But let us now turn to what I have called a second broad feature of the settlement of 1662. The rubrics of this date are often appealed to as though they allowed of *choice* in the adopting of ceremonial acts. A great point is made now of liberty and toleration. All that is claimed, in fact, even by extreme Ritualists, is freedom of choice. They reiterate again and again (and, no doubt, with perfect truth) that they have no wish to interfere with others if only they may be allowed to do what they themselves think right. This always seems to me a very suspicious circumstance. For surely if there is any one characteristic of the great Act of Uniformity it is that it was *imperative*.[1] If there could have been an authorised option as to the wearing of the surplice or as to kneeling during the administration of the

---

[1] It is possible that some of the earnest advocates of choice in matters of Ritual have not read the preamble of the Act of Uniformity, which begins thus: "In regard that nothing more conduceth to the settling of the peace of the nation, nor to the honour of religion, than *an universal agreement in public worship*, and to the intent *that every person may certainly know the rule to which they are to conform, &c.*" And this is in harmony with one of the answers of the Bishops to the Presbyterians at the Savoy Conference: "There is no such way to the preservation of the peace as for all to return to *the strict use and practice of the form.*" — Cardwell's *History of Conferences*, p. 336.

Holy Communion, the history of Dissent in England would have been very different from that which we know it to have been. Nothing, as it appears to me, could be more contrary to the whole spirit and genius of 1662 than the sanction of alternatives in such matters, and the allowance (as men speak now) of a *maximum* and a *minimum* in ceremonial acts.¹ I shall have occasion to refer to this subject again at the close of this volume; but it is of great consequence to call attention to it here, for it bears intimately on every part of the question before us. If I am right in this general view, then either the Eastward Position during the consecration prayer is compulsory upon us, or it is not legally allowable at all.²

But let us come at once to that modification of

---

¹ This has been well pointed out by the Rev. R. W. Kennion in his Letter on *The Vestments and the Rubric*, reprinted (1867) from the *Times*. What is said there in reference to the costume of the officiating priest is at least equally applicable to his position : " A notion has been suggested by a leading advocate of Ritualism that though it was not intended to compel anything but the surplice, the Rubric was left as it is in order to allow an alternative, so that the vestments might be worn by those who liked them. Surely no one could say this who reflected what the principles of the High Church party of that day were. The words of the Rubric give not the slightest colour to the notion. Whatever particular things are to be understood by the word ' ornaments,' they are all prescribed with the same absoluteness. If albs and tunicles are included, they are not permitted, but ordered, just as the surplice is ; and the man is as truly a Nonconformist who omits the one as the other," p. 20. And Mr. Kennion proceeds to quote what Lord Clarendon says in his *Autobiography* (ii. 296) of the Act of Uniformity. " By this Act there was an end put to all the liberty and licence which had been practised since His Majesty's return. Whatever clergyman did not fully conform to whatever was confirmed in that Book was *ipso facto* deprived of his benefice, and the patron might present as on a lapse, so that it was not in the King's power to give a dispensation to any man."

² I am not here arguing in favour of extreme stiffness in the law of ceremonial, but only contending that there was this stiffness in 1662, and that therefore the Consecration Rubric must have had a definite meaning.

the question before us, which inevitably arises on our reaching the time when the position of the Lord's Table was really changed, and when it became customary, not only "at the Communion time," but at all times, to fix it against the east wall. That the change did take place is certain. We see the results of it in every church which we enter. That the change took place gradually and silently, and that, with a few exceptional cases, it became very general, after no long interval below the great date of 1662, is most probable.[1] It is obvious that it would be convenient: for the removing of the Holy Table, from time to time, for the administration of the Lord's Supper, must have caused trouble to churchwardens and others. Moreover, those who would be likely to raise objections to a customary eastward placing of the Table, were not now, for the most part, within the Church of England, but organised into systematic Nonconformist bodies outside; and as to any illegality which might be committed in thus setting aside the directions alike of the rubric and the canon, this would not attract much attention, and the Bishops would not be likely to interfere. The eighteenth century was, on the whole, an easy time in matters ecclesiastical.

The question before us, however, at the present moment relates simply to the position of the "celebrant" under the changed circumstances of the placing of the Lord's Table. We have seen that the intention of the rubric of 1662 was that he should look southwards in this part of the service. Did it now become customary that he should look eastwards at

[1] See above, pp. 38, 39.

this time, in consequence of the changed position of the Table? We have the most distinct evidence that nothing of the kind took place, but, on the contrary, that consecrating in the Southward Position was still the recognised rule in the Church of England: and some of this evidence is very curious.

Let me refer, first, to the Nonjurors. They certainly in the early part of the eighteenth century represented the theological opinions of Laud and Cosin, more nearly than did any other persons in the country. Moreover, being trammelled by no connection with the State, they were free to adopt any ecclesiastical arrangements and to make their own rubrics. On examining their Prayer Book, printed in 1718, we at once observe two very significant changes. The Lord's Table is now again an "Altar;" and this "Altar" is to be placed, and *fixed*, so far as we see, at the east end of the church or chancel. And yet what do we read concerning the position of the priest? We read the following very remarkable rubric:—"*Note, that whenever in this Office the Priest is directed to turn to the Altar, or to stand or kneel before it, or with his face towards it, it is always meant that he should stand or kneel on the North side thereof.*"[1] This rubric conclusively settles two things of very great importance. First it gives a decision as to the use of words. To stand or to kneel "before" the Altar or Table is to stand or to kneel "with one's face towards it," just as I have con-

[1] Hall's *Fragmenta Liturgica*, vol. v. p. 10. In the *Directorium Anglicanum* (p. 38) is a sentence, which, I confess, I do not understand. "The corresponding rubric in the Nonjurors' Office explains their north side to mean the north end; and thereby shows by implication that the then practice of the Church of England *did not.*"

tended above.¹ This condition would be satisfied on any one of its four sides. Here it is ordered to be fulfilled by standing on the north, though the "Altar" is placed north and south. But a second point is determined here. These truest representatives of Laud, who had restored the "Altar," and replaced it in its old fixed position, still found it natural to direct the priest to stand and kneel during the Communion Office, with his face towards this "Altar," but on its north side.² It is somewhat remarkable that Mr. Beresford Hope, who is seldom at fault in minute points of ecclesiastical archæology, should not have noticed this liturgy of the Nonjurors.³ Mr. Morton Shaw does make mention of it, admitting that they "represented pre-eminently that section of the Revisers of 1662, who did their best, at that time, to give a higher tone to the worship and ritual of the English Church;" and he endeavours to meet the case by urging that the Nonjurors were inconsistent with themselves, and that in some of their liturgies of a subsequent date it is directed that consecration is to take place in front of the Lord's Table with the face eastwards.⁴ This is interesting as an historical fact; and nothing could be more natural than that the Nonjurors, set free from the law and custom of the Established Church in this respect, should have drifted back to that which was the rule before the Reformation. But this

---

¹ See pp. 58, 59, and the *Notes*.

² As an illustration of the spirit of this Prayer Book, it is enough to quote the first sentence of the Preface : "The Eucharistic Sacrifice, being the most efficacious means for pardon and grace, ought to be performed with proportionable care and solemnity."

³ Neither does Mr. MacColl take any notice whatever of this important evidence.

⁴ *The Position of the Celebrant*, &c., p. 47 and Appendix B.

is no refutation of the inferences which I have drawn above from this rubric. It still remains true that in the Church language of about 1700 "before the Table" was not understood to mean "in front of the Table facing eastwards," but "on the north side of it facing southwards."

The next reference shall be to a very well-known book by a learned and loyal member of the Church of England, but to a particular edition of that book. In the second edition, dated 1714, of "The Church of England's Man's Companion, or a Rational Illustration of the Harmony, Excellency, and Usefulness of the Book of Common Prayer," I find a frontispiece which represents a priest in the act of consecration at the Holy Communion. In the chancel are the people reverently kneeling eastwards: the Holy Table is fenced off by rails, and standing as we are accustomed to see it stand: the priest is at the north end, standing and facing southwards: above is a representation of our Lord in the heavens, an addition which is worthy of mention, because it is hardly consistent with any mere Zuinglian view of the Holy Eucharist.[1] A picture of this kind supplies, as it seems to me, very important evidence, because it shows to us what was customary at the time to which it belongs.[2]

But it is further important to mark the explanation given in words of that which is represented in a picture; especially since Wheatley was recognised as the standard liturgical writer of his day in the Church of England. His words on this subject

---

[1] Over the head of the Saviour is the text, Heb. vii. 25, and under the altar before which He stands is the text, Rev. viii. 3, 4.

[2] See Appendix K. (Evidence from Engravings.)

have often been quoted; but they acquire freshness and force by being placed in juxtaposition with this picture.

"If it be asked," he says, "whether the priest is to say the prayer standing *before* the Altar, or at the *north end* of it,[1] I answer, At the *north end* of it; for, according to the rules of grammar, the participle *standing* must refer to the verb *ordered*, not to the verb *say*;[2] so that whilst the priest is ordering the bread and wine, he is to stand before the Altar; but when he says the prayer, he is to stand, so that he may with the more readiness and decency break the bread before the people, which must be on the north side. For if he stood before the Table, his body would hinder the people from seeing, so that he must not stand there, and consequently he must stand on the north side, there being in our present Rubric no other place mentioned for performing another part of this office." And Wheatley adds: "In the Romish Church, indeed, they always stand before the Altar during the time of consecration, in order to prevent the people from being eye-witnesses of these operations in working their pretended miracle."

And this became the recognised interpretation of the Consecration Rubric, the theory and practice corresponding with one another, throughout the eighteenth century, and during the present century, till about five-and-twenty years ago.[3] Thus, to quote very

---

[1] We should note here how Wheatley assumes, as a matter of course, that "north end" is synonymous with "north side."

[2] See below, p. 98, on the grammatical analysis of the sentence.

[3] Besides Bishop Mant and Professor Blunt, who are quoted here, Mr. Bardsley adduces, to the same effect, Dr. Nicholls, whose notes on the Book of Common Prayer were published in 1710. Archdeacon Yardley

eminent liturgical writers of the later part of this period of nearly a hundred and fifty years, Bishop Mant, adopting Wheatley's view, says: "This seems to have been ordered for the purpose of avoiding the fashion of the priest's standing with his face towards the east, as is the Popish practice:"[1] and Professor Blunt observes of the priest's position, after the elements have been ordered, "This done, he returns to the north side, and breaks the bread and takes the cup, 'before the people,' i.e., *in their sight*—the Church not wishing to make the manner of consecration, as the Romish priest does, a mystery. .... So that they mistake this Rubric altogether, I apprehend, and violate both its letter and spirit, who consecrate the elements with their backs to the people, after the manner of the Church of Rome."[2] It must be added further that this is the view of the matter upon which the "Purchas Judgment" is based.

In the preceding paragraphs notices of opinions and practices, in regard to the position of the consecrator, have been mixed together; but the purpose of this section is to show that both opinion and practice in the Church, through the whole period between the Restoration and our own day, pronounce most distinctly for the Southward Position. I do not at all doubt that there were sporadic cases of the Eastward Position, both of earlier and later date, throughout the whole of this period. I frankly confess that in our own times there has been a larger

---

(1728) "who even in our day would be called a very high Churchman," and Mr. Procter, one of our best recent commentators on the Prayer Book. *Eucharistic Vestments and the Eastward Position*, pp. 20, 21.

[1] *The Book of Com. Pra. with Notes.* I quote from Mr. Bardsley.
[2] *Lectures on the Duties of the Parish Priest*, p. 334.

number than I at first supposed. Many, too, have adopted this position without any doctrinal intention at all. It was most natural that, looking simply at the words "before the Table," and being ignorant or forgetful of those details of history which environ this phrase and fix upon it another meaning, they should have honestly believed that they were thus obeying the law of the Church. I myself know an instance of this belief and this practice in conjunction with religious convictions distinctively "Evangelical." Still such cases of "orientation" have been, comparatively, very few. Clergymen of great age and wide experience, and connected with no "Evangelical" partizanship, have recently asserted that till within these last few years they never knew of one.[1] All put together are of no argumentative value whatever when placed side by side with the general practice and clear intention of the Church and the deliberately expressed opinion of the weightiest writers; and there is special force too in the fact upon which Bishop Charles Wordsworth has laid great stress, that in our Cathedrals, until very recently, there has been an absolute agreement of practice, condemnatory of the Eastward Position.[2]

[1] See Appendix L. (Novelty of the Eastward Position).
[2] In a published letter addressed to Mr. Beresford Hope (June 4th, 1874) by the Bishop of St. Andrew's.

XI.

CRITICISM OF THE PURCHAS JUDGMENT.

Mr. Morton Shaw's verbal arrangement of the Consecration Rubric—Correct grammatical analysis of the sentence—The late Professor Selwyn—The parenthetic view not necessary—Speech of Lord Cairns—The Purchas Judgment substantially correct and just.

BEFORE I make a few remarks on the Purchas Judgment, it is necessary to encounter an objection raised by Mr. Morton Shaw on the ground of the mere verbal and grammatical meaning of this rubric. He says that in order to arrive at "the proper solution" of the problem before us, "we must obviously look at the order in which the words of the rubric are placed, for here alone we can expect to find the true key to their instruction."[1] I cannot agree in so restrictive a principle of interpretation. No doubt it is important to observe the order of the words; but it is no less important to observe the drift and aim of the rubric, and the point to which it tends. If this sentence were given by one of Her Majesty's Inspectors, in an examination of pupil-teachers, as an example of "analysis" (and it would be a very good example) I feel sure that neither the more intelligent pupil-teachers nor the examiner would come to Mr. Morton Shaw's result. He proposes, by the abolition of two commas, to group together certain words which in the rubric are thus separated, and to make "The-priest-standing-before-the-Table" the

P. 13.

subject of the sentence. But, in fact, the words "standing before the Table" are a part of what the grammatical analysts of our day term an adverbial sentence, of which the verb is "hath ordered," and which is connected with another adverbial sentence of which the verbs are "may break and take," while both are subordinated to the principal sentence, of which the verb is "shall say." Thus Mr. Morton Shaw's theory is thrown to the ground by a due regard to this double subordination in the grammar of the rubric.[1]

But instead of following further my own reasoning on the subject I will turn, for confirmation of my view, to a great master of language, whom it is a painful pleasure to quote, the late Professor Selwyn. How is it possible to refer to his name without a pang in the thought that so bright a star is extinguished in our dark night of theological debate? Some of his private letters are before me at this moment; and I desire to pause as I write, to lay my tribute of admiration and affectionate respect upon his grave. We shall not soon see again such a combination of learning and epigram, of noble-hearted charity and steadfast adherence to truth. That which brings his honoured name into this part of my book is his letter to the "Three Deans,"[2] in which he argues (p. 7)

---

[1] See the common-sense language of Wheatley, as quoted above, p. 94.

[2] *Letters to the Very Rev. the Deans of York, St. Paul's, and Manchester, with Historical Documents, showing the Origin and Meaning of the New Rubrics of* 1661 *in the Communion Office.* 1874. We should not fail to notice Professor Selwyn's motto, "Behold how good and pleasant it is for brethren to dwell together in unity;" and the quotation from Bishop Patteson which follows: "It is clearly better not to view such holy subjects in connexion with controversy; but then comes the thought, How is Christendom to be united, when this diversity exists on so great a point? (Written on Holy Innocents' Day, 1867.)"

that while some of the Clergy hold and express the belief that by the position facing eastward "is signified and expressed the solemn oblation and sacrificial presentation made by the celebrant, after the example of Christ,"[1] and others celebrate the Lord's Supper as "a continual remembrance of the sacrifice of the death of Christ" and a communion of His Body and Blood, there can be among us no real unity. As respects the rubric before us he says (pp. 13, 17,) that having regard to historical facts, remembering that in 1549 and 1552 the priest was in the same position for all the prayers, and bearing in mind also Bishop Cosin's MS. draft, he regards the words "standing before the Table," as parenthetical, and as referring only to the time of ordering the Bread and Wine, and he adds (p. 23) that in order to express the view of "the three Deans," the rubric would have run thus: —*When the Priest hath so ordered the Bread and Wine, that he may with the more readiness and decency break the Bread before the People, and take the Cup into his hands, standing before the Table he shall say the Prayer of Consecration, as followeth.*

And yet I must beg leave in some degree to criticise both the Purchas Judgment and the *consensus* of such writers as Wheatley, Mant, and Blunt, even with the great authority of Professor Selwyn to support their view. In their determination that the officiating minister's position during the prayer of consecration is on the north side, facing southwards, they are perfectly correct. This does not admit of a question. But they adopt a verbal interpretation of the rubric, which

[1] Professor Selwyn told me that these words were quoted from Archdeacon Freeman, and I find them in *Rites and Ritual*, p. 73.

is not really necessary to secure this end. If my view
of the meaning of the preposition "before" is correct,
the priest is equally "before the Table" on the north
side or the west side.[1] The position he is to assume
in ordering the elements is merely a matter of convenience. The essence of the matter is that he is to
"*stand* before" the Table during this part of the
service, in contradistinction to his "*kneeling* at" the
Table during the prayer of humble access. The
interpretation here criticised is unnecessarily technical,
though it secures that one point which is really
essential—the breaking of the bread and the taking
of the cup at the north end. The performing of these
acts and the saying of the prayer of consecration by
the minister, with his face to the east, is of all possible interpretations of the rubric the most contrary
to its spirit and meaning.

It will be observed that in adopting the simple
view here advocated we steer clear of the difficulty,
which in a speech of great importance, at a very
critical moment, the present Lord Chancellor laid
before the House of Lords. The most is made, very
naturally, by Mr. Beresford Hope,[2] of this utterance
of one who, both personally and officially, has so
high a claim on our respectful attention. The essence
of the matter, I apprehend, is this. In the rubric
which we are considering either the words "standing
before the Table" belong to the whole sentence or they
do not. If they do not, how could Mr. Mackonochie
be justly condemned, on the ground that they do
belong to the whole, for kneeling at this part of the

---

[1] See again pp. 58, 59, and the *Notes*, with p. 92.
[2] *Worship in the Church of England*, p. 175.

service? If they do, what fault could be justly found with Mr. Purchas for doing what the sentence, as a whole, told him to do throughout the consecration prayer? When we look at the matter in this way we become conscious of a certain haziness, uncertainty, and faltering, on comparing the two judgments; and this, I imagine, is the fact which Lord Cairns wished to bring to view.

And yet is it not obvious, on a rough and general view of the case, that the Purchas Judgment is, in its substance, just and correct? I do not presume to give any opinion upon the merely legal aspect of the question; and I am very sensible of the great importance, in all such matters, of legal exactitude. But looking at the subject with unprofessional eyes, I cannot see any inconsistency between the two judgments. In the one case the matter at issue was a question of *posture*, in the other a question of *position*. In the one case it was decided that, during the prayer of consecration, Mr. Mackonochie had no right to *kneel*; in the other case, that Mr. Purchas had no right to direct his face *to the east*. The two decisions are not inconsistent with one another. The reasons given by the judges in either case are mere matters of opinion, and are not part of the judgments themselves. Nor is the drawing of this distinction any fancy of my own, or merely an ingenious method of escaping from a difficulty. I fall back here upon the words of Canon Trevor, who, I am quite sure, has a better understanding than I have of the legal bearings of this subject.

Canon Trevor tells us that we must draw a clear and well-marked distinction between that which is termed the "Judgment" of the Lords of the Council and that which is really "the Decree of the Court."[1] "The Final Court of Appeal is not the Judicial Committee, but the Queen in Council. The Judgment of the Court is her Majesty's Order in Council, passed on the Report of the Judicial Committee; and this Report is required by the statute to be read in open Court. The (so called) *Judgment* of the Judicial Committee is not the Report, and is not embodied in it—it is not even communicated to the Court. It is simply the *argument or reasoning* of the majority of the Lords, read to the parties before the Report is made, and published for general information. . . . . It follows that a large number of propositions, which have been hastily quoted as 'the law of the Church, declared by the highest Ecclesiastical Tribunal' are of no legal force. Their authority is that of the *obiter dicta* of the greatest Judges, presiding in one of the highest Courts of the realm." He adds that we are under no obligation to attempt the reconciliation of apparently conflicting cases of judicial reasoning, "since none of these expositions have been introduced into the Judgment of the Queen in Council:" it is a well-known principle of law, that "no judgment is to be pressed beyond the issue determined by the court."

Hence, while I do not agree with that which may be termed the *parenthetic* view of Wheatley, Mant, and Blunt, as expressing, literally and exactly, the true intention of the rubric, I venture to contend that this view is substantially just. If it is untenable, it is not because the priest was intended to stand "before"

---

[1] *On the Disputed Rubrics*, pp. 31—36, see p. 43.

the Lord's Table with his face towards the east, but because the Lord's Table was intended to be so placed, as to put this turning towards the east out of the question. Grammatically this view is quite tenable; and it is in harmony with the spirit and the meaning of the Prayer Book. Our Communion Tables, too, being now customarily fixed at all times against the eastern walls of our chancels, it is a most natural and reasonable view to regard the act of standing before the Table to order the bread and wine as a parenthesis in the process of consecration, or, in the words of what is popularly termed "the Purchas Judgment," to regard the Priest as "set free" to move at this time, for convenience, to the front of the Table. But if the Table itself were placed according to the rubric and canon which relate to this subject, perfect clearness and consistency would result, in letter as well as spirit. In short, the "Purchas Judgment" is only to be blamed, because it is not so strong and decisive as it might have been made, if more account had been taken of law and history in regard to the placing of the Holy Table in 1662 "at the Communion time."

XII.

THE DOCTRINE OF THE NEW TESTAMENT.

Exaggerated language concerning the Eastward Position—Determination to obtain a victory, if possible—The first three Evangelists and St. Paul—St. John VI.—The natural interpretation of words on this subject used in the New Testament—No trace there of a sacrificial Christian priesthood—The Holy Communion as an act of worship.

Having now dealt, as I hope, sufficiently, though by no means exhaustively, with the historical aspect of our question, and believing that I have established the fact that the saying of the Consecration Prayer eastwards is entirely contrary to the intention of the Prayer Book, I will turn to the religious meaning of the rubric which contains our rule to this effect. To omit this side of the subject would evidently be to leave the matter very incomplete. For it is abundantly clear that this rubric is viewed not merely as containing a rule, which has been long misapprehended and which requires that the right practice be restored, but as involving a great principle, which requires a struggle to be made, so that a victory, if possible, may be won. Both Mr. Morton Shaw and Mr. Beresford Hope write upon the subject with the utmost warmth. The former, having argued in favour of a certain doctrinal view of the Holy Eucharist, to which I shall presently turn, says, "If we regard the Eucharist in this light—and it is certainly, at the very least, an admissible[1] Church of England view of it,—such a view must surely justify, must absolutely demand, the use of the Front position, on the part of the celebrant, for its adequate and suitable expression;" and again: "I am unable to contemplate the prospect of having the north end explicitly and definitively forced upon me, and upon those who think as I do, with any sort of feeling in the least degree resembling equanimity or resignation . . . . I cannot think of being myself compelled to use the other position but with the most profound repugnance and aversion."[2] To this let me add the words with which Mr. Beresford Hope concludes his fifth chapter: "I feel more deeply on this question of the priest's position than upon any other question of controverted ceremonial . . . . If the authorities in whose hands the ultimate solution of all such questions lies were to refuse and to prohibit a distinctive Eucharistic dress, I should regard their decision as a mistake, a misfortune, and a loss; but I should wait in patience for days in which reason might have the advantage of prejudice. But if, at the highest moment of Christian worship,—when God's priest most impressively pleads Christ's sacrifice in Christ's own words, in Christ's own ordinance —loyal and peaceable children of the Church of England were to be forbidden to unite themselves with that priest in the great act, according to the

---

[1] If a doctrine is *admissible* as an opinion of individuals, it does not follow that it has a claim to be inculcated in the ritual of a congregation. There is the greatest difference between holding an opinion and expressing it in *a ceremony*. If all doctrinal opinions had a right to ceremonial expression, we should be in danger of ecclesiastical dissolution. See below, pp. 130—132, and the *Notes*.

[2] *Position of the Celebrant, &c.*, pp. 96, 112.

order in which the Holy Catholic Church has, from the first, been wont to show forth the Lord's death, while thoroughly acknowledging that the efficacy of the Sacrament was in no way affected, I should in my inmost soul, feel that there was a great wrong done."[1]

The tone of this language may be exaggerated, and no doubt it is; but it evidently implies a deep feeling and a very determined resolve. We have much more before us here than the interpretation of a misunderstood rule for the settlement of an attitude in itself indifferent; nor is there any doubt that the idea present to the minds of those who write and feel this is the idea of sacrifice[2]— that the Eucharist is viewed here as an offering to God, and not merely as a gift to man. That this great Sacrament is a gift to man no one indeed denies; though such writing as this has a tendency to throw deeply into the shade

---

[1] *Worship in the Church of England*, p. 211.

[2] I often find it extremely difficult to apprehend the exact meaning of those who, while repudiating the Roman Catholic view of this subject, and those near approximations to the Roman Catholic view which are now current amongst us, still view the Eucharist as in itself a sacrifice. Some more exact definitions would be of great advantage in this controversy. That there is a sacrifice of prayer and praise and of ourselves, concomitant with the partaking of the Holy Communion, is allowed by all; and on this point the Book of Common Prayer is very emphatic. That there is an "oblation" of the bread and wine in the Church of England Service is believed by many; but this is quite a different subject from that with which we are concerned in the Consecration Prayer. Many persons speak of a "commemorative sacrifice," when they mean simply "the commemoration of a sacrifice;" but surely there must be great confusion of thought, if these two phrases are treated as having the same meaning. The very fact which we commemorate is the fact that the sacrifice is complete. If in our commemoration we still offer the same sacrifice which we commemorate, we are brought back to the Roman view. If it is a different sacrifice, then we are entitled to ask what that sacrifice is.

that which, to say the least, is the most prominent, in regard to this subject, alike in the New Testament and in the Prayer Book. Let us now look at these two authorities, reverently recollecting which of them is primary and which secondary.

Reverting, then, in all simplicity to the New Testament, let us remember, in the first place, what information we find there on this subject, and what we do not find. A proper reverence for Holy Scripture requires us to be very careful not to introduce into the Sacred Volume that which was not in it when it came from God. We have four accounts of the institution of this Sacrament, one from each of the first three Evangelists,[1] and one from St. Paul, in the First Epistle to the Corinthians,[2] in which letter he also gives some instruction concerning this Sacrament.[3] In no other Epistle by any one of the sacred writers is this subject mentioned at all. There are likewise allusions in the Acts of the Apostles to the reception of the Holy Communion as a fact and a custom.[4] I will add, also, what we find in the sixth chapter of St. John's Gospel.[5] Though, as is well known to all theologians, it has been forcibly argued by weighty commentators that the Eucharist does not at all come within the scope of what is said in this chapter,[6] yet I would rather assume the opposite view to be correct, partly because I myself think there

---

[1] Matt. xxvi. 17—30; Mark xiv. 12—25; Luke xxii. 7—21.
[2] 1 Cor. xi. 23—26.
[3] 1 Cor. x. 16, 17, 21; xi. 20—34.
[4] Acts ii. 42, 46; xx. 7—11.
[5] John vi. 26—63.
[6] I may simply here combine a reference to the note of Maldonatus on St. John vi. 53, with one to a sermon in Dr. Arnold's third volume. See also *The Life of Dr. Arnold*, Vol. ii. p. 331.

must have been in our Lord's words on this occasion some anticipatory reference to that which He was purposing to ordain, partly because in an argument like this it is a good policy to concede as much as possible, partly because by the utmost concession on this point I gain the more for my argument. For what is there in this solemn discourse that points in the least degree to the thought of a sacrifice, as offered by man to God? Throughout it is the reiterated assurance of a gift from God to man. Let us touch, one by one, with reverent fingers, the sacred links of this golden chain: "Ye seek me because ye did eat of the loaves—labour for the meat that endureth unto everlasting life—my Father giveth you the true bread from Heaven—I am the bread of life—I am the bread which came down from Heaven—he that eateth of this bread shall live for ever." If I were disposed in the presence of such a passage to use a mere *argumentum ad hominem*, I would urge that they whose views of the Sacraments lead them to limit the scope of this passage to the Eucharist, prove to themselves that the main aspect of that ordinance is not sacrifice but communion.

But let us turn to those passages about the reference of which to the Eucharist no doubt can be entertained. They tell us of this Sacrament as a most lively, affecting, and eloquent remembrance of Christ—as a perpetual proclaiming, from age to age, of the death of Christ—as a communication of Christ Himself to our souls—as an act of communion which, by virtue of their union with Him, Christians have one with another—as a solemn ordinance, which is to be diligently purged from all irreverence and carelessness. As to those words ἀνάμνησις and καταγγέλλετε in St. Paul's First Epistle to the Corinthians, I am, for my own part, firmly convinced that they would never have been interpreted as denoting the reminding God of the sacrifice of Christ, if an argument had not been wanted for a sacrificial view of the Eucharist, which had become current, and which it was necessary to justify. Let any one dispossess his mind of conventional theology, and try to reproduce in imagination the scene of the Last Supper when the Lord was addressing those whom He was about to leave; and can he doubt how τοῦτο ποιεῖτε εἰς τὴν ἐμὴν ἀνάμνησιν were meant and understood?[1] Let any one call to mind that the other word is one of St. Paul's customary phrases for preaching Christ or proclaiming the Gospel; and can he doubt that τὸν θάνατον τοῦ Κυρίου καταγγέλλετε is the "setting forth" of "Christ crucified" in the congregation and to the world. Nor in the Acts of the Apostles is there any trace of a sacrificial view of the ordinance, or any title anywhere in the New Testament given to the ministers of the Christian Church, Apostles or others, that would in the slightest degree suggest such a view. This last point seems to me to contain an argument on this subject which cannot be answered. The Apostles and Ministers of the Christian Church receive various

---

[1] As regards the phrase τοῦτο ποιεῖτε, and the sacrificial interpretation sometimes given to it, see Dr. Vogan on *The True Doctrine of the Eucharist*, p. 364, and his Appendix FF. He shows that when ποιέω in the Septuagint denotes the offering of a sacrifice, it has some other word connected with it, as in Levit. vi. 22, 2 Kings x. 21. Let it be remarked, too, that in St. Paul's account of the institution of the Lord's Supper, the words are: "this *do*, as often as ye *drink it.*" His account and St. Luke's are substantially identical. The words τοῦτο ποιεῖτε do not occur in St. Matthew and St. Mark.

designations, but never one which is identical with, or similar to, the customary designation of the sacrificing priests of the Jewish Church.[1] To take only a single contrast by way of illustration, see the Old Testament overflowing, as it were, into the New, where mention is made of the "Priest Zacharias" at the "altar of incense;"[2] and then see how the Apostle of the Gentiles, discarding all literal application of such language to himself, is free to apply it allegorically, and to speak of his Gentile converts as the "sacrifice" he offers to God.[3] And in this particular the whole of the New Testament is absolutely consistent with itself. Is it not a very bold proceeding—might I not almost say it is a great irreverence—to insist on presenting the Holy Eucharist chiefly in that aspect in which it is not exhibited by the New Testament at all? Is it not strange to make that a distinguishing feature of the Christian Religion, which is not even revealed in Scripture? How can a human interpolation command for us the same respect as those original writings which we regard as Divine?

But it will be said that the Holy Communion is our highest act of worship, and that therefore it was to be a sacrifice, and our greatest sacrifice. Now, I doubt

---

[1] In one of the most comprehensive passages of the New Testament (Eph. iv. 8—16) we are told that after Christ ascended, He gave to the Church "apostles, prophets, evangelists, pastors, teachers." If He gave also "priests," how can the omission be accounted for by those who contend that the office of strict priesthood is essential "for the perfecting of the saints, for the work of the ministry, for the edifying of the body of Christ"?

[2] Luke i. 5, 11.

[3] Rom. xv. 16. The mere fact that St. Paul uses this sacrificial language *allegorically* is, to my mind, a very strong proof that it could not be *literally* applicable to his own office.

whether it is wise to institute comparisons as to the relative value of different means of grace. If it were necessary to follow any line of reasoning of this kind, the analogy of Scripture would suggest to us that we ought to set "the Word" in a higher place than the Sacraments.[1] And again, as to nearness of approach to God, the Sermon on the Mount and other passages of the Gospels seem to say to us that this approach is nearer in private prayer than on any other occasion. I should suppose that St. Paul's communion with God was quite as intimate, when on his solitary way to Assos, as when he had broken bread with the congregation at Troas.[2] But, as I have said, I doubt the wisdom of such comparisons. Most certainly, when we "draw near" to receive the blessing of this Sacrament, there must be supplication and homage. I should be quite willing to admit that at this time we are engaged in the highest act of our public worship. But is there not some confusion of thought in speaking of the Holy Communion as *in itself* an act of worship? It seems to me that worship in this case is collateral and coordinate, and that the Lord's Supper itself is a memorial, a communion, a proclamation of truth, and a conveyance of grace. Remembering Christ, calling His great atonement to mind, receiving of His fulness

---

[1] Not only do we find no mention of this Sacrament in parts of the New Testament, more especially the Epistle to the Hebrews, where, on what I will venture to call the ultra-sacramental theory of Christianity, such mention must have occurred; but throughout its books the mention of "the Word" meets us everywhere, and always in a position of high supremacy. Let the *consensus* of such passages as the following be carefully marked: John xv. 3; Acts xx. 32; 2 Cor. v. 19; Col. iii. 16; Jam. i. 21; 1 Pet. i. 23; 1 John ii. 14. No such *consensus* of pervading supremacy can be traced in the New Testament, as regards the Eucharist.

[2] Acts xx. 11, 13.

by His own appointed way, we must worship, we must offer the sacrifice of our prayer and praise, of our hearts and our lives. I recognise it, too, as highly fitting that such an occasion should be surrounded by circumstances of reverence, solemnity and dignity. But all these considerations put together cannot alter what we find in the New Testament, or transform a gift to man so that it becomes an offering to God.

This must suffice for an allusion to the Scriptural aspect of the case. We are still more closely concerned, in the present discussion, with the view taken of the matter in the formularies of the Church of England. That which abstractedly is secondary becomes to us in this instance primary. Even if our Prayer Book were, in this matter, out of harmony with the Bible, still the subject with which we should be obliged to deal would be the doctrine of the Prayer Book.

XIII.

TEACHING OF OUR COMMUNION SERVICE.

Final exclusion of the word "Altar" from the Prayer Book—True meaning of the word "Priest" in the Prayer Book—Teaching of the rubrics in the Communion Service—Teaching of the prayers and thanksgivings in that service—Doctrine of the Consecration Prayer.

In endeavouring to state the doctrine of the Book of Common Prayer in reference to the question of Eucharistic Sacrifice, I am disposed, first of all, to urge the immense significance of the absolute and final removal of the word "Altar" from that Book. The force of this argument is shown, partly by the anger with which it is received, and partly by the ingenious and circuitous replies by which it is met. The opinions and habit of various writers in the Church of England are quoted in favour of the use of this term; but still the fact remains that it is excluded from our authorized ecclesiastical vocabulary. Those who are most vehement in their dislike of Erastianism are sometimes so far able to overcome this repugnance as to adduce the retention of this word in the Coronation Service (the variations of which depend on the government of the day), in order to overbear the deliberate rejection[1] of the word by the

---

[1] It is not meant to assert that there was a struggle for the reintroduction of this term in 1662; but it is important to observe that if there was any effort of this kind, it was defeated, and that if there was no such effort, then Cosin, and those who were like-minded with him, were willing to dispense with the term.

Convocation of 1662.[1] It is a policy, more diplomatic than candid, with some writers, to throw into the shade the great fact that from 1552 to that year, the ecclesiastical battle, swaying this way and that, till finally it was decided, was between the principles represented by the two words "Altar" and "Table." The worst course of all is the contention that the two terms are synonymous. I could not write with any honest sincerity if I did not repudiate this as utterly untenable. This theory is an absolute contradiction, alike to correct etymology and to the facts of English Church history during its most exciting time.[2] The

[1] The form and order of the Queen's Coronation has recently been republished by Mr. Fuller Russell under the title of *The Coronation Service according to the use of the Church of England*, though this service has never received the sanction of Convocation. It is clear in this service that, as regards the position of the Queen's Chair, the *south* side of the Altar is used in a general way for the southern part of the West side; and it is urged that thus "south *side*" is not synonymous with "south *end*." But what we are concerned with is the *north* side, and it is overlooked that when the Archbishop takes his place at the "north side" (p. 5), and again pronounces the blessing over the Queen (p. 13) from the north *side*, he is really at the north *end*. See also p. 27, where the Queen is said to retire from the Church "through the door on the *south side* of the Altar, into King Edward's chapel." This cannot be on any part of the west side.

[2] The distinction, as seen from the historical point of view, was laid down in 1857 by eminent lawyers of calm minds, independently of the heat of the clerical mind. "The distinction between an Altar and Communion Table is in itself essential and deeply founded on the most important difference, in matters of faith, between Protestants and Romanists. By the latter the Lord's Supper was considered as a sacrifice of the Body and Blood of the Saviour; the Altar was the place on which the sacrifice was to be made. The Reformers, on the other hand, considered the Holy Communion not as a sacrifice, but as a feast to be celebrated at the Lord's Table." The Judges on this occasion were Lord Chancellor Cranworth, Lord Wensleydale, Mr. Pemberton Leigh (afterwards Lord Kingsdown), Sir John Patteson, and Sir William Maule. They proceed to bring forward various authorities of greater or less weight, as, for instance, the injunctions of Bishop Ridley, that, "in order to move and turn the simple to the right use of the Lord's Supper, Curates and Churchwardens are to erect and set up the Lord's board in the form of an

argument derived from a comparison of our Prayer Book of 1662 with that of 1549 is so decisive, that I need not dwell on it further. The historical truth of the case comes down on this whole controversy with the force of a hammer.

But it is urged that the word "Priest," and the word "Altar," are correlative; that the one implies the other; and that having "Priests" recognised in our Prayer Book, we have literally "Altars" in our churches. If this were really a just and full statement of the case, it would be one of the strangest occurrences in history that the word "Altar" should have been utterly and finally excluded from the Book of Common Prayer, and that the very thing which was intended by our last revisers to be clear, should have been made obscure. It is quite true, indeed, in a certain sense, that the words "Altar" and "Priest" are correlative. The latter term is ambiguous, and may denote either, according to its derivation, the Christian Presbyter of the New Testament, or, according to the usage of our Authorized Version, the Sacrificing Minister under the Jewish system. If a doubt were to arise as to the meaning of the word in any particular instance, the doubt would naturally be settled by inquiring whether the word "Altar" is associated with it. A Sacrificer must have an Altar. If the word "Altar" remained in our Book of Common

honest Table," and the injunction of Queen Elizabeth, that "the Holy Table in every Church be decently made and set in the place where the Altar stood;" and finally, near the close of the judgment, in answer to observations made on the other side, the great general principle is seriously and strongly laid down again : "To these observations," say these eminent lawyers, " the answer is that the distinction between an Altar and a Table is in itself essential." *Ecclesiastical Judgments of the Privy Council*, by Brodrick and Fremantle, pp. 144—152.

Prayer, it would be fair to say that the Church of England took the word "Priest" in that sense, however inconsistent we might feel this to be with the New Testament. But as the case stands, the meaning of this term in the Prayer Book is narrowed to the other sense. Thus the Bible and the Prayer Book are in this matter consistent. The "Priest" of our English Church Services is the "Presbyter" of the New Testament, as indeed must be the case if these Services are Scriptural.

There is nothing new in these statements. They are quite commonplace. But it has become necessary to repeat them. The case does not really admit of any doubt. If any necessity existed for bringing forward authorities, I might quote such unexceptionable writers as Hooker[1] and Mede.[2] But perhaps it is more to my purpose to mention Archbishop Laud himself. Whatever his private opinions may have been, he has given the most public sanction to our making the words "Priest" and "Presbyter" synonymous; for in every part of his Scotch Prayer Book of 1637 the latter is employed and not the former.[3]

---

[1] See Keble's edition, vol. v. c. 78, pp. 471—2.

[2] "Our Curates of holy things in the Gospel are not to offer Sacrifice, and therefore ought not to be called *Sacerdotes*. . . . . If it be well examined, *Priest* is the English of *Presbyter*, and not of *Sacerdos*, there being in our tongue no word in use for *Sacerdos* : *Priest*, which we use for both, being improperly used for a *Sacrificer*, but naturally expressing a *Presbyter*, the name whereby the Apostles both call themselves and those which succeed them in their charge."—Mede's *Works* (1672), p. 27.

[3] In Hall's *Fragmenta Liturgica*, vol. v., are editions of the Scotch Liturgy of various dates; and in all of them, though in some of the later the word "Altar" has stealthily crept in, the word "Presbyter" holds its ground throughout. In editions of this Liturgy, dated 1800 and 1844 (pp. 272 and 302) we find "then shall the Presbyter, turning him to the Altar, kneel down and say," instead of Laud's original form in 1636," then shall the Presbyter, kneeling down at God's board, say." The change seems to have taken place, by authority or otherwise, between 1743 and 1755.

But, though the removal of the word "Altar" from our formularies sums up in itself nearly the whole of our present controversy, let us go into the matter a little further. There are several tests by which we can try the Church of England as to its doctrine of the Holy Eucharist. Our Communion Office itself supplies the first and most obvious.

Let us look through the rubrics, the prayers, and the thanksgivings of this Service. If it is the doctrine of our Church that the Eucharist is inherently, and in itself, and by Divine appointment, a sacrifice, we should expect this doctrine to be expressed in some part of our authorized office. But I search for any such expression in vain.

First let us glance at the rubrics.[1] In them we are met immediately by such phrases as "*partakers* of the Holy Communion," "*partakers* of the Lord's Table." Even as regards the rubric which gives directions for the placing of the bread and wine on the Table, though an effort was made to introduce into it the word "offer," and thus to convert the bread and wine into an "oblation," as in the Scotch Prayer Book of 1637, yet this was overruled by Convocation and Parliament.[2] So resolute was the determination to exclude from the Priest's part in the service the semblance of sacrificial acts. And if we pursue the rubrics further, we find both exhortations addressed to those who *receive* "the Holy Sacrament" or "the Holy Communion," the confession made in the name of those "who are minded to *receive*," and the prayer of humble

---

[1] It ought to be carefully borne in mind that the authorized designation of the service is "the *Order* of the *Administration* of the Lord's Supper."
[2] See Procter *On the Book of Common Prayer*, p. 351.

access said "in the name of all them that shall *receive.*" Finally, it is ordered that there is never to be any celebration of the Lord's Supper at all, "except there be a convenient number *to communicate with* the Priest;" and so tenaciously is the principle which this implies maintained, that it is added : "If there be not above twenty persons in the parish of discretion to receive the Communion, yet there shall be no Communion, except four (or three at the least) *communicate with* the Priest."

And now from the rubrics that regulate this service let us turn to the prayers and other parts of the service itself. No word is used denoting that this Divine institution of the Eucharist is a Sacrifice; but everywhere it is presented to us as a Communion. It is particularly important to observe that the true character of the ἀνάμνησις prescribed to us in the institution of this Sacrament is *defined* for us in our service. In the first of the two forms for giving notice of the celebration of the Holy Communion, we are told that it is to be "*received* in remembrance of Christ's meritorious cross and passion;" in the second we read with stronger emphasis, "It is your duty to *receive* the Communion in remembrance of the sacrifice of His death, as He Himself hath commanded." This is the explanation authoritatively given to us of the "perpetual memory" which is prominently named in the Consecration Prayer; and in harmony with this are the words of the administration, "*Take, eat* in remembrance," "*Drink* in remembrance." The idea of *reception* runs like a thread through every part of the Office. In every form of expression this is set before us. In the Eucharist we have "spiritual food and sustenance:" it is a "heavenly feast," a "rich feast," a "table decked with all kind of provision," "a banquet of heavenly food." If we express our unworthiness of so great a benefit, it is in the touching words of the Syrophenician woman concerning "the crumbs under the table." And while there is so great a wealth of words to indicate this aspect of the Lord's Supper, there is absolutely not a syllable to present it in the character of a sacrifice. The thought of the sacred "Table" is at every moment before us. The thought of the "Altar" is not perceptible. No mention of sacrifice occurs at all till we reach the prayers at the close of the service, when the Communion is complete,[1] and then it is the sacrifice of "praise and thanksgiving," the sacrifice of "ourselves, our souls and our bodies"—in strict harmony with what we read in the Epistle to the Hebrews (after the mention of Christ's great completed sacrifice) concerning the offering of the "sacrifice of praise to God continually," and those "sacrifices of doing good and communicating," with which God is "well pleased."[2] To all which must be added this significant fact, that this particular prayer, in which all the sacrificial expression of our Eucharistic Service is concentrated, is itself an optional prayer.

When I compare this presentation of the Lord's Supper in our service with that different presentation of it in books and tracts all around us, for which this service gives no sanction, I am utterly astonished and made very conscious of the peril in

[1] This ought to be very carefully noted. Even *this* presentation of the Holy Eucharist in a sacrificial aspect does not occur in the *Consecration* Prayer.
[2] Heb. xiii. 10, 15, 16.

which we are placed. And here let us look carefully at the Prayer of Consecration, in which the notion of sacrifice, if it was characteristic of the service itself, would surely be found. Let us see what this prayer really is. In some of the arguments I am combating it is assumed that it is an act of sacrifice to Almighty God: that which requires to be proved is taken for granted; and then from this assumption the writers reason backwards to the rubric. But there is not a word in the prayer which expresses or implies the offering of a sacrifice to God at this moment of the service. At the beginning of the prayer the completed sacrifice of Christ is, with the strongest emphasis of which language is capable, laid down as the justification of the supplication which is to follow. At the end of the prayer the historical recital of the institution of this Sacrament is combined with the Priest's manual acts. In the midst, thus framed by two great historical statements, the supplication is simply this, that our merciful Father will be " pleased to grant that we, *receiving* His creatures of Bread and Wine according to His Son our Lord Jesus Christ's holy Institution, *in remembrance* of His death and passion, may be *partakers* of His most Blessed Body and Blood." The minister, at this moment of the service, is not making an offering to God on behalf of the congregation, but invoking a blessing on that of which the congregation are about to participate.[1]

[1] Let it also be marked that, " if the consecrated Bread or Wine be all spent before all have communicated, the Priest is to consecrate more according to the form before prescribed; beginning at [*Our Saviour Christ in the same night*, &c.] for the blessing of the bread; and at [*Likewise after Supper*, &c.] for the blessing of the cup." This then must be the consecration; and we see that it is simply a recital. This, too, is a rubric of 1662.

XIV.

TEACHING OF OUR OTHER FORMULARIES.

Language of the Ordination Service—Doctrine of the Church Catechism—
The Articles—The Homilies—The Canons.

BUT the Communion Service in our Prayer Book is not the only instruction which is supplied to us in the Church of England concerning this serious question. We find the same subject set before us, and with perfect consistency, in the commission given to priests at Ordination, in our Catechism for the instruction of the young, in the Articles which are signed by the Clergy, and in our authorized Homilies for the people. We may with advantage glance at each of these in order, before we turn to the conclusion of this argument.

And first, the "Form and Manner of Ordering Priests." In this part of the Prayer Book no dishonour is done to the Holy Eucharist. On the contrary, the "Service for the Communion" is interwoven and incorporated with the Ordination Service. The Sacraments, too, are—as is fitting—prominently mentioned in the commission given to those who are admitted to the order of priesthood. But what is the language used on this subject? All the stress is laid on *ministration.* Not a word is said concerning sacrifice, or any allusion made, however remotely, to any sacrificial aspect of the Holy

Communion. In the course of his solemn questioning, the Bishop asks:—"Will you give your faithful diligence so to *minister* the Sacraments as the Lord hath commanded, and as this Church and Realm hath received the same?" During the act of ordination these words are used, "Be thou a faithful *dispenser* of God's Holy Sacraments;" and when the Bible is delivered into the hands of each one, it is said, "Take thou authority to *minister* the Holy Sacraments in the congregation." But this is not all. If we compare the Roman Pontifical with the English Ordinal, we find that a most significant change has been made, as regards this subject, both in ceremonial and in words. In the ordaining of a Roman Catholic Priest, the Bishop delivers into the hand of each "the Chalice and the Paten, with the Host," saying the words "Receive power to offer sacrifice to God, and to celebrate masses, as well for the living as for the dead;"[1] and the final benediction is as follows, "The blessing of God Almighty, the Father, the Son and the Holy Ghost, descend upon you, that you may be blessed in the priestly order, and offer propitiatory sacrifices for the sins and offences of the people to Almighty God, to whom be honour and glory for ever."[2] It is needless to add any commentary on this contrast, except just to observe that the change is in remarkable harmony with one of the Thirty-nine Articles to be mentioned below, and expresses the same historical truth. How

---

[1] *Pontificale Romanum* (Par. 1664), p. 50.

[2] We find the same forms, with a slight verbal difference, in the Sarum Ordinal. See Maskell's *Monumenta Ritualia*, iii. pp. 214, 222. We should note, too, the form of blessing the hands "to offer sacrifice," p. 212.

can it be consistent to urge that a sacrificial office of the Clergy should be expressed by a ceremony, when in the whole Ordination Service there is no reference to any sacrificial office at all?

And now reference must be made to the Church Catechism. That which a Church holds in a matter of grave and fundamental doctrine will surely be seen by the teaching on the subject which that Church directs to be given to the young. We do not indeed expect complete teaching to be given on any subject to the young; but we do expect the main points to be made clear to them. And we are dealing here with a main point; otherwise those are inexcusable who have raised this controversy. Now the latter part of our Catechism is looked upon even by some Churchmen with suspicion, as tending to exalt the Sacraments unduly, and to inculcate extreme views of their efficacy. It is certain that those by whom this part was compiled cannot be accused of undervaluing the efficacy of the Sacraments. Hence their questions and answers are the more important for this argument. Now we are there directed to teach to the young absolutely nothing concerning the Eucharist viewed as a sacrifice. It is affectionately set forth to our youthful Christians as a communion, as a special blessing to the soul, as a help to the recollection of Christ, as an incentive to charity. Everything points to *reception*, as that by which "the continual remembrance of the sacrifice of the death of Christ" is to be maintained. Everything in this Catechism indicates in this ordinance a great gift to man; nothing suggests that we are to see in it an offering to God. Let this be compared with the language of the Roman Catholic Catechisms on the same subject; or, what is more to the point, let it be compared with some recent manuals compiled by those who, having accepted English doctrine, employ much activity in teaching a doctrine very different.

It is not worth while to spend many words on the Thirty-nine Articles, partly because there can be no doubt of their paramount authority, and partly because, in the matter before us, they are very clear and explicit, both positively and negatively. On the one hand, "the *ministering* of the Sacraments in the congregation," "the *receiving* rightly and by faith the Sacraments *ministered*," are set forth several times as the characteristic features of these ordinances:[1] on the other hand it is said, as though a commentary were to be added to the above-mentioned omissions from the old Ordination Service: "The Sacrifices of Masses, in the which it was commonly said that the Priest did offer Christ for the quick and the dead, to have remission of pain or guilt, were blasphemous fables and dangerous deceits."[2]

The Homilies, however, deserve a special notice apart from the Articles. No one, indeed, supposes that every phrase of the Homilies is binding upon the conscience of every member of the Church of England. But they are stated in the Articles, which were contemporary, to contain a godly and wholesome doctrine necessary for those times;[3] and "those times" were specially occupied with the Eucharistic question. Moreover the Books of Homilies were reckoned in the Canons of 1603 among the "ornaments" appertaining

[1] Art. xxiii.—xxvi.   [2] Art. xxxi.   [3] Art. xxxv.

to Churches;[1] and thus the sanction of the seventeenth century was given, in this respect, to the doctrinal teaching of the sixteenth.

It is natural to turn here especially to the two parts of the Homily "of the worthy receiving and reverent esteeming of the Sacrament of the Body and Blood of Christ," where it is to be noted, in the first place, that the very title lays upon *reception* the same stress which we have seen elsewhere in the Prayer Book. In this Homily it is said that "the great love of our Saviour Christ doth not only appear in that dear-bought benefit of our redemption and salvation by His death and passion, but also in that He so kindly provided that the same most merciful work might be *had in continual remembrance*, to take some place in us, and not to be frustrate of its end and purpose. . . . . Our loving Saviour hath ordained and established the *remembrance* of His great mercy in the institution of His heavenly supper. . . . . So then of necessity we must be ourselves *partakers of this table*, and not beholders of other. . . . . This we must be sure of especially, that this Supper be in such wise done and *ministered*, as our Lord and Saviour did, and commanded to be done, as His Apostles used it, and the good fathers in the Primitive Church frequented it. . . . . Neither can he be devout that otherwise doth presume that it was given by the Author. *We must then take heed lest of the memory it be made a sacrifice.*[2] . . . . It followeth to have with this knowledge

---

[1] Canon lxxx.

[2] Compare what we find in the Second Part of the "Homily for Whitsunday:" "Christ commended to His Church a sacrament of His Body and Blood: they have *changed* it into *a sacrifice for the quick and the dead.*" There is in the 81st of the *Tracts for the Times* (pp. 43, 44), a

a sure and constant *faith*, that Christ hath made upon His Cross *a full and sufficient sacrifice* for thee. . . . . Herein thou needest no other man's help, *no other sacrifice or oblation, no sacrificing priest,* no mass, no means established by man's invention. . . . . Seeing that the name and thing itself doth admonish us of thanks, let us (as St. Paul saith, Heb. xiii.) offer always to God the *host* or sacrifice of praise by Christ." And with this exact and careful teaching the language of the other Homilies on the same subject is quite consistent. Thus when the topic is "the Right Use of the Church or Temple of God, and of the Reverence due unto the same," it is declared that the Church is "the house of the Lord, for that the service of the Lord (as teaching and hearing of His holy Word, calling upon His holy name, giving thanks to Him for His great and innumerable benefits, and due *ministering* of the sacraments) is there used."[1] So, too, in regard to "repairing and keeping clean, and comely adorning of Churches," we have the following sentence:—"Like as men are well refreshed and comforted, when they find their houses having all things in good order, and all corners clean and sweet; so when God's house, the church, is well adorned, with places convenient to sit in, with the Pulpit for the preacher, with *the Lord's Table for the*

most curious comment on the passage quoted in the text. The writer of the Homily is said to employ "popular" language, and to use the simple word "sacrifice" in the Popish sense, while he uses "that of the memory" for what was anciently designated by "sacrifice:" and then he refers to Courayer's free translation, which might more properly be termed an ingenious alteration, "Cavendum, ne sacrificium commemorationis convertat in sacrificium proprium et materiale."

[1] For these words see the end of the first part and the beginning of the second part of this Homily; and compare the similar words at the beginning of the first part of the "Sermon against Peril of Idolatry."

ministration of His Holy Supper, with the Font to christen in, and also is kept clean, comely, and sweetly, the people are more desirous and the more comforted to resort thither, and to tarry there the whole time appointed them."[1]

And to all this may be added, in conclusion, a reference to the language of the Canons. The rule regarding the Communion Table [2] has regard to "ministration" or "administering," thrice repeated; and the phraseology is similar which deals with Divine service on Holy Days and in College Chapels, with the duties of Ministers, whether they be Lecturers or Preachers, and with the Communion in Private Houses. In fact, wherever we question our authorized formularies for their teaching on this subject, the emphasis they lay on *reception* in the Holy Eucharist, and their silence in regard to *sacrifice* in this Sacrament, are alike remarkable.[3]

---

[1] I am not aware of a single passage in the Homilies which gives any countenance to our viewing the Eucharist as a sacrifice. As a precaution indeed (knowing how some of our modern controversialists argue) I refer to the quotation, in the Homily on "Common Prayer and Sacraments," of a constitution of Justinian, in which bishops and priests are said to "celebrate the holy oblation." This quotation, however, is not brought forward for the purpose of any reference to "oblation," but to illustrate the duty of using audible language in the Communion Service. In *Tract* xc. neither this passage nor any other from the Homilies is adduced in favour of a "Catholic" view of Eucharistic Sacrifice. See Appendix M (The Perpetual Oblation in Heaven).

[2] Canon lxxxii. See above, p. 27, *note*.

[3] Canons xiv., xvi., lvi., lviii., lxxi. See also iv., xxii., xxiv., &c. The reiterated allusion to the Holy Communion in the Canons is very observable; and it is incredible that it should not once be presented there in a sacrificial aspect, if those who sanctioned these Canons intended this view to be a doctrine of the Church of England.

XV.

PERMISSIVE ORIENTATION.

The School of Jacobean and Caroline Divines—Freedom to hold an opinion does not imply freedom to express it by a ceremony—Liberty in this respect would disturb the balance of doctrinal expression in the Church—This mode of introducing doctrinal change not fair—Option, in this respect, contrary to the principles of the Prayer Book—And full of peril for the future—Would foment religious discord—Further results to be feared.

It follows from the preceding remarks that a perfect consistency runs through the whole of our authorized formularies in regard to this subject; and it is a consistency harmonious with that of the New Testament in the same particular. In neither is there any sanction for the opinion that the Holy Eucharist is inherently and itself a sacrifice.

But it will be urged that English Divines have held, with full toleration and allowance, the sacrificial view of this ordinance, that there has always been such a school of thought in the Church of England, that the Reformers would not have repudiated those who maintained this opinion, and that it was strongly maintained by theologians, who were in this country the pride of the seventeenth century. It is contended, further, that this aspect of the Eucharist was prominent in the early ages of Christianity, and reflected in the Primitive Liturgies.

I very willingly concede nearly all that the opponents of my argument will require under this head. As regards Primitive Liturgies, however, I suspect that no part of our early ecclesiastical literature requires more careful criticism and revision. Moreover, those to whom for the most part we owe our present editions of them, have been concerned, in the interest of their opinions, to make the most of the sacrificial aspect of these documents.[1] As regards the writings of the Fathers, it is very difficult, whenever they deal with this subject, to distinguish between rhetoric and sober statement of doctrine. Moreover, we are not to expect, in a period before the beginning of sacramental controversies, a caution which to us is imperative. There is no doubt, however, that the apprehension of the Holy Eucharist as a sacrifice began at an early date. The question is, whether such a view is a deviation from primitive truth and the precursor of serious and gradually-increasing error, or a standard of primitive truth which is to override the obvious meaning of Scripture. Into this question I will not enter; for I think that free toleration ought to be given to this view of the Eucharist, so long as it is maintained as a pious opinion, and not asserted to be an express doctrine of the Church of England. I was once asked, when putting forward the view which I am here endeavouring to justify, whether I would exclude such a man as Bishop Andrewes from our Church; to which I

[1] I cannot help hoping that we may gain much in these respects from the researches of the Old Catholics of Germany, who are engaged, I believe, in the revision of existing Liturgies, with the view of producing Books of Public Devotion for use in their own congregations. These men have the possession of great learning and the habit of critical inquiry; they are free from the disturbing influence of our English controversies; and while they cling to the traditions of the past, they have obtained a new starting-point, which is full of promise for the future of Christendom.

K

replied that I should regard the thought of such exclusion as a sacrilege. I should never dream of not tolerating within our communion a large range of variety of opinion on a subject so mysterious as the Holy Eucharist; and I know how much weaker the Church of England would have been than it is, if such men as Bishop Andrewes had never belonged to it.

But then it is asked—If I am free to hold such doctrines within the Church of England, why may I not be free to express them by a ceremony? Why may not liberty of opinion and liberty of ritual be co-ordinated together and of equal extent? Here I join issue at once. It is not at all the same thing to be free to hold an opinion within the Church, and to be free to express it by a ceremony. Nor indeed is the ceremonial freedom at all necessary for the holding of the opinion. Those who in past times cherished the views in question, did not attain any corresponding ceremonial freedom.[1] "While we are taught in the Prayer Book that the Eucharist is a communion; men are quite at liberty, if their convictions impel them, to hold that it is something more. As regards Bishop Andrewes, I imagine that when he said the consecration prayer in the parish churches of his diocese, he did this with his face to the south, at a Holy Table entirely disengaged from the east wall. Therefore his doctrine, whatever it might be, did not require on his

---

[1] I do not mean to say that in 1662 there was any deliberate effort to obtain license for the Eastward position. But, even if we assume that there were those who earnestly desired this change for the purpose of expressing their doctrine, still, though doctrinally free, they obtained no corresponding ceremonial liberty. See above on the word "altar," p. 113, note.

part the introduction of a new ceremony. But I contend further that there is the greatest difference between the ceremonial expression of a theological opinion and its expression by means of words. Nor is the statement of this difference a mere random utterance of a perverse opinion of my own. I will here quote the words of one who, though silent, is still eloquent.

This question was raised in the Upper House of the Convocation of Canterbury in 1868, and the Bishop of Oxford then said: "I do not hold that the liberty of introducing unusual rites into the Church stands in the least on the same footing as the liberty of preaching doctrine. Now that is an important distinction, and one which the persons concerned seem to me to forget. When a ritual long established, and standing on the *mos pro lege*[1] principle, is altered in a church, it is not only that the man who does it advances his views as a teacher of the Church, but taking advantage of his position to make actual manual alterations in the services, he makes all the congregation of the church who acquiesce in these alterations parties with him in his particular view;[2] and there must be a distinction between the larger licence given in preaching, and the smaller

---

[1] In this essay very little has been said of the question of *usage*, as modifying the question of mere statute law and rubrical law. But the common sense of the English People has decided that, in case of divergence between usage and statute, the former ought to have very great weight. I may refer here to some remarks on this subject by Archdeacon Sharp—*On the Rubrics*, pp. 53—56.

[2] It should be added that those who, under such circumstances, do not agree with the Clergyman will either take open action against him, in which case the congregation will be scandalously divided, or will nurse a smouldering discontent, to the impairing of their allegiance to the Church and the injury of their religious life.

licence given in any alterations of an existing ritual."[1] I might have quoted other words of equal authority to the same effect: but the sentences of Bishop Wilberforce are likely to exercise persuasion in quarters where the same argument from other lips would receive little attention.[2] Let me now illustrate, in more particulars than one, the importance of this distinction in its reference to the topic before us.[3]

---

[1] *Chronicle of the Convocation of Canterbury*, Feb. 1868, p. 1154. I quote the passage from the Rev. W. G. Humphry's excellent essay on "The Revision of the Liturgy," in *Principles at Stake*, p. 266.

[2] I have given above the opinion of a distinguished Bishop. Let me here add the utterance of a Judicial Court, to the same effect. In the case of Sheppard v. Bennett, the Judges speak thus:—"If the Minister be allowed to introduce at his own will variations in the rites and ceremonies that seem to him to interpret the doctrine of the service in a particular direction, the service ceases to be what it was meant to be—common ground on which all Church people may meet, though they differ about some doctrines. But the Church of England has wisely left a certain latitude of opinion in matters of belief, and has not insisted on a rigorous uniformity of thought which might reduce her communion to a narrow compass." Brooke's *Six Privy Council Judgments*, pp. 231, 232.

[3] The following remarks in the Bishop of Exeter's Charge of this year seem to me to be at this crisis of high importance. I quote from the report given in the *Guardian* of July 14th:—"I wish very much indeed that my brethren the clergy would lay to heart how very serious a responsibility rests upon them if they give occasion for all this disagreement. I do not think that they sufficiently consider this matter. I do not think that they sufficiently consider how very much we are losing daily by the fact that those controversies, which always have prevailed and always will prevail in the Church of Christ, have during the last twenty years passed from the printing press and the pulpit, to which they were formerly confined, into that public worship which used to be at any rate the stronghold of our unity. Forty years ago it was certainly the case that if any clergyman went from one parish to another, if he went for a long time, or only for a single day, go where he would, the service was practically the same. That cannot now be said; but, on the contrary, very often it is quite difficult to recognise the fundamental unity in the great variety. Now, variety, of course, has its merits. There is good in variety itself; but I am quite sure that no merit which can be assigned to such variety can be compared with the loss which we sustain when the variety has gone so far as to separate us from one another. It is most deeply to be

The doctrine of sacrificial presentation in the Eucharist not being hitherto an explicit part of the system of the Church of England, a ceremony understood to express this doctrine would make it explicit. The doctrinal basis deliberately adopted in 1662 would be disturbed. The lines, which are now clear, would at least be made obscure. The change would not precisely amount to the adding of a fortieth article to the Thirty-nine; but it would introduce a new element of obscurity among the Thirty-nine. The proportions of our religious teaching would be altered. That which had previously been merely a permitted private opinion of individuals would now have found an official exponent. Something would have been introduced amongst us, which we had not before. The centre of gravity of the Prayer Book would have been shifted; and it is probably the consciousness that this result would be secured which makes some so eager for the optional use of the Eastward Position.[1]

regretted that what was once the means of bringing us so close together has now been changed into the very means and occasion of our disputes with one another. We can find unity in this matter only by steadily endeavouring to the utmost of our power to come closer to the law as we find it laid down in the Church's rubrics, and as we find it interpreted by the courts to which the Church calls us to submit. I deeply deplore that it should be necessary to speak on this matter, because I do not think that the clergy feel the importance of it as they should. I do not think that when a man adopts one practice or another which he thinks edifying to the people, which he thinks will assist his own work, it is always sufficiently considered whether it does not tend to bring in an amount of disagreement between brother and brother, and whether we do not lose far, far more by these miserable disagreements than we gain by the slight increase of apparent edification."

[1] It is obvious likewise that those who have hitherto contended that the Prayer Book Services (in harmony with the Articles and Homilies) present to us the Eucharist as a Communion and not as a Sacrifice, would be placed, for the first time, at a disadvantage. This change in the field of argument is probably well understood.

It will be urged at this point that nothing more is claimed than a merely optional use. It is contended in the most ingenuous manner (and, I am sure, quite honestly), that no notion is entertained of interfering with others who desire still to consecrate at the north end. No one proposes to make the other method, whether it be new or old, compulsory. But here, as I have said before, is one of the most dangerous and suspicious parts of the whole case. To claim only an optional use seems to show that the claim of right is weak. The rubric does not say to the Clergy "may," but "shall." I should feel far less repugnance to what is proposed, if it were to be made compulsory on all. If it were the rule that we are to say the Prayer of Consecration with our faces towards the east, I should most cheerfully acquiesce. I should then fall back upon the doctrine of the Prayer Book, which is unchanged, and which I should assume to be consistent with its authorized ceremonial. If the door is closed upon all choice, I make no objection. What I so strongly object to is this proposition to set the door ajar. If a door is ajar, it is open. This door was opened very quietly at first, but it is now creaking uneasily on its hinges; and attention is inevitably called to the change and to the consequences it may involve.

But, further, this is a very unfair method of bringing about a changed condition in our balance of Church teaching. Such things ought not to be done by a side-wind, but by open contention—not, to use Mr. Gladstone's phrase, by the " silent, steady suasion of ceremonial,"[1] but by the deliberate decision of the

---

[1] In the Article on "Ritualism," published in the *Contemporary Review* for October, 1874, p. 663.

Church, after full argument and discussion. The change of ceremony ought to follow this change of doctrine, not to precede it for the sake of introducing it. If a religious opinion, which is not to be found in the words of the Prayer Book, is to be forced upon us by help of a ceremony, how can we be expected to submit without resistance? Something like indignation takes possession of the mind, when, with such ends in view, a point of ritual is first asserted, then persevered in, notwithstanding remonstrance, and then claimed from us under the plea of conciliation.

But now, further, I venture to argue that the adoption of an alternative ceremony, in a case like this, is wrong in principle, and full of peril.

It is wrong in principle, because we have no instances in the Prayer Book, hitherto, of this kind at all. The instances which might, on merely looking at the surface of the subject, be adduced from the Burial and Baptismal Services, are not cases in point. They involve no doctrine. Moreover an exception to a rule is not an alternative rule. The liberty given to the "Priest and Clerks," at a funeral, to precede the corpse "either into the church or towards the grave," is granted, I presume, through sanitary considerations. So at a christening, the prescribed rule is immersion, the exception, however customary, is allowed for the safety of health. Thus neither case affords any parallel for that which is before us. Again, it is quite true that we have the choice of alternative prayers, on two occasions, in the Communion Service itself, and prayers too with perceptible differences in their sentiment and tone. I allude, of course, to the Collects for the Queen said immediately after the Commandments, and the Collects which succeed the Lord's Prayer near the close of the Office. But alternative prayers are not alternative ceremonies; and it may be said with some confidence that an authorized choice of position at the saying of the Prayer of Consecration in this office would introduce a principle unknown hitherto in the Church of England.

And to confirm this view, that the choice of alternative ceremonies is an expedient hitherto foreign to the Church of England, I may refer once more to the settlement of 1662.[1] The great characteristic of that settlement was, that it imperatively decided all questions of ritual observance and allowed of no exceptions. This may have been both harsh and inexpedient; but of the fact there can be no doubt.

A friend, learned in the history of constitutional law, puts the matter to me thus in a private letter:— "Throughout the whole of my reading on this subject I have found no traces of the *maximum* and *minimum* theory.[2] The whole idea of Parliament and Convocation was to fix the ritual and ceremonial of our communion on a strictly uniform basis. For my own part, I wish more concession had been made in 1603 and 1662; but the very stiffness of the opposition proves the fallacy of any such theories as the above." This great constitutional fact ought not to be forgotten by those who plead for choice in

---

[1] See above, p. 89.

[2] I had put my question with special reference to this theory of *maximum* and *minimum*, which finds much favour with some persons. I presume that this theory, applied to the position of the "celebrant," would give the Eastward position as the *maximum* and the Southward as the *minimum;* and this distinction, as it appears to me, would be grotesque, except on the hypothesis of a *doctrinal* distinction between the two positions.

the "celebrant's" position, on the ground of what took place soon after the Restoration.

But besides being wrong in principle, such a course would be full of peril for the future. We are not left in ignorance as to the purposes for which, and the spirit in which, such a permission would be used by unscrupulous partizans. We have to deal with some men whose power of assertion is astounding: and others, whose own sentiments are quite moderate, have fallen into the habit of accepting persons of the former class to be their spokesmen. As an illustration of what I mean, I will refer to what caught my eye when I was preparing to write this paragraph. Seeing my name quoted in a letter printed by a well-known paper, I was induced to read, and I saw it stated that the Bennett Judgment had affirmed Mr. Bennett's teaching on the Eucharist to be the doctrine of the Church of England: whereas the Judgment laid down a totally different doctrine, and that gentleman was saved from penal consequences merely because his words were *possibly* capable of a satisfactory explanation.[1] So in the case before us, can we doubt that if the Eastward Position is made authoritatively optional, this permission will be paraded as a triumph, and claimed as asserting the most extravagant doctrine? and have we any ground from experience for expecting that moderate High Churchmen will protest against such inference from the change? Moreover, is it not certain that those who continue to say the Consecration Prayer on the north

[1] At the close of the Judgment it is stated that the Respondent's words had been "perilously near a violation of the law," and that—the proceedings being "highly penal"—"every reasonable doubt" had been "construed in his favour." Brooke, p. 248.

side of the Lord's Table will be led to view this *their* position as a protest against error? And can such rivalries at this most holy ordinance be conducive to the edification of the Church? At present the north side is a neutral position,[1] and this is one of its great claims for permanent acceptance. But under the change supposed it would cease to be neutral. Thus, so far from tending to peace, such intentionally-contrasted diversity of usage would be the incitement and perpetuation of civil war within the Church: one congregation would be at enmity with another: idle gossip and uneasy suspicion would permeate the community: families would be divided; and I should fear that our well-meant but futile effort after conciliation would have prepared the way for a definite schism at no very distant date.[2]

And all this would be true, even if there were not in the background that further peril, which was mentioned in the earlier pages of this volume.[3] Choice in regard to one ceremonial act immediately suggests choice in other ceremonial acts. Party-spirit is not limited to one side, when different sections of the ecclesiastical community are arrayed in opposition to one another. If the extreme men of one party insist on

---

[1] Some recent papers of great interest by the Rev. Dr. Hayman suggest the question whether our Reformers, in fixing on the *north side* of the Table, were not partly influenced by the fact that there is evidence of authority for this side in very primitive times. The same papers bring us into contact with the question of the *Basilican* position of the "celebrant," a subject which seems to me to have been most inadequately treated by Mr. Morton Shaw. See Appendix N. (The Basilican Arrangement.)

[2] Instead of dwelling further in my own words on this grave aspect of the subject, I will refer at this point to the Supplement which I am allowed to place at the close of this volume.

[3] See above, pp. 23—25.

the Eastward Position, in the face of both usage and law, for the sake of a doctrinal victory, can it be supposed that the extreme men of another party will not employ the law, when it has been clearly expressed both by rubric and by canon? There may have been great forbearance hitherto on the part of Evangelicals and Low Churchmen. No widely spread wish exists to disturb those arrangements of our chancels which for many years have been customary. But if "orientation" during the Consecration Prayer were to become authoritatively permissible,[1] I fear this forbearance might be at an end. I will not dwell on this alarming prospect, but will simply repeat some words which I have used elsewhere.[2] "It is often said that no one now wishes to disturb the customary position of the Holy Table in any English church, at the east end of its chancel ; and this is quite true, if other things are allowed to remain as they were. But it is not true, if the desuetude as regards one rubric is to be made the shelter for acting on another rubric in a manner contrary to its proper meaning. Already we hear the mutterings of the storm. Some of the Clergy are very seriously beginning to consider

[1] I must repeat that the whole of this argument is directed against what I regard as the *fatal gift of choice*. If the Eastward Position were made imperative, and not permissive, I should take a very different view of the whole subject. By being made imperative, it would be denuded of doctrinal significance ; for in such case it would not be possible to use it for the purpose of declaring a doctrine not found in the words of the Prayer Book. I do not regard the Eastward Position as having inherently any doctrinal significance at all. Some have urged that the Southward Position has more of a sacrificial meaning ; and this may be quite true. But this is not a practical question.

[2] In a letter which was published in the *Times* of July 12th, and for which occasion was given by Mr. Gladstone's recent article in the *Contemporary Review*, "Is the Church of England worth preserving?"

whether it may not be their duty to obey the 82nd canon and the corresponding rubric in the Prayer Book, as regards the placing of the Lord's Table.[1] If this were done by one party, while another party insists on 'orientation,' can we contemplate without alarm the results that would follow to the Church of England? The permissive use would thus become, not what is fondly hoped for, a peaceful platform under which we might forget our differences under a clear and cheerful sky, but the erection of hostile batteries in every part of the country, with the smoke of angry debate always hanging over them. Would the Church of England be worth preserving on these terms? Could it be preserved at all?"

[1] By a very friendly critic these words have been regarded as a threat. Nothing could be further from their meaning. I deprecate extremely the moving of the Lord's Table from time to time, though I believe our Church law strictly requires it to be so moved; and it is because I deprecate this, that I think it necessary to indicate a real danger. The Archbishop of Canterbury, in addressing his recent Conference of Clergy and Laity (held at Maidstone on Jan. 27, 1875), pointed out that persistence in a new interpretation of the Consecration Rubric might force others to do what His Grace hoped his words would not encourage in the Diocese of Canterbury—to act on the Rubric which prescribes the removal of the Communion Table. The report in the *Guardian* states that these words were received with "laughter." But would not the peril arising from such increased divergences of practice be very serious?

XVI.

CONCLUSION.

Bearing of this subject on the question of the Reunion of Christendom—Its connection with other parts of the Romeward movement of the day—The Confessional—Party combinations—Changes in our religious phraseology, our devotional manuals, and the arrangements of our churches—Appeal to Moderate High Churchmen—The lesson of Whitsuntide—Duty of maintaining the right proportion of the Faith.

ONE most serious aspect of the subject which has been under our consideration is this, that the question of the Eastward Position at this part of the Communion Service[1] is inextricably mixed up with the thought of the Church of Rome.

The circumstances of the time render this quite unavoidable. Many persons, indeed, who have no Romeward tendency at all, cling with a strong pre-

[1] The assuming of the Eastward Position at other parts of our service is quite a different matter. Into the question of general orientation I do not enter. I will only say that I would far rather see the Eastward Position generally assumed by our ministers and their congregations in all the precatory parts of our service, than see the use of it concentrated on the Consecration Prayer. I have referred above (p. 64, *note*) to the difference between turning to the East during the recitation of the Creed and turning to the East during consecration in the Communion Service. In the former case no rubric is touched, no doctrinal meaning is involved, and no suggestion is given of any localized presence of the Deity at the Holy Table. As to the words used by the Bishops at the Savoy Conference (Cardwell's *Hist. of Conf.*, pp. 320, 353), it is to be remembered that the question of the moment regarded, not the turning to the East, but the turning to the Table, and that the Table then stood free from the east wall—and, further, that, though they quoted a passage from Augustine having reference to the East, which very probably expressed their own preference, still they were far from obtaining in 1662 all that they desired. See above, p. 65, *note*.

ference to this ceremonial act, because they view it as a link between the English Church and the Church Catholic; and with such feelings I must confess I have a very strong sympathy. It is quite true also that in past times, for a long period, it was customary that the consecrator in the Service of Communion should during the Prayer of Consecration face the east, and that such is the custom now with the Lutherans, both of Germany and Scandinavia. But is there not an unreality in clinging very strongly to a sentiment of this kind, especially when our Church has decided for us otherwise? The Oriental communions are too remote, and their liturgical usages too different from our own to touch us in this matter very closely in the West. As to assimilation with the Protestants of the Continent, the recommendation of it comes with a very bad grace from those at least who execrate the very name of Luther. And ought we altogether to forget those other large Christian communities, by which we are surrounded? The drawing together of the English-speaking Presbyterians from various parts of the world is becoming a remarkable feature of our times. Nor ought we to forget the vast organisations and spreading influence of the Methodists and Baptists in the New World, or the large amount of spiritual life which surrounds us in the Nonconformist bodies at home. On the whole, if thoughts of ultimate reunion[1] are in our minds, (and surely such thoughts ought to be familiar and dear), the adopting of Sacramental Orientation is more likely to be a hindrance than a help. Practically and popularly this ceremonial act will be viewed as an intentional resemblance to the Modern Church of Rome.

[1] See Appendix O (The Reunion Conferences at Bonn).

It must be carefully remembered that this matter is inevitably complicated with other very grave questions. Though circumstances do tend just now to isolate the ministering Priest's position at the Lord's Table, and to single it out for separate consideration, it is by no means in itself really an isolated subject. There are certain collateral topics belonging to our time, which we cannot reasonably forget, and which colour this whole inquiry. A few years ago the position of the minister at the Lord's Table might have been viewed, and would by most persons have been viewed, as a matter of little consequence.[1] Not so now. The change that has recently been creeping in amongst us is connected, not alone chronologically and by accident, but organically and by natural affinity, with a great religious movement which has been productive of very grave results.

The trumpets of the "Catholic Revival" are perpetually sounding in our ears; and I must be allowed to say in passing that I question whether the habit of boastfulness is a good symptom of any religious movement. It seems to me that humility and thankfulness are the proper states of mind to foster under the consciousness of spiritual success. So far as my own experience extends, I am continually shocked and

---

[1] And this I found to be the prevalent view when I was in America in the year 1871. I well remember how, in a small congregation of coloured people at Baltimore, two American Clergymen, with myself, knelt at different parts of a small Communion Table (I think in shape it was oval) made of white marble. In fact, doctrinal questions had not been connected in the public mind with the form or material of the Lord's Table, or the Priest's position in regard to it. Thus the references which have been made to our Sister Church in America, as though the permissive use of either the west or the north side of the table had been formally granted, rest upon a mistake.

pained by the harsh and intolerant language of the partizans of the school, by their unjust assumptions, by their taking credit for what belongs to others, by sarcasm or contumely according as the writer or speaker may be refined or vulgar, and especially by (what is perhaps more to be blamed than anything else) an air of patronage and infinite superiority. I make no grudging admission that much good has resulted to the Church from the movement which we commonly associate with the Oxford Tracts. Elsewhere I have expressed this very freely and strongly.[1] But it is still true that much that has been good would have been better, if it had not been hindered by the bad features of the movement; and that much too of its good has been borrowed without due acknowledgment of the source from whence it came. How many things are done now with applause by extreme High Churchmen, which were sneered at when they were done by Evangelicals! This however is not the point towards which my remarks were tending. I only felt it necessary, in honesty, to say something to this effect by the way.

One most serious fact is, that this movement, whether it be called "Tractarian" in its earlier phase, or "Ritualist" in its later, or by whatever other designation it may be known, has led to many and deplorable secessions to the Church of Rome. There is a close resemblance, in some respects, in the position of Church questions now with the state of things of which we read in the middle of the seventeenth century. Then, too, defections to Rome from the ranks of the Lau-

---

[1] I may be allowed to refer to an essay on "Parties and Party Spirit," in *Principles at Stake*.

dian divines became the cause of much uneasiness and suspicion; and these feelings were not altogether allayed because Laud and others of his school wrote strongly against the Church of Rome.[1] That is a pathetic passage in Bishop Cosin's life, in which we can trace his sorrow on account of his son's defection to that Church, and in some degree, his change of tone, after that time, in writing upon theological subjects.[2] We have the same state of things amongst us now, with these differences, that the evil is on a larger scale, and that the maintenance of Roman doctrine and Roman practice within the Church of England is bolder and more unreserved than it was then.[3]

---

[1] Many of us must remember how strongly both Cardinal Manning and Dr. Newman used to write and preach against the Church of Rome.

[2] See above, p. 83, and compare Dr. Droop's highly-important pamphlet on *The North Side of the Table*, p. 33.

[3] Two very serious facts must be carefully kept in mind in this controversy. First we have to deal with a much closer and larger approximation to Romanism within the Church of England than any which was found in the Jacobean and Caroline divines; and secondly, Romanism itself is developed to a much higher level than was the case then. As to the former point I will refer to a learned and candid Nonconformist, who is free from our own party attitudes. Dr. Stoughton, in his *Church of the Commonwealth* (1867), says that most of that work was printed before the present controversy on Ritualism arose; but he adds, "Judging from ceremonial worship now performed in certain quarters, and from the publications of persons who represent the party, we may say that Archbishop Laud never attempted to go so far in the adoption of Roman Catholic rites and vestments as his modern successors have done" (p. 547). With this compare the *Church of the Restoration* (1870), where, speaking of the architecture and ornaments of churches, he says that at this period they "indicate a feeling totally at variance with mediæval Catholicism; and nowhere does it appear that in those days the accompaniments of mediæval Ritualism were in any case employed: on the contrary, a keen jealousy of Romanism extensively prevailed" (ii. p. 183). See, too, the *Church of the Revolution* (1874). "Nothing like what is now called Ritualism had then any existence. No coloured vestments were worn by Anglicans either within or without the Establishment, nor were there any attempts at extraordinary ornamentation of either altars or

L

The sorrow and discord in many families, in consequence of conversions that have taken place, sometimes very unexpectedly, are too familiar amongst us to require description. And as to the easy way in which this is sometimes disposed of by saying that these are simply the conversions of "Evangelicals," who have been brought up without any training in "Church principles," this is a very feeble and inaccurate explanation.

Nor is it at all likely that these troubles are yet at an end. One of the most serious facts of the time is the silent preparation which is going on within the Church of England for the adoption and naturalization of views which are distinctively Roman. Those who read this pamphlet are sure to have fresh in their recollection the recent correspondence between Monsignore Capel and Canon Liddon. How can we wonder, when our eyes are opened to see what is going on around us, that the fruit, on trees so cultivated, gradually ripens and then falls? Conversions which we hear of, one by one, of clergymen here and there, or members of aristocratic families, are like minute guns in the night, warning us of our danger. It seems to me madness at such a time not to be explicit in matters of theology. When we know that we are on the edge of a precipice, that is not the time when we ought to desire to be in a mist.

In illustration of the combinations in which we are forced, by the circumstances of the day, to take even this question of the Eastward Position in consecrating

---

churches" (p. 323). As to the Non-jurors, "pomp, such as is now so fashionable, was to them an impossibility; not," adds the writer, "that I find them manifesting any cravings in that direction" (p. 398).

at the Communion, I will make a slight reference to the subject of the Confessional. It is quite true that in the practice of what is commonly understood by that term the attitude assumed by the Priest is not sacrificial, but judicial :[1] and the two ought carefully to be distinguished. Still it is also true that the same persons who are excessive in the one claim are excessive in the other. We cannot practically disentangle the efforts of those who wish to introduce the systematic confessional into the Church of England from efforts to introduce by means of ceremony such sacrificial views of the Eucharist as are inconsistent with the Reformation. Whatever helps the one forward helps the other also. Not only are the same powers claimed for the English Clergy that are claimed within the Church of Rome for the Roman :[2] but Roman methods of administering the practice of confession and absolution are introduced: the Roman phraseology on these subjects is made familiar: the same modes adopted of preparing the Clergy, so far as it can be secretly done, for their mysterious duty,

[1] I have endeavoured to state this popularly in a little book recently published under the title of *Sacramental Confession*.

[2] This has been done with the strongest emphasis and in at least one quarter deserving of the highest respect. Let us then look at the language of the Council of Trent on this subject. "Since Bishops and Priests are, as it were, God's authorised interpreters (*interpretes et internuncii quidam*), who in His name teach men the Divine law and the precepts of life, and represent (*gerunt*) on earth the person of God Himself, it is manifest that their office is such that none greater can be conceived: wherefore they are rightly called, not only angels, but also gods, because they hold among us the Divine power (*vim et numen*) of the Immortal God." And then follows a co-ordinate sentence in regard to the Eucharist : "The power of making (*conficiendi*) and offering the body and blood of Christ, and also of remitting sins, surpasses human reason and intelligence : nay, nothing equal to it or like to it can be found in the world."—*Catech. Concil. Trid.* de ordinis sacramento c. vii."

which are provided by Roman manuals;[1] and there is beginning to result, in consequence, the same kind of uneasiness and suspicion which in Roman Catholic countries terribly separates the Clergy from the Laity.

I know that I shall be blamed for introducing here the mention of this subject. It will be said that it is unjust to mix up together two things which are not necessarily connected, and that this is done to create a prejudice in the public mind against the Eastward Position. I am quite innocent of any such intention. The true injustice consists in refusing to see that things which are inextricably combined together must naturally strengthen one another. Why do not those who advocate the Eastward Position without any sympathy with these grave and alarming tendencies, boldly separate themselves, define their own ground, and enable us to see wherein they differ from others? Why is a common ceremony made the silent bond between those who differ so widely? If this great Romeward movement is repudiated in heart, why, instead of being encouraged, is it not publicly rebuked? Why are all the hard words reserved for "Evangelicals," and for the few independent men who, without any connection with party, endeavour to call attention to the peril in which we are placed? The impression must inevitably be created that large numbers of our Clergy care very

---

[1] I must especially refer to Part II. of *The Priest in Absolution*, which is printed without any publisher's name, cannot be procured by any ordinary clergyman, and is privately distributed among those who are in confidential communication with one another. I am far from saying that this book, which is now before me, is fit for general perusal. I only refer to it as an exemplification of the clandestine difficulty with which we have to deal.

little for the undoing of the Reformation, if only they can remain under the vague general classification of "High Churchmen." If men are combined together in this way before the public eye, the most extreme among them must gain the advantage of the momentum derived from numbers. Illustrations without number could be given of the harm which is resulting from this cause on every side. I will content myself with one, which came accidentally before my eye. It may be taken as a sample of all the rest.

In a well-known organ[1] of those whom we may, without exaggeration, term "Ritualists," I read the following words :—" If the Eucharist is really *the great Sacrifice that taketh away the sin of the world*, the due celebration *of a single Mass* is of infinitely greater consequence than a hundred general elections, or liquidation of a hundred national debts. Priests say they do not use the chasuble because it offends the well-meant prejudices of some of their people. Why are these people offended? Simply as a matter of taste and fancy? Certainly not ; but because they do not believe in *the Sacrifice of the Mass*." And then on another page of the same paper I find the following : "A very important meeting was held at Oxford yesterday week : it was attended by about sixty gentlemen, who represented almost *every shade of thought in the High Church School*, and who remained in deliberation the live-long day :" and the practical impression of the occasion is said to have been this, that the party was *united* "*in a manner that it never could boast of before*." It is the juxtaposition of these things which illustrates our present danger ; and examples of the same kind

[1] The *Church Times* of Oct. 23, 1874.

might be gathered every day from materials in print scattered over the country.

There is, I am persuaded, a crisis in our present position, with risks hanging over the Church of England of the future, quite unperceived by many excellent Church-people, who float along the stream of the current theology without being at all aware of the direction in which it is moving. This state of things might be elucidated at some length from various symptoms, which are in truth both cause and effect, arising out of these evils and extending them further,—symptoms in our theological language, in the devotional books of the day, and in the structural and decorative arrangement of our churches. A very few words may be permitted on each of these points.

As to language, there is growing up side by side with the sober and sound phraseology of our Prayer Book a religious vocabulary very different. As regards the subject specially before us here, new modes of speech, of various gradations, are beginning to be more or less in vogue. The policy of familiarizing the public mind with language formerly unaccustomed is well understood; and the less startling novelties lead easily up to those which would at first cause a shock, such as "the sacrifice of the Altar" and "the Mass." The solemn Scriptural designation of the Eucharist—"the Lord's Supper"—is treated with contumely. To speak of it as "a celebration" is more in favour, because we are thus reminded more of the priest and less of the congregation. Even barbarous uses of language are commended to us, if they are used by us in common with the rest of the Latin Church. The priest is said by Anglicans as well as Roman Catholics to "communicate" those who come to receive the consecrated elements at his hands. In themselves many such things are extremely trivial: but in the aggregate they may produce a considerable and serious change. "Minuta sunt, sed multa sunt," as St. Augustine says of repeated acts which result in habits. A process of this kind is going on, which threatens to alter the whole outward expression of the Church of England, though its old internal structure remains the same.[1] There is (if my memory is correct) a part of Gloucester Cathedral, where the solid and simple Norman architecture is reticulated, so to speak, with elaborate panelling of the Perpendicular period, and by this process an extraordinary change has been produced, while yet the old work remains. Not very dissimilar is the transformation now in progress with much of our theological vocabulary.[2]

With this change is closely connected a similar change in the character of many of our devotional books, which are published and used side by side

---

[1] Another illustration comes before me casually, as I correct these pages. At the public institution of a clergyman into a new parish, it was recently said (according to the report of a local newspaper) that the office of the Parish Priest in the Church of England is "to instruct the people and to *plead the Holy Sacrifice.*" The language of the Ordination Service is different. If phraseology drawn from thence were used, we should say that his office is "to instruct the people and to *administer the Holy Sacraments.*" See above pp. 121—123.

[2] With the copying of Roman phraseology must be classed the copying of Roman costume, which has caused so painful a sense of division among us, without (so far as I can see) any religious advantage whatever. Mr. Beresford Hope (p. 163) finds fault with "exchanging the old familiar full and graceful surplice for the little scamped article in vogue in certain churches." It may or may not be true, as some suppose, that the Roman fashion, in this respect, grew out of the cutting off of lace from the bottom of the surplice; but great discomfort is caused to many minds by such little imitations of the French *sacristie.*

with our Prayer Book, but are very different from it in tone and teaching. These are parasitical growths which tend to stifle and kill that on which they grow, and the danger of this result is very serious. The contents of some of these publications are brought before the public eye in the correspondence to which allusion has been made; but a large amount of this evil is only privately known; and, for my own part, I am disposed to think that the greatest danger lurks in some of those books which at first sight deviate least from our common standards; as, for instance, when the instructions concerning confession are printed from the book of 1549 along with those which finally superseded them in 1662; or when suggestions of sacrificial presentation in the Communion are interpolated among those prayers and rubrics of our authorised manual which contain nothing of the kind.

As to other suggestions of the same nature, which result from changes in the structure and decoration of our churches, I can enter on this subject with a very clear conscience. When a man has been occupied during a large part of some busy years in earnest efforts to restore a dilapidated cathedral to its ancient beauty and dignity, he can afford to be very indifferent to imputations of disregarding propriety and solemnity in the condition of our sacred fabrics. It is, however, one thing to act in the spirit of our Homily for "Keeping clean and repairing of Churches," and quite another thing to promote the transformation of their chancels into a condition not intended or contemplated by the Prayer Book. Our architects, following their instinct of taste and consistency, and in some cases impelled by clergymen who have doctrinal ends in view, have done much towards effecting this transformation.[1] I hope I am sensible of the great obligations under which many distinguished members of a noble profession have laid the Church of these days. Nor is it fair that, while following æsthetic aims, they should be held responsible for the theological results of their efforts to bring back our churches to the mediæval pattern, and for the peril in which we are consequently placed. It is most natural that they should wish to secure harmony and completeness in the churches which they restore, or which they build in the styles of the past. Still it is true that those churches were originally erected, and that those styles flourished, when the old Basilican method of celebrating the Holy Eucharist had passed away, and when those doctrines, against which the Reformation was directed, had begun to reach their position of commanding power. The glorious era of our ecclesiastical architecture was the age of Innocent III. The expression of the Eucharistic doctrine of that age cannot be at home in the Church of England; and no one can for a moment believe that a Church can be in a safe position, when its service-books and authorised formularies, on the one hand, and the structural and

[1] There is, however, another side of the subject, which ought in fairness to be stated; and the statement shall here be made in the words of a friend who has given close attention to the question. He thinks that in many cases our modern architects have almost forced the Eastward Position on the Clergy, by ordering altar-like Communion Tables of great size, and by erecting "foot-paces" of such a form as to leave convenient room for kneeling on the west side of the Tables only. He adds, that such things are often not observed on the plan, and that thus churches are consecrated before the evil is remedied. At the beginning of this century the Communion Tables were small, and the "foot-pace" not common.

artistic arrangements of its houses of worship on the other, are not in agreement and harmony together. I press this subject, however, no further than to invite attention to the inconsistency which now troubles us in this respect, and to ask that it may be considered.

In concluding this essay, I venture to make an appeal, respectfully but very earnestly, to those of the Clergy whose place is among the Moderate High Churchmen. They probably hold, more than any other class of persons, the future destinies of the Church of England in their hands. This party (not that I have any wish to term it a "party") will always be the most numerous among the parties of the Church. The conservative spirit of the Universities, the traditional feelings of country gentlemen, the love of quiet and order, the dread of vulgar fanaticism, will combine to swell their numbers and to make them strong; and, hitherto, it must be admitted with regret, that, not actively, but by passive encouragement, their strength has been largely used to shelter those, of whom even these Moderate High Churchmen would say that their Romeward tendencies are dangerous. The appeal is here made, not to those who view the Eastward Position, because of its high doctrinal and devotional significance, as a matter of principle, but to those with whom it is only a matter of preference, or who, not having this preference, are unwilling to invade the liberty of those who have it. To the clergy of this class who have adopted this position, so that it now becomes a point of honour to maintain it, surely it may be urged that to stand on a point of honour, when the peace and comfort of others are at stake, is no part of the Christian code.

There is, however, one part of the Christian code strictly characteristic of our religion and most imperative: it is that which charges us to beware of causing "offence," of giving needless pain, of exciting groundless suspicions, of wounding the consciences of those who are weaker than ourselves. From whom ought the concession in a case like this to come? Is it not from those who are invited to resign a preference, without the gratifying of which they can live religiously and serve God effectually, rather than from those whose consciences must be disquieted by a course of action which they cannot help viewing as in the highest degree perilous to the Church?[1]

But rather let us, each and all, irrespective of party combinations, make an appeal to one another for charity and candour, for mutual forbearance and the love of truth. The writing of these pages, begun at Christmas and continued afterwards at intervals, amid many difficulties and with many anxious thoughts, is brought to a close at Whitsuntide. It would be a most irreligious forgetting of the sacred season, if, in such a crisis of our Church history, there were no desire for that teaching of the Holy Spirit which alone can keep us free from prejudice and bitterness, alone can enable us to see the revealed truths of the Gospel in their true balance and proportion. In the light of Whitsunday, we ought more clearly than at any other time to see this true balance and proportion. This festival is the perpetual testimony of the Catholic Church against a merely ceremonial religion — the perpetual opportunity of coming back to the right

[1] See Mr. Kennion's paper, which I have been allowed to print in the Supplement to this volume.

standard, when we have deviated from it; of restoring the symmetry of our Christianity, when through controversy that symmetry has been marred.

It cannot be too carefully and constantly recollected that our duty is not simply to be faithful to the religion which has been revealed, but to the right analogy of all parts of that religion: and that right analogy cannot be preserved except by keeping the lower in subordination to the higher. The great topic, too, of this festival sets forth a commanding feature of this law of subordination. Can any one, who reads the New Testament simply, fail to observe how far the direct action of the Divine Spirit upon the soul is placed above all positive outward observances, even if those positive outward observances are Divinely-appointed Sacraments? Is it not most clearly revealed that it is in and through the Holy Spirit that the soul is united to Christ? And is not some of our present trouble due to this — that we have intruded the Eucharist into the place which the Holy Spirit ought to have occupied in our system?[1]

And one other concluding thought is proper at this season of Whitsuntide. In the Eucharist we call Christ to *remembrance:* but we *are living* in the dispensation of the Spirit. While Christ is absent the Spirit is present.[2] We cannot make a mistake in using such words:

---

[1] Above (p. 111) attention is invited to the *consensus* of the New Testament as respects the supremacy of the "Word" and the absence of any such testimony to the supremacy of the Eucharist. The same line of argument might be followed here. But instead of naming any texts I will simply refer to a most edifying book by the Rev. E. H. Bickersteth, entitled *The Spirit of Life,* pp. 23—35. See also pp. 155 and 182.

[2] Mr. Gladstone (*Contemporary Review* for 1875, p. 211) speaks, apparently with strong disapproval, of some who view the Eucharist as expressing the *Real Absence* of Christ. I am not aware that this phrase has

for they are the Lord's own. His departing was the condition of this abiding spiritual presence. St. John makes no mention of the Holy Eucharist in connection with the Last Supper; but in our Bibles three chapters are filled with the discourse which St. John relates to have been addressed to the Apostles after that Supper. Might it not be wise for us always to read this discourse, before we speak or write in controversy concerning the Eucharist? Our Lord says that He is departing, but that He will give them "another Comforter that He may abide with them for ever, even the Spirit of Truth." Again He says, "These things have I spoken unto you, being yet present with you; but the Comforter, which is the Holy Ghost, whom the Father will send in My name, He shall bring all things to your remembrance, whatsoever I have said unto you:" and again, still more strongly, "It is expedient for you that I go away: for if I go not away, the Comforter will not come unto you : but if I depart, I will send Him unto you . . . . When He, the

obtained any theological currency. But, after all, would it not express the teaching of our Blessed Lord in these passages? It seems to me that the introduction of the word "presence" into our controversies on the Eucharist has led to much confusion of thought. There is no Scriptural authority for the use of the word in this connection, and the phrase "Real Presence" is ambiguous. Our Lord promised something more than His presence to the believing recipient : He promised Himself. At the same time I feel that we cannot make rules for one another as to our apprehension of Christ's communicating of Himself in this ordinance. There must be much mutual toleration in regard to so mysterious a subject. It is in combination with the doctrine of *Sacrifice by a human priest* that the doctrine of the *Real Presence* becomes so serious. Archdeacon Wilberforce said, in his work on the subject, that "the doctrine of the Eucharistic Sacrifice has its root in the truth of the Real Presence," p. 364. I will add that he said in the same work that the Communion Service in our English Prayer Book had been "divested of its sacrificial character," p. 440.

Spirit of Truth is come, He will guide you into all truth .... I came forth from the Father, and am come into the world: again I leave the world and go to the Father." And in harmony with this teaching is the teaching of the whole body of the Epistles. That which is supreme in the system of doctrine there exhibited is not any sacramental presence, but the indwelling of the Holy Spirit Himself, in the Christian Church and the Christian soul.

APPENDIX.

A.

(*Page* 8.)

THE BRIGHTON CHURCH CONGRESS.

CANON RAWLINSON occupies a position of considerable responsibility in regard to this present controversy; and for his wide historical learning, and the great service he has rendered to Biblical Science, as respects the Old Testament, he deserves to occupy such a position. When men of inferior note insist on connecting a high doctrinal meaning with the Eastward Position, and use violent and exaggerated language on the subject, this might be treated as a mere rivulet of controversy, which, however noisy, is harmless. But when men of mark, like Canon Rawlinson, and others who might easily be named, insist, in the strongest terms, on this particular connection of ceremony and doctrine, then we see that it is a powerful stream of opinion with which we have to do, and that if the stream is not stemmed or diverted, serious harm will result to the Church.

Canon Swainson expressly says that it was a speech from Canon Rawlinson in the Lower House of the Convocation of Canterbury which changed his attitude in reference to this controversy, so that, having previously been willing to concede the use of the Eastward Position, he now feels bound to resist this change. Professor Rawlinson had said "that little acts might involve the greatest doctrine; and there was no disguising the fact that the observances of the Ritualists were

used for that very purpose; they declared that they set
doctrines before the people by those external acts; the whole
question was, in fact, that of the *Real Presence;* there was
no use in blinking the matter." He proceeded to say that, as
regards the position of the priest, "relaxation" must be "in
favour of the non-ritualistic party."[1] At this language Professor
Swainson naturally took alarm. He found that mode
of "ministering the Sacraments," which had been the almost
universal tradition of the Clergy of the Church of England,
and which was adopted by the very bishops who assisted in
making the laws of 1662, treated as an action "now merely
allowed by the favour of the Ritualists," and this in the cause
of "a doctrine which is not the doctrine of the Church of
England;" and part of the result we see in his excellent and
highly important pamphlet on "the Rubrical Question of
1874."

Consistent with his course in Convocation was that which
Canon Rawlinson followed at the Brighton Church Congress.
The subject there on the third day was the "Fabrics and
Services of our Church," on which the two leading papers,
both containing excellent suggestions, but both tending
strongly in one direction, were read by Mr. Beresford Hope
and Mr. Street. So far as I remember (I was not present the
whole time), these papers were listened to with polite and
decorous attention; and yet they both had this characteristic,
that they reiterated, again and again, with marked emphasis,
the word "altar," which has been excluded from the Prayer
Book, and of that word which is authorised there, made no use
at all, except in one sentence, where it was used in concession,
I might almost say in condescension.[2] But when Professor
Donaldson called attention to this remarkable fact, adding
that "every sensuous impression of the Lord's Table" is far
"inferior to the innate sacredness of the solemn rite" which is
there celebrated, he was received with a rudeness, which I
cannot recollect without extreme pain, when I consider his
venerable years, his eminence, and his great services to a

---

[1] The quotation is given by Canon Swainson from the *Guardian.*
[2] *Authorised Report of the Church Congress held at Brighton,* p. 282.

noble art.[1] From this moment there was evident uneasiness in the meeting; and the feeling was brought to a crisis when Canon Rawlinson said, "The important thing in the Church is the altar and the services in connection with it. I have used that word, and I will just say that I have used it because I found it to be the name given in the Bible. It is so termed in every place but one, when it is called the table. That it is the Lord's Table I am most willing not only to allow, but to affirm most strongly; but in the one place where it is called the table, it is called so in contrast with the Table of Devils, which was the heathen altar." Such criticism of the New Testament appeared to many persons at the time as very startling; but that occasion did not seem to me the proper opportunity for discussing so serious a question. Feeling, however the gravity of the subject, I wrote afterwards, and was allowed to publish in the *Standard* of Oct. 26 and Nov. 16 two letters entitled "Altar or Table?" These letters I hope to republish, after the most careful consideration of all the correspondence (so far as it is known to me) which resulted from them. Many persons did me the favour to write to me privately on the subject. I hope they will accept a very busy life as an excuse for some delay. I will only add here that St. Paul's avoidance of the word "altar" both in 1 Cor. ix. 13, 14, and in 1 Cor. x. 18, 21, when it would have been the natural word to use, if there had been in the Christian system a literal "altar" correlative to the Jewish, seems to me decisive against Canon Rawlinson's exegesis, especially when consideration is given to the whole analogy of the teaching of the New Testament on this subject.

---

[1] At the age of eighty it is hardly likely that he is less wise than some of the Clergy who were rude to him. It should be added that he is the founder of the "Royal Institute of British Architects," of which Sir G. Gilbert Scott is now the President.

B.

(Page 34.)

ELEGY UPON AN ALTAR.

APPENDED to Ley's letter to Bishop Bridgeman is "a Postscript to the precedent Letter, for further satisfaction to the Reader touching the publication of it, and some other points of moment that appertain to it." Among other contents of the postscript is "an Ironical Elegy," bearing this title: "A sad complaint of the late Altar newly erected, and prepared for a new sacrifice, by the Lord Bishop of Chester, in the upper end of the Chancell of the Cathedrall Church of Chester, in the new intended Chapell there, newly pulled downe (as it was high time)." Some of the lines in this Elegy are as follows:—

> "I, who from those faire banks of *Tyber* came,
> A stranger here by nature and by name,
> I, whom the reverend Father here had placed
> And with the name of *Altar* had me graced,
> * * * *
> Am now become the object of all scorne,
> My members and materials rent and torne.
> Come, holy Fathers of the Convocation,
> See and lament my wofull desolation:
> Come, Deanes and Prebends, in your surplice clad,
> From whose examples I much reverence had;
> Loud Petty Canons, come, roare out your cryes,
> Make up your Chorus in sad elegies
> For my departure * * * *
> Come, Conducts, Choristers."

I quote these lines, not because I have any sympathy with this mode of treating a grave subject, but because such documents, preserved from the past, are a serious warning for us in the present. I cannot but think that one peril involved in the great movement of the day within the Church of England, if it is recklessly urged on in disregard of both usage and law, is the risk of a violent Puritan reaction.

C.

(*Page 36.*)

THE PLACE OF THE LORD'S TABLE BETWEEN 1640 AND 1662.

I THINK I should have avoided the use of the word "whimsical," if, when I wrote the sentences on p. 36, I had known who had maintained the unbroken continuity of the altarwise position of the Lord's Table from 1640 onwards. Still some very strong expression is necessary to denote my conviction of the utter inconsistency of such a view with both the probabilities and the facts of the case. The Dean of Bristol (*Letter to Rev. F. V. Mather on the Ornaments Rubrics*, p. 30) quotes Dr. Liddon as saying in a pamphlet entitled *The Purchas Judgment* (p. 12), "Since the Reformation, the Position of the Holy Table has been what it is now. . . . the position which the Holy Table has continuously occupied since the Primacy of Laud;" and Dr. Bright as saying in the same pamphlet (p. 13) "The revisers of 1661, who framed this Rubric (the Consecration Rubric) were thinking of a table set, as was then the case, altarwise, along or in front of the east wall. This arrangement of Charles the First's time had made good its ground: it was established in practice, though not enjoined by law." I have not seen the pamphlet to which the Dean of Bristol refers; and it may contain sentences which modify the impression produced by those which he quotes. If not, I cannot help expressing my earnest hope that these statements may be reconsidered. We look to our Theological Professors for guidance in the reading of Church History, and a sound argument cannot be erected on an erroneous historical basis.

D.

(*Page* 40.)

CATECHISM OF CHURCH DOCTRINE AND CHURCH PRACTICE IN 1674.

THE full title of this Catechism is "'Ενιαυτός; *or, a Course of Catechising, being the marrow of all orthodox and practical expositions upon the Church Catechism, and of all controversies upon Church Customs and Observances, digested into LII. heads for LII. Sundays in the year, useful for Ministers and their People, Schoolmasters and their Scholars, Parents and their Children, Masters and their Servants.* Second edition, enlarged and illustrated with forty-eight Copper-pieces, fitted to the several occasions. London: Printed by F. C., for Fra. Kirkman, and are to be sold at his shop over against the Robin Hood in Fenchurch Street, near the Aldgate. 1674."[1] The general character of the book is this—that it is a very carefully prepared manual of catechetical instruction, based in the earlier part on our authorised Catechism, and illustrated throughout by engravings. It is to be observed, moreover, that the book is no mere expression of Puritan opinion, but very much the contrary. This is made evident by the approving references throughout to such authors as Hammond, Sanderson, Mede, Bilson, Morton and Sparrow. It is further made evident by various incidental phrases, which are full of meaning, as, for instance, "No form of good words is dead to me if my heart be not dead;" and again, "If we cast off everything that Rome hath, we must throw away our Bibles." The sacraments in this volume are spoken of as

[1] This volume is the property of the Rev. G. T. Horn, Rector of Haverfordwest, who described it briefly in a letter published in the *Guardian* of December 16th, 1874, and to whose courtesy I owe the opportunity of examining it carefully. The book must be very rare, since no copy of it is found in the University Library at Cambridge. I have, however, seen a second copy in the library of the Master of Jesus' College in that University. The first edition, as we learn from Mr. Fuller Russell, seems to have been published in 1664.

"conveyances" of the grace we pray for. Its advice to the devout Christian is that, after his private prayers, he should "go, if he can, to Church, to receive absolution of the Minister, who hath power to declare the will of God concerning poor penitent sinners." But especially I am disposed to lay stress on the prominence which, in harmony with the plan of our Prayer Book, is given to Saints' Days. In the questions on the Fourth Commandment, it is asked whether there are "no other days to be set apart by Christians except the Lord's Day?" And at the end of the volume a large space is given, with illustrative engravings, to the days thus set apart, which are described as "the ornaments of Religion, the witnesses of ancient Truth, motives to serious Devotion, lasting Records on earth, and shadows of everlasting felicity in Heaven." The substance of what is here written has been published previously in the *Guardian*; and I must adhere to the opinion I have expressed of the book, notwithstanding a criticism published by Mr. Fuller Russell in the *Church Review* of May 29th. This being the general character of the work, the following question and answer, having reference to the position of the priest during the Prayer of Consecration, assumes a very high importance, especially when we consider the date of publication: "*Q. Why doth the Priest stand on the North side of the Table? A. To avoid the Popish superstition of standing towards the East.*"

E.

(*Page* 42.)

BISHOP NICOLSON'S VISITATION IN 1703.

THE title of Bishop Nicolson's Manuscript Journal, preserved in the Chapter Library at Carlisle, is as follows:—"*Miscellany Accounts of the Present State of the Churches, Parsonage and Vicarage Houses, Glebelands, &c., in the several Parishes within the Diocese of Carlisle, as they appeared to me by view on the*

[1] See L'Estrange, as quoted in the Preface.

credible information of witnesses hereafter mentioned, A.D. 1703." The volume is 8vo., and consists of 404 pages. The writing is close but very legible. Besides the instances of the Lord's Table being placed East and West, which are named above, Orton, Bongate, and "several other places" in the Deanery of Westmoreland are mentioned as exhibiting the same arrangement in their churches. In many cases rails are noted being wanting; but it is to be observed that though directions are repeatedly given by the Bishop for the providing of rails, no order is found for the setting of the Table in what he himself doubtless viewed as the most suitable position. My information regarding the contents of this MS. volume is derived from two of the Canons of Carlisle.

F.

(*Page* 44.)

FURTHER INSTANCES OF CHANCELS REMAINING IN THEIR OLD CONDITION.

SINCE the earlier pages of this book were written I have received most obliging communications from various Clergymen, who mention several existing or recent illustrations of this part of my argument. It would seem that the county of Gloucester is peculiarly rich in examples. The most remarkable is that of Deerhurst, which possesses "one of the oldest and most interesting churches in the kingdom: Mr. Parker calls it the earliest *dated* church." Here, in the chancel, which is, proportionally, very large, is "a continuous row of seats, running round on the North, South and East sides; on the West side comes a low railing with a gate: the Holy Table stands, unattached to any wall, in the centre: the communicants arrange themselves in the seats, and the Minister goes to them with the elements, white cloths being placed along the desks of the seats, all round—no doubt an ancient practice." Till within the last thirty years the Table seems to have stood "longitudinally." The same correspondent states that a similar arrangement was recently found in the church of Winchcombe, "a small country town among the Cotswold Hills, giving its name to a Rural Deanery." A second correspondent states that at Hailes near Winchcombe he " saw about thirty years ago a Communion Table, which he was able to walk round, and which the Clergyman of the place said had remained in that position since the days of Cromwell :" a third, that in the parish church of Ogleworth in the same county, he has " seen the Communion Table with its end to the East wall of the Chancel ;" and a fourth gives the instance of the parish of Toddington near Winchcombe as " one in which the Communion Table has never, so far as can be ascertained, stood against the East wall of the Church," adding the following remarks :—" When I came here in 1854 I found it placed nearly equidistant between the East wall and the chancel rails, and it so continued until the church was pulled down, and will probably be so placed again when the building is completed." A Clergyman in Worcestershire names Rock Church near Bewdley, in that county, as one where a monument, with an effigy of life-size, was placed in 1554 against the East wall on the floor, and adds that he believes that in the adjoining parish of Abberley, a pew used to intervene between the East wall and the Communion Table. I may conclude these notices by quoting what a friend writes to me from Kent: " At Hollingbourne in this county there is a very well-known and handsome cloth for the Holy Table. It was elaborately embroidered by the Ladies Culpepper during the exile of Charles II., and given by them to the church at the Restoration. The peculiarity of this cloth is that the very rich embroidery is the same on all *four* sides; and the dimensions prove that the table and cloth were made one for the other, so that the cloth should hang down on each and every side alike."[1]

[1] Since this was written I have received further illustrations from the county of Kent, the most important being the fact that till the beginning of this century the Mayor and Corporation of Dover used to have their seats on the East of the Communion Table.

G.

(Page 47.)

THEORY THAT THE NORTH SIDE IS THE NORTHERN PART OF THE WEST SIDE.

Though I regard the debate on this subject as an extinct controversy, I will mention (after referring, by the way, to the "Directorium Anglicanum," p. 38, where the theory in question is taken for granted) the following treatises, where the arguments derived from Jewish ritual are effectually disposed of:—"The North Side of the Table," by Canon C. J. Elliott, pp. 3—10 ; the "Christian Observer" for July 1874, pp. 515—519; and the "Altar Question in the light of the Mosaic Ritual," by Rev. R. W. Kennion. In the second article which Canon Simmons published in the "Contemporary Review" (Jan. 1867), it is stated (p. 3) that Dr. Littledale had announced a new edition of his treatise on the "North Side of the Altar," "revised and expanded, and containing answers to the ingenious arguments of Mr. Droop and Mr. Elliott;" but though eight years have since elapsed, I have not heard of the appearance of this new edition.

H.

(Page 67.)

THE BREAKING OF THE BREAD BEFORE 1662.

In Cosin's "Notes and Collections on the Book of Common Prayer," he speaks of this subject in such a manner as to show his own opinion very clearly, and also to make it probable that the public breaking of the bread at consecration was frequently practised before our present rubric was inserted in the Prayer Book. "At the words *He took the bread and He brake it, and He took the cup*, no direction is given to the priest (as in King Edward's service-book there was, and as in most places it is still in use) to *take the bread and cup into his hands*, nor to *break the bread before the people*, which is a needful circumstance belonging to this Sacrament; and therefore, for his better warrant therein, such a direction ought here to be set in the margin of the book." *Works* in Anglo-Catholic Library, vol. v. p. 516. In another part of the same volume (p. 342) we find Cosin quoting with approval the following passage from Calixtus:—" Voluit Dominus Corpus et Sanguinem suum eo modo sumi, quin panem quoque et vinum, cum quibus exhibentur, eo modo tractari, qui *ad passionem animis fidelium imprimendam* esset idoneus. Nempe voluit Sanguinem seorsim et tanquam a Corpore separatum accipi, et voluit benedictum panem, qui *κοινωνία* est Corporis, frangi, et vinum calici infusum effundi, ut ita et passio et mors, ac Corporis cruciatus et Sanguinis effusio *repræsentaretur*, et non modo menti, sed *ipsis quoque oculis* per hujusmodi *signa et actiones* efficaciter ingenerentur."

I.

(*Page* 72.)

BISHOP BEVERIDGE ON SEEING THE BREAD BROKEN.

NEAR the end of his treatise on "The Necessity and Advantage of Frequent Communion," Beveridge points out how "that incomparable office which our Church hath made for the administration of this Holy Sacrament" is so contrived that "from the beginning to the end of it there is matter and occasion given us all along for the exercise of our faith in Christ." Then he proceeds to show in detail throughout the office "how we should act our faith all the while that we are at the Lord's Table, so as to receive spiritual strength and comfort from it;" and when he reaches the Prayer of Consecration, he writes as follows:—" And now there is nothing either seen, or said, or done, but what puts us in mind of something or other whereupon to employ and exercise our faith in the highest manner that we can. When we see the bread and wine set apart for consecration, it reminds us of God's eternal purpose and determinate counsel to offer up His Son as a sacrifice for the sins of the world. The minister's reading the Prayer of Consecration and performing that whole work alone, none of the people speaking a word, or any way assisting him in it, may put us in mind how the whole work of our salvation was accomplished by Christ alone, no mere creature contributing anything at all towards it; and therefore we should believe in Him as our only Mediator and Advocate. When we hear those words, 'Who in the same night that He was betrayed took bread,' we are then by faith to behold our Lord at His last supper, there instituting this Sacrament which we are now to receive, and distributing it to His apostles with His own most blessed hands. When we see the bread broken, we should then call to mind that grief and pain, those bitter agonies and passions, which the eternal Son of God suffered for our sins, and in our stead. How ' He was wounded for our transgressions and bruised for our iniquities;' how His blessed body was broken, His hands and His feet fastened to the cross, with nails drove through them, and all for our sins—even for ours. And so when the minister takes the cup into his hands, or pours out the wine, we are then by faith to behold how fast the blood trickled down from our dear Lord and Saviour's head when crowned with thorns, from His hands and feet when nailed to the cross, from His side when pierced with the spear, and from His whole body when He was in His agony, and all to wash away our sins."[1]

[1] Hartwell Horne's ed. of Beveridge's *Works*, vol. i. p. 602. To the evidence furnished under this head several additions might be made. I will here only mention three devotional books, to which a friend refers me, containing passages of the same kind. The first is Jeremiah Dyke's *Worthy Communicant* (1645 and 1661). This book is dedicated to Thomas Earl of Winchilsea and Cecil Countess of Winchilsea, which fixes the date of the first edition between March 1633, when he succeeded his mother, and November, 1634, when he died. The other book is *A Familiar Guide to the Lord's Supper*, by Theophilus Dorrington (1695), and *Reformed Devotions* by the same author (1704), the latter of which had, I believe, a preface by Dr. Hickes.

J.

(*Page* 76.)

THE CONSECRATION OF ABBEY DORE CHURCH.

MUCH stress has been recently laid upon a form for the Consecration of the Church of Abbey Dore in Herefordshire, published from a MS. in the British Museum, collated with another MS. at Lambeth.[1] It is stated on the authority of a Rector of Dore, who wrote in 1727, that this ceremony was performed by Field, Bishop of St. David's, under a commission from Wren, Bishop of Hereford. On the form of the Consecration ceremony, as thus published, I beg leave to offer the following remarks.

This ceremony, inasmuch as it took place in 1634, can be no illustration of the meaning of our present Consecration-rubric, which did not then exist, but was introduced into the Prayer Book in 1662. Nor is there any proof that it represented the general custom of the time to which it belonged: it may only indicate the kind of service which Field, an obscure Bishop (or perhaps Wren, a very distinguished one), desired to introduce. Moreover it prescribes various ceremonial acts not authorised even by the Prayer Book as it stood in the reign of Charles I.[2] On the other hand, it is to be observed that though the people are directed to turn eastwards at the saying of the Apostles' Creed,[3] the Chaplain and Priest officiate during the Communion Service at the North end and South end of the Lord's Table, which are also termed the

---

[1] The eagerness with which Mr. Beresford Hope and Mr. Malcolm MacColl have seized on this publication is as remarkable as their omitting to notice some other publications which have a far more important bearing on the question before us. The pamphlet was published last year by the Rev. J. Fuller Russell.

[2] Thus the direction that the Table is to stand at the East end of the chancel (p. 15) is in violation of a rubric and a canon, both of which were extant in 1634.

[3] P. 19.

North part and South part.[1] Even as regards the Bishops' position in the Consecration Prayer, there seems to me to be a certain haziness in the instructions for his position: for he is directed to stand not "before the Table, with his face eastwards," but "with his face to the Table, about the midst of it."[2] And finally I must observe, that not only are the "oblations" in this service distinguished from the placing[3] of the Bread and Wine on the Holy Table, but that the word "*altar*" is not used once in the service, though the word "*table*" occurs nineteen times.[4] This fact, considering the general spirit of the service, and the motives for its present publication, appears to me of no light importance. If the two terms had been then viewed as ecclesiastically synonymous, it seems incredible that, at least, some modest alternation in the use of them should not have occurred in a service for the Consecration of a Church.[5]

---

[1] Compare p. 27 with pp. 25, 28, and 30.

[2] P. 30. The words in the note "he himself staying at the end of the Table" should be remarked.

[3] This act is described here by the word "offer," the introduction of which Sancroft and others in vain endeavoured to secure, at this point of the service, in 1662. It should be added that a distinction is drawn (p. 27) between those offertory sentences which are applicable to "Alms," and those which are applicable to "Oblations." This is in harmony with what we find in Bishop Wren's *Notes*, as recently published by the Bishop of Chester.

[4] It ought to be noted that in the most emphatic place it is termed "communion-table" (p. 15), and surely it might be fairly argued that if this book is of authority in regard to ceremony it is of authority in regard to the use of words.

[5] I observe a very strange circumstance on the page which follows the Preface in Mr. Fuller Russell's pamphlet. Certain rubrics of the Prayer Books of 1549 and 1662 are there co-ordinated, with the view of proving that "before the Table" in the latter is synonymous with "afore the midst of the Altar" in the former. To this end the *Consecration* Rubric in the Communion Service of 1662 is co-ordinated with the last *initial* rubric of 1549. But the author has overlooked the fact that in the last initial rubric of 1662, which furnishes the true parallel, the old words have been changed into "at the North side of the Table."

K.

(*Page* 93.)

EVIDENCE FROM ENGRAVINGS.

The evidence from pictures is a very interesting and by no means unimportant part of this inquiry. Many engravings, especially frontispieces to books of devotion, have been brought into notice in the course of the discussions which have taken place on the general subject. I will refer only to some which I have myself seen.

Certain abatements must in candour be made in estimating the weight of testimony of this kind. Engravers may be very careless and inaccurate in points of detail. Pictures belonging to one period of Church history may, for the sake of economy, be bound up in books belonging to another period; so that the former do not strictly illustrate the latter. We must remember, too, that the latter part of the seventeenth century with the early part of the eighteenth, notwithstanding the peremptory legislation of 1662, was a period of transition. The usage of one diocese or district might not be absolutely identical with the usage of another. Moreover there were difficulties then, which do not now exist, impeding communication among different parts of the country.

Great stress has been laid upon the well-known frontispiece to Sparrow's *Rationale upon the Book of Common Prayer*. The picture indeed represents, not any part of the celebration or administration of the Communion, but the saying of the Litany. It is argued, however, that because the Lord's Table in this engraving has a white cloth upon it, and a book in the midst, open to the west, the Communion is about to take place and the Priest about to consecrate in the Eastward Position. Now, as to this, I have to observe that no flagon or chalice or paten appears on the Table, the northern part of which is not shown at all,[1] and that no kneeling cushion is

---

[1] Dr. Blakeney remarks very truly that this engraving does not show the "north side" in *either* sense, p. 451.

shown such as that which indicates the position of the Priest in the plan of Archbishop Laud's Chapel.[1] But further, this picture cannot be adduced as an illustration of the Consecration Rubric of 1662; for that rubric did not exist when it was engraved. Sparrow's *Rationale* was first published in 1622,[2] and this frontispiece was prefixed to various subsequent editions. My copy is the Oxford reprint (1840) from the edition of 1684, with a preface bearing the initials "I. H. N." But I have a curious circumstance to add, which seems to me worthy of attention. In a copy (dated 1676) of that volume of Comber's *Companion to the Temple*, which contains a Commentary on the Litany, is a frontispiece, exhibiting the saying of that part of the service, and extremely similar to the other, but with this marked difference, that, though the Holy Table in this case also has a white cloth, the north side is shown, and the book is *there*, open to the *north*. If the cloth and the open book are sufficient grounds for assuming eastward consecration in the former, then they are sufficient for assuming southward consecration in the latter. Are we then to conclude that the new rubric of 1662 had, in the interval between 1657 and 1676, settled this point in favour of the north end?

Another picture, from which a photograph has been taken and circulated in certain quarters, is prefixed to a very rare book, entitled *The Whole Duty of Receiving the Blessed Sacrament*, by the author of *The Whole Duty of Man*. I have been told that only one copy of this book is known to exist; and this copy (the fifth edition, published in 1717) is at this moment, through the great kindness of the owner, in my keeping. Here are two flagons and a paten on the Table, and an open book on a cushion in the middle of the west side, giving the impression that consecration had taken place there in the Eastward Position. The Priest is administering the cup, moving northwards. I will not attempt to dilute the value of the picture, as an argument for "orientation." I will simply add the following extract from *The Whole Duty of Man*,

---

[1] See above (p. 79).
[2] See Mr. MacColl's *Lawlessness*, &c., p. 203.

which seems to show that the author, whatever pictures might be bound up in his books, contemplated *visibility* to the congregation in the Priest's act of breaking the bread during consecration:—" When thou art at the Holy Table, first humble thyself. . . . Then meditate on the bitter sufferings of Christ, which are set out to us in that Sacrament; when thou *seest* the *Bread broken*, remember how His Blessed Body was torn with nails upon the Cross; when thou *seest* the Wine *poured out*, remember how His precious blood was spilt there; and then consider that it was thy sins that caused both." [1]

[1] A friend who has paid careful attention to the literary history of *The Whole Duty of Man*, expresses a doubt whether this Companion to the Lord's Supper is really by the same author. The evidence is of two kinds.

The Preface to the works of the author of *The Whole Duty of Man* (Oxford and London, 1684), after referring to various attempts to pass off other works as by the same author, says: "To avoid like attempts and impostures for the future, it is here solemnly declared, that these tracts which we here exhibit are the genuine and only writings of our author." The next sentence, "Indeed had Almighty God lent longer life to this eminent person," &c., implies that the author was then already dead. *The Whole Duty of Receiving Worthily the Blessed Sacrament* is not in the volume to which this preface is added, and which consists of tracts printed in 1683 and 1684, and shown to be complete by lists of *errata* and of texts for the whole at the end of the volume.

Again, there are in these two volumes discrepancies of language and of doctrinal view, such as the following. The former devotes several pages to direction for self-examination and only at p. 33 suggests an "advice," that "*if* any person cannot satisfy his own soul in sincerity" he should "make known his case to some discreet and learned minister;" and says nothing whatever about "absolution," while the latter (p. 14) directs us "for better preparation, as occasion is, to disburthen and quit our consciences of those sins that may grieve us, or scruples that may trouble us, to a learned and discreet Priest, and from him to receive advice and the benefit of Absolution." And, to take another instance, *The Whole Duty of Man* says (p. 34) "When thou art at the Holy Table," *The Whole Duty of Receiving*, &c. (p. 155), says "When you are come to the Altar."

L.

(Page 96.)

NOVELTY OF THE EASTWARD POSITION.

I HAVE been accused of exaggeration in what I said last year at the Chester Diocesan Conference concerning the novelty of the Eastward Position. I had used the phrase "ecclesiastical microscope" to describe the difficulty of discovering any sufficient number of instances to justify the claim of a continuous practice co-ordinate with the practice of the Southward Position; and I am quite willing to withdraw this phrase, if it causes offence, though I cannot see how any blame attaches to me for the use of it, when due allowance is made for the freedom of extemporaneous speaking.[1]

Instances of this ceremonial act, previous to the changes of the last thirty years, have been sought out with the utmost diligence; but all of them put together, as it seems to me, are of no argumentative value. The Dean of St. Paul's, in a letter addressed to the *Times* about fifteen months ago, spoke of this position as a novelty within his recollection. The Bishop of Manchester, speaking in Convocation at York of his reminiscences of Oxford, said that Dr. Newman, when at the height of his University influence, did not consecrate in this way at St. Mary's. As to the instances of the practice which have been very confidently brought forward, many of them break down on close inquiry. Mr. Morton Shaw (pp. 8-9) adduced the example of Mr. Simeon; but I was able to furnish the express testimony of a clergyman who regularly attended Trinity Church, Cambridge, and frequently gave help in the service there, from 1823 till Mr. Simeon's death in 1836, and of another clergyman who was Mr. Simeon's curate there from 1829 to 1836, to the effect that this venerable man always "ordered the elements" at the front of the Lord's Table, and then returned for the Prayer of Consecration to the

---

[1] See p. 56 of the official Report of this Conference.

north side.[1] Another case is that of Bishop Law, who occupied the see of Chester from 1812 to 1824. It was first stated in a letter to the *Guardian* (published July 16, 1873), that on Easter Day in 1814, at an ordination in St. James's, Piccadilly, this prelate consecrated " standing before the midst of the altar," and the same testimony was recently brought forward by Canon Gregory in a speech before the Lower House of the Convocation of Canterbury. On being asked to try to ascertain Bishop Law's practice, and after using my best endeavours, I was able to produce the following evidence which cannot be questioned :—" I was Bishop Law's chaplain from the day of my ordination. I was constantly by his side during his episcopate at Chester and Wells. On countless occasions I have seen him officiate at the Lord's Supper. He invariably stood on the North side of the Table. I never witnessed a single deviation. I am ignorant of the incident, which is said to have occurred in 1814. If it occurred at all, it must have been exceptional in reference to the position of the Table." Another name which has been brought forward in the same way is that of Dr. Routh; but I have letters now before me, written by those who were resident in Magdalene College, Oxford, during his life, which refute the allegation. Even with regard to Bishop Maltby there seems to be some doubt, though I have, on more than one occasion, heard his practice very confidently urged. However this may be, I cannot think that even extreme High Churchmen would be disposed to lay great stress on that prelate's authority in matters of doctrine and ritual.

I may be allowed here to quote some words (printed in the *Guardian* of May 12) by Canon Harvey, whose evidence is of peculiar value. "The speech of Canon Gregory," he says, " was generally felt to be able and effective. But as a clergyman more than twenty years his senior, and connected from the first with well-known High Churchmen, I can say, from my own experience, and after the fullest inquiry, that the Canon has not been correctly informed." He then refers especially to his first rector, Archdeacon Watson, the brother of

---

[1] See the *Guardian* of Jan. 6, 1875, p. 19.

Joshua Watson, and to Bishop Blomfield; and adds in a postscript:—"*I should be glad to see a list of those clergymen who used the Eastward Position at the commencement of their ministerial career, if ordained before 1832.*"[1] To this I am allowed to append the testimony of my honoured friend Canon Blomfield, who tells me that, though he has been present at discussions of all kinds on Church questions in his brother's house, he never heard the Eastward Position referred to, or ever saw it adopted till recent times. I will conclude this note with an extract from a private letter addressed to Canon Harvey, which he kindly permits me to use: "I have been in Holy Orders fifty-three years—was brought up in a Cathedral Church, of which my late father was a member—was educated at a College in Oxford, the head of which was a Bishop of no mean repute—and have been blessed with various opportunities of attending Divine Service at several Cathedrals—and yet I never saw the practice of the Eastward Position adopted."

M.

(*Page* 127.)

THE PERPETUAL OBLATION IN HEAVEN.

PARTLY for the sake of escaping, for a moment, from the personalities of our present conflict in England, and partly for the satisfaction of quoting the well-considered words of one, who, besides being a Bishop, is a distinguished theologian, it may be useful to recall the troubles which disturbed the Episcopal Church of Scotland in 1859 and 1860. I do not refer to the case of Mr. Cheyne, which is handled in Bishop Charles Wordsworth's Charge of 1859:[2] though for

---

[1] This and some other questions were very pointedly put by Canon Harvey, in a letter to the same paper, at least a year ago.

[2] The doctrines condemned in this case were—(1), that the Sacrifice of the Eucharist is substantially the same as the Sacrifice of the Cross; (2), that in the Lord's Supper we kneel to the Lord Himself, invisibly present under the form, or the veils, of bread and wine; (3), that the only thing necessary to the completion of the sacrifice is the Communion of the Priest.—*Charge*, p. 11.

another reason that Charge ought here to be specially mentioned. In the course of it he states that, whereas previously he had been in the habit of saying the Consecration Prayer in the Eucharistic Service with his face towards the East,[1] believing it to be prescribed by the Rubric in the English, and allowed by the Rubric in the Scotch,[2] Prayer Book, he should thenceforward, having been convinced by Professor Blunt's arguments, discontinue the practice, more especially as he feared this position was encouraging wrong doctrines concerning the Sacrifice in the Eucharist, as well as the practice of non-recipient attendance, which is connected with those views. Such a change of opinion and action, in one so eminent, learned, and thoughtful, appears to me a fact of no slight importance, more especially as the Bishop's career can by no possibility be identified with any "Evangelical" or "Low Church" partizanship.

The chief purpose, however, of this note, is to refer to the case of the Bishop of Brechin, and to the "Opinion" which was delivered by the Bishop of St. Andrews in the Episcopal Synod held in Edinburgh in 1860, and which was published in the following year. Among the points at issue in this controversy were the identification of the Sacrifice in the Eucharist with the Sacrifice on the Cross, and the argument in support of this view derived from the belief that there is a perpetual Sacrifice of Christ in Heaven. The Bishop of Brechin had said that "no words of man can strengthen the tremendous and absolute identity of the two sacrifices," or "of the one sacrifice" in its two aspects.[3] Now, in order to establish this identity, it has long been a commonplace in Roman Catholic theology (and the same mode of arguing has been, during the last thirty years, used by some Anglican

---

[1] The Bishop had gone so far in concession and conciliation at St. Ninian's, as to say there in the Eastward Position the whole of the devotional parts of the Communion Service, commencing with the first Lord's Prayer, though the Rubric of the Scotch Prayer Book is as follows:—*The Presbyter standing at the north side or end shall say the Lord's Prayer*, &c., p. 21.

[2] The Scotch Rubric runs thus:—*The Presbyter, during the time of Consecration, shall stand at such a part of the Holy Table where he may with more ease and decency use his hands.*

[3] *Opinion*, &c., p. iv. in the Supplementary Note.

theologians) to employ the priesthood of Melchizedek as the link of connection. Christ is "a priest for ever after the order of Melchizedek:" hence He must have a sacrifice to offer; and that sacrifice must be the sacrifice of Himself. To this a most carefully-reasoned reply is furnished by Bishop Charles Wordsworth; and, using his materials, I may put the matter briefly thus:—Neither in the Epistle to the Hebrews, nor in the Book of Genesis, nor in the 110th Psalm, is any mention made of any offering by Melchizedek. Bishop Andrewes says of Melchizedek, *sacrificium nullum obtulit*.[1] It was in fulfilment of the type of the *Aaronic* priesthood, that Christ offered the sacrifice of Himself. Melchizedek, as King and Priest, receives tithes and dispenses blessing.[2] Thus the link which it is sought to find in the Melchizedek-priesthood of Christ entirely disappears. How far, even if it were otherwise, it would be possible to identify, except by an assumption, a sacrifice in the Lord's Supper with a perpetual oblation in Heaven, I do not stay to inquire.

I must further ask attention to the reference made in this argument by the Bishop of St. Andrews (an accomplished Greek scholar, as well as a learned theologian) to the exact meaning of the Greek words in the Epistle to the Hebrews. Our Lord is not said to have ascended into the true Holy of Holies, Heaven itself, *with* His own blood, but *by* His own blood. The preposition is διά (Heb. ix. 12). Christ *hath perfected* for ever (not *is perfecting*) them that are being sanctified. The word is τετελείωκεν (Heb. x. 14). Christ does not *stand* at the right hand of God, but *sat down, and continues to sit*. The word is ἐκάθισεν (v. 12). The Bishop adds that he thinks the εἰς τὸ διηνεκὲς (v. 12)

---

[1] From Bishop Pearson's *Treatise on the Creed*, which is here quoted at length, it is sufficient to give these sentences:—"When Jesus *had given* Himself a propitiatory sacrifice for sin, He ascended up on high. . . . Nor is He prevalent only in His *own oblation once offered*, but in His *constant intercession*. . . . . We read of no other sacerdotal act performed by Melchizedek, the Priest of the Most High God, but only that of *blessing*."

[2] If we regard Christ, in His Melchizedek-priesthood, as "blessing God" in our name, and offering our sacrifices, we see in Heb. xiii. 15, 16, what those sacrifices are.

belongs rather to the "Session for everlasting," than to "the one Sacrifice for everlasting," more especially as the phrase is repeated presently afterwards (v. 14). "The Session is εἰς τὸ διηνεκὲς, because by one Sacrifice Christ hath perfected εἰς τὸ διηνεκὲς them that are being sanctified."[1]

N.

(*Page* 138.)

THE BASILICAN ARRANGEMENT.

I AM perplexed by a passage quoted above (pp. 105, 106) from Mr. Beresford Hope's Book. He seems to say there that the use of the Eastward Position is "the order in which the Holy Catholic Church has, *from the first*, been wont to show forth the Lord's death." But surely it is a well-authenticated fact of history that on the Basilican method, when public buildings for Christian worship took their place among the established institutions of the Empire, consecration at the Eucharist took place in the *Westward* position, and an equally well-authenticated fact that the inversion of the mode of consecration became customary afterwards, co-ordinately with the development of Roman doctrine. Mr. Morton Shaw, admitting the Basilican custom as a fact, harmonises it, in a manner which to me is astounding, with the view which he advocates. He says that "this position of the celebrant was

[1] I had intended to refer to the Bishop of Brechin's treatment of our 31st Article; but in the near presence of death disputation must become silent. This Appendix was written before the decease of that eminent theologian. The note, however, may be used for a quotation from a letter written in 1866 by the late Bishop of Argyll and the Isles, and just published (Oct. 16) in the *Buteman and Advertiser for the Western Isles.* "I have been much pained in my journeys to find the increasing prevalence of a practice which is as foreign to the experience of our elder Clergy as it is opposed to the laws and principles of our Church. I mean the practice of the officiating clergyman performing portions of the Divine Service having his back turned towards the people, and accompanying this posture with actions which can have no intelligible meaning but the conception of a Creative Priestly Act, whereby a Presence and Offering are supposed to be made of our Lord's body, and to which adoration is paid."

not at the back of the Holy Table, but at what was then believed to be the front; and although in one sense, he faced the people in that position, yet he was in truth *practically ignoring them as a part of the congregation*, and his position at that side of the Holy Table was adopted simply with a regard to the clergy who were behind him, and not with any regard to the laity who were before him" (p. 107).[1] But *the whole question with which we are concerned is that of the relation between the priest and the congregation*. We certainly can get over many difficulties in such matters by "ignoring" the congregation:[2] but in this case the point at issue appears to me to be conceded. I must be allowed to add that the part of Mr. Morton Shaw's argument, which relates to the Catacombs, is to my apprehension altogether cloudy and unconvincing.

The papers by Dr. Hayman, to which reference is made in the text, appeared in the April, May, and June numbers of the *St. James's Magazine* in the present year, under the title of "Altar or Table? and the Eastward Position." To his argument in favour of *choice* in position, which is stated with much seriousness and ability, I will not offer any further answer than that which is contained in the pages of this volume. But I desire to call attention to the use he makes (pp. 198—201) of the description given by Eusebius (*Hist. Eccl.* x. 4) of the Church of Paulinus (probably in its main features a reproduction of an earlier Church) at Tyre. This church did not "orientate," but its great porch "fronted the rising sun:" its "altar" was not against the wall, but stood "in the midst;" and the officiating priest "stood beside the altar on the right." I may also refer to a passage quoted

---

[1] The same answer is sometimes given when the present practice of the Pope on great occasions is brought forward as a surviving proof of the early silican method. Are we not sometimes apt to patronize Roman Catholics by explaining their practices for them, when they could explain them better themselves? I find the *Tablet* of June 3rd saying, quite simply, "When the Pope himself officiates at one of the great Papal altars he celebrates with his face to the congregation."

[2] Is it not a serious charge against the clergy of the Church, during the period between Constantine and Charlemagne, that in the celebration of the Eucharist they *ignored the congregation?*

from Augustine (p. 325), which seems to show that in his time the "altar" or "table" stood detached from the wall (*Serm.* cccx. 2). As to the two terms, Augustine appears to have employed them indifferently. Dr. Hayman confirms Bingham in his statement that Chrysostom's usual word is "table" (p. 327).

It is hardly necessary to say that throughout what I have written I have used "Eastward" in its conventional sense, *i.e.*, "in the direction of the Lord's Table," whether the church in which the table is placed orientates or not. There is the greatest difference between the "orientation" of a church, according to our common use of the word, and the "orientation" of the priest within the church, according to the use of the word which has recently been suggested by Mr. Gladstone,[1] and which I have adopted in my fourteenth section. By attending to this distinction we dispose at once of any difficulty caused by the answer of the Bishops at the Savoy Conference, who quoted a passage from Augustine which recommends, on a somewhat fanciful ground, *standing* in prayer towards *the literal East* (see p. 65, *Note*). These Bishops probably shared the common English feeling in favour of the orientation of churches. It is worth while, however, to show that this custom represents no general law of Christendom. I have now before me the letter of an accomplished architect, who says that "the whole of Rome repudiates the custom: the front of St. Peter's is nearly due East, and consequently the altar is to the west of the church generally: nevertheless the priests in the *Coro* have it on the east of them; but in the Sistine Chapel, where there was perfect liberty to choose either end, and where the altar is quite at one end, that end is the West." He adds that St. John Lateran is placed just like St. Peter's, and that Santa Maria Maggiore and Santa Croce in Gerusalemme turn their backs exactly on one another, one looking N.W. and the other S.E., and that the Corso, running almost N. and S., has several churches on each side of it, those on the west having their altars to the west, and those on the east being reversed in

[1] *Contemporary Review* (July 1875), p. 195.

this respect. I may observe that at Caen, a city famous for its churches, I lately remarked that the Abbaye Aux Hommes, which contains the tomb of William the Conqueror, is nearly at right angles to the Abbaye Aux Dames, which contains that of his queen.

O.

(*Page* 142.)

THE REUNION CONFERENCES AT BONN.

THAT recent and important article in the *Contemporary Review*, to which reference has been made more than once in these pages, contains the following passage:—" One of the strongest freaks of human inconsistency I have ever witnessed is certainly this—we are much (and justly) reminded with reference to those beyond our pale, to think little of our differences and much of our agreements; but at the same time, and often from the same quarters, we are taught and tempted by example, if not by precept, within our own immediate 'household of faith,' to think incessantly of our differences and not at all of our more substantial and weighty agreements."[1] I do not know whether these words have any intentional reference to recents events or particular persons; but they clearly might be viewed as applicable to some of those who, in the recent Reunion Conferences at Bonn, went very far in endeavouring to find provisional forms of theological agreement with those who have been long separated from us, while yet at home they have been firm in adhering to what they believe to be the true legal sense of our own formularies, and have deprecated the introduction of new interpretations by means of ceremonial. Mr. Beresford Hope has made a distinct reference to this subject, which I am bound to notice. He says: "It is a curious coincidence that amongst those

[1] P. 212. I hope I have never seemed, in my frequent reference to this article, to forget the respect which is due from the Clergy to all Mr. Gladstone's utterances on theological subjects.

who have made themselves prominent in claiming both by declaration and otherwise the distinctive Eucharistic dress and the Eastward position, Canon Liddon holds a foremost place, while the Dean of Chester is one of the most prominent signers of the declaration on which I have just been commenting against both these incidents of sacramental ceremonial. In the name of Christian charity and of common sense, why cannot the parties in the Church of England agree to differ in their Eucharistic ritual? Dr. Liddon has expressed no desire to interfere with Dr. Howson's practice; why need Dr. Howson interfere with that of Dr. Liddon? Dr. Liddon may prefer the west side and the distinctive dress, Dr. Howson the north end and the simple surplice, but as both could combine in framing a document to embody the doctrine which the Church of England holds upon the 'sacrifice' and the 'sacrificial character' of the Eucharist, each may well leave the other to adopt the rites which most tend in his own eyes to carry out views on which they both agree." [1]

Now I am bold enough to say very confidently that the two cases are very different. In the one we are working down from a fixed point; in the other we are working up to a point not yet ascertained. Here, in England, we are living together in the same house on certain understood and recognized principles; at Bonn we were, as Dr. Döllinger said, merely building a bridge, so that those who had dwelt far apart might make acquaintance with one another. Ambiguous phrases, used by members of the same Church, may hide a discord which is sure to break out hereafter; whereas ambiguous phrases, used by members of separated Churches, may be the shelter under which they creep on to a gradual agreement.[2] But instead of defending myself I will refer to a defence which was made for me by a friendly hand early this year, in the course of some criticisms on Mr. Beresford Hope's book:—" We never

[1] *Worship in the Church of England*, pp. 88, 89.
[2] Hence I have absolutely refused to mix up our home controversies with these international, or rather inter-ecclesiastical, discussions. English battles must be fought on English, not on German ground ; and among ourselves, not in combination with Old Catholics and Greeks.

have attached, as our readers are aware, much importance to the carefully-balanced compromises of the theologians of Bonn. If they have any value, it is as articles of peace between distinct communions. Mr. Hope talks as if the parties in the Church of England had as little need to interfere with each other as have the Churches whose representatives met at Bonn. All might be well if we could divide England as King Knut and Edmund Ironsides divided it. But in the single church of a parish, how can both parties agree to differ in their Eucharistic ritual? Mr. Hope's appeal is practically confined to Dean Howson, who has to concede everything, and whose common sense is insulted by supposing that he was inconsistent in signing both the articles of Bonn and the memorial against the Eucharistic Vestments and the Eastward Position. It is, of course, from the other party that concession ought to be asked. A genuine desire for peace would command the relinquishment of everything except what is essential to the validity of the Sacraments."[1]

As to the specific question which gave occasion to the remarks both of Mr. Beresford Hope and of his critic, it was closely connected with the subject of these pages of my own. We came in 1874 to a provisional agreement on an article regarding Eucharistic sacrifice, and in the framing of this article I was permitted to take a part. In the published report the sense in which some Greek Churchmen understood it was stated, and it seemed to me very important to state, this year, the sense in which it is understood by some English Churchmen, a course to which two of our Bishops have given their approval.[2] But as I hope in due time to publish some thoughts on these Conferences, I need not at present say more on the subject.

[1] *The Spectator* (Jan. 16, 1875), p. 86.
[2] See the *Guardian* of Sept. 22, 1875.

SUPPLEMENT

I.

THE EASTWARD POSITION: A Letter addressed to the Editor of the *Times* by the BISHOP OF ST. ANDREWS.[1]

SIR,—As we have been told upon very high authority, both Lay and Clerical, that it is wrong to import into the Eastward Position any "doctrinal significance," I am inclined to ask—Can *any one* of your many thousand readers inform me why it is that so much stress—involving, in many instances, disobedience to the law—is laid upon this usage in regard to the administration of Holy Communion, and not to any other portion of our Church Services?

In a letter which you did me the favour to publish some three months ago upon the debate on the same subject in the Convocation of York, I ventured to put this question, and I have looked in vain for any answer to it in any quarter. The Lower House of the Convocation of Canterbury have indeed assured us in their Resolution, proposing to legalize the position, that no alteration of Doctrine is intended by it; but they have not informed us *what is intended*. It would seem to be obvious that every reason *not doctrinal* for placing the Minister with his back to the congregation at the altar, applies with *still greater force* to his occupying a similar position in the Prayer Desk, because the latter is not so far removed from the people. And yet I know of only one

---

[1] Many readers will join with me in thanking the Bishop of St. Andrews for complying with my request for permission to publish this letter. It was written, without any understanding or communication between us, at a distance of 500 miles from London, on the very morning (July 12, 1875), when a letter of mine on the same general subject appeared in the *Times*.

clergyman who has been consistent in this respect. Mr. Keble, during the latter part of his ministry at Hursley, was accustomed, I believe, to use the Eastward Position *in the Desk*, for Morning and Evening Prayer, as well as at the altar for the Communion Service. But any general attempt to follow his example would, we may be sure, be at once resisted, though *there is no Rubric to forbid it;* and would, I have little doubt, be disapproved by many who have adopted the usage for the Consecration Prayer.

I may be reminded of the position of the Minister at the Faldstool in the use of the Litany. But this is scarcely a case in point. The proper place for the Litany Faldstool is "between the porch and the altar;" or, in other words, "in the midst of the church;"[1] and in cathedrals it commonly stands nearer to the west than to the east end of the choir, while the congregation, instead of kneeling eastwards, generally face each other from the opposite sides.

I am quite as much averse as Mr. Gladstone himself can be, from importing into this vexed question anything which does not properly belong to it; and I no less willingly admit that a large proportion of the clergy who have adopted the Eastward Position have done so without any consciousness of a doctrinal intention which is not perfectly legitimate, according to a just interpretation of the teaching of our Reformed Church; but nevertheless, I am quite unable, *from mere æsthetical considerations,* to account for the fact that, whereas, before the Reformation, in every cathedral, and in every parish church throughout the land, the Eastward Position, and no other, was unquestionably used, ever since the Reformation that position has not been used in any one cathedral till within the the last thirty years, or less, and in very few, if any, parish churches.

How, then, is this fact to be accounted for? If we are to exclude all doctrinal significance, I can only account for it in one of two ways. Either it was thought, when Latin was given up and the service as reformed began to be said in the vulgar tongue, that *what the priest said could not be sufficiently heard,* or that *what he did could not be sufficiently seen* if he

[1] See the Frontispiece to Sparrow's *Rationale*.

were to continue to stand at the altar with his back to the people. Our predecessors ever since the Reformation have been influenced by both these considerations (whether they have not been also influenced, and perhaps in a still greater degree by doctrinal considerations is a point which I am now waiving); and, for my own part, I am not prepared to maintain that they acted upon improper or insufficient grounds. This however *must be maintained*, I conclude, by the non-doctrinal advocates of the Eastward Position; and further, they must maintain, *if they are to be consistent*, that the minister in the Prayer Desk ought to adopt the same position which he has already adopted (we suppose) at the Altar.

It is manifest[1] that a drifting to some extent *both doctrinal and practical*, from the moorings taken up by our Church at the Reformation, is being pressed upon us by a mixed multitude—some of them influenced by doctrinal, others by æsthetical considerations, and some by the mere love of novelty and excitement; and all I plead for in this letter is that we *weigh well the nature of the change we are urged to make; the grounds upon which*—if it is to be made—*we are prepared to make it; and the effect which it is likely to produce upon those without*—I mean, more particularly, our Nonconformist brethren.

The Bishops on the English Bench have been selected more or less, from all parties in the Church, and may fairly be supposed to represent all parties. Very few of them, I believe, are even now in the habit of using the Eastward Position on any occasion; and it may be doubted whether *any one of them* was in the habit of using it when he was first ordained priest. This fact, if it be so, added to the fact before mentioned, of the universal practice of our cathedrals since the Reformation, would indicate still further that the *advocates of the position are advocates for Innovation*, and that we ought to know from them more distinctly than we yet do *what their motives are and what the ends they desire to gain*. As at present informed, I can imagine *several motives against the usage*, such as the supposed reasons of our Reformers for giving it up; and, in addition to those, the danger of giving

---

[1] See the recent proceedings of the Church Union, and of the C.B.S.

encouragement to the superstitious notion of *vicarious worship* (that is, of the Priest worshipping not only *with*, but *instead of* the congregation), and, again, the danger of leading men to substitute a *materialistic localization* of the Divine Presence for the true spiritual belief which the Scripture teaches : but I can imagine *no motive for going back to the usage* which would not logically involve a complete change in the relations of the clergyman to the congregation throughout all the devotional parts of our Public Worship; *unless, indeed, it be the doctrinal, or semi-doctrinal one*, which many of its advocates, as we know, do not scruple to avow. That is, they wish to shift the existing balance of our Church teaching—a procedure which Mr. Gladstone so strongly, and so justly deprecates—by giving *greater* prominence to the notion of a *Sacrifice*, and consequently *less*, in comparison, to the notion of a *Communion*, in the celebration of the Holy Eucharist. That there is something, not altogether immaterial, to be said in favour of such a change, I am well aware ; but there is, in my opinion, more—very much more—and of greater weight to be said against it.

If, however, it shall be decided by competent authority, reversing the Purchas Judgment, that the usage all but universally prevalent amongst us since the Reformation till within the last fifteen or twenty years, has been the result of ignorance, or carelessness and irreverence, and *not of a right understanding and due observance of the Church's mind and law upon the point*—however much I must regret the virtual condemnation, which such a decision would involve, of the great and good of all parties in our Church who have gone before us for three centuries—I shall be prepared to acquiesce in it, both as a Scotch Bishop (though in that capacity it will not be directly binding upon me), and as a clergyman still holding place, through my connection with Winchester College, in the Church of England.

I am, Sir,
Your obedient Servant,
CHARLES WORDSWORTH,
Bishop of St. Andrews,

FORFAR, *July* 12, 1875.

II.

THE EASTWARD POSITION: Whether it would be right to permit it; and what would be the consequences of its being permitted. By the REV. R. W. KENNION, M.A.

THE permission of this ceremonial act, not its enforcement, is now proposed. But as to the way in which this permission is to be given, its proposers differ. Some hope it may be effected by a reversal of the Purchas Judgment; though it is not easy to understand how a permissive rule can result from any true interpretation of a stringent Act of Uniformity. Others propose an alteration of the Rubric, or an explanatory note appended to the Office; though it may be observed that the legislative enactment of an alternative, in a matter on which opinions differ and strong party-feeling exists, is a new thing to our Church, and seems to require very great consideration, as to the persons to whom the license should be given, and the way in which it should be exercised. But these questions of form I pass by, and proceed to ask whether it would be right for the Church to grant this license?

First, I remark that the Eastward Position is not a new matter of controversy. It is an old custom of the Church of Rome; and, though used also in other Churches, it is in England chiefly known as belonging to Rome. As connected with Romish doctrine, it was rejected by our Reformers. As connected with Romish doctrine, it was resisted by the Puritans in the time of Charles I., and discarded by *some at least* of the High Church party under Charles II.[1] Disused for many generations, or only used in some obscure places, it was revived a few years ago by a party of men who were (many of them at least) confessedly approximating to Romish doctrine; and its doctrinal significance has been publicly proclaimed by Dr. Pusey, Canon Rawlinson, and others.

[1] See Swainson's *Rubrical Question*, p. 117.

Thus, however unmeaning in itself, it has in common repute acquired a doctrinal significance. It is so regarded, not only by a large number of men of various parties in the Church, but also by all the Methodists and Nonconformists.

It is true that *some* who advocate the Eastward Position deny that there is any doctrinal significance in it; and they propose that the Church shall make a declaration to that effect. But the meaning, whether of words or actions, depends, not on authority, but on use and custom and popular acceptance. And a doctrinal meaning has been so long and so widely attached to this position, that no disclaimer of it has now any more chance of being believed and accepted, than if the Legitimists in France were to say that the white flag had no political meaning. Whatever we may mean, our permission of the Eastward Position will be taken for a retrograde step towards Rome.

And this imputation will be all the more widely spread and more deeply felt, because of the principle of reserve, which is thought to be held by some of the advocates of the Eastward Position, and which gives rise to the impression that men mean more than they say.

Indeed we are distinctly told that the innovation desired is not confined to the Prayer of Consecration. Mr. Morton Shaw's pamphlet begins with that, but he does not end with that alone. He is dissatisfied with the old arrangement of our choirs, as well as with the old position of our reading-desks: and it is evident that nothing will satisfy him except such an adoption of the Eastward Position in all our prayers, as would, I fear, give people the notion that they were praying to a localized Deity.

Is this extension of the license generally understood by those who propose it?

Be this as it may, the Eastward Position gives great offence to many, who think the doctrine symbolized by it erroneous, and feel bound to offer to it the most strenuous opposition.

What then ought to be done? Ought the one party to give up their wishes, or the other their objections?

I think the Word of God gives us the principle by which

our answer should be determined. "Let all your things be done with charity." "If thy brother be grieved with thy meat [*or position*] now walkest thou not charitably" (1 Cor. xvi. 14; Rom. xiv. 15). We are so constituted that it is as a general rule easier for us to *do without* something which we wish for, (not being necessary) than to *bear* a positive offence or pain. We have all our lives to do without many things which we much wish for, and the want does not materially curtail our powers either of enjoyment or usefulness. But to bear an actual offence or pain is a much more serious trial. Hence the rule is that a man who wishes for a thing which offends his neighbour ought to give it up. If my wife's piano gives me a headache, and my pipe makes her ill, the pipe and the piano ought both to be put down. By the same rule of Charity, the Eastward Position ought to be given up by those who wish for it, for the sake of those who would be offended by it.

But this is not the whole case. The offence is not a mere personal feeling, which a strong effort or a long habit might overcome. Those who oppose the Eastward Position do so on the ground, that as it is understood to represent a doctrine which they consider false, they *must* oppose it, and must *all their lives continue* to oppose it. And they feel that as the giving of the license would be the act of the whole Church, the whole Church would be compromised by it, and not merely the individual parishes in which it might actually be used. On this point, therefore, they cannot consent to any compromise.

Whereas the case of those who wish for it is quite different. Even those who hold the doctrine symbolized by it cannot say that this particular way of symbolizing it is necessary, or that they would be *committing a sin* by standing with their faces southward. And certainly those who disclaim its doctrinal significance, can have no reason for it sufficient to justify their giving offence to their brethren.

There is no doubt in our times a prejudice against any restriction on individual liberty. But what we are contending against is not men's liberty to act as they please in their own private capacity, but their being allowed to compromise the whole Church by their way of conducting its public services. In this case the liberty granted to the few is an oppression over the many.

I now ask what consequences would be likely to ensue if the license were granted?

There would be an end to all the hopes which some of us have entertained of a reunion between ourselves and the Methodists and Nonconformists. Whatever we may say, they would see in it a fresh proof of what they are always ready to suspect, a leaning of the Church towards Rome: and instead of joining us, they would become more and more hostile to us. The Liberation Society would rejoice over our fall; and the Church of Rome would be filled with new hopes of a successful issue to the effort she is making for our subjugation.

Then we must also be prepared to see a secession of large numbers from our Church, if not a complete division of it into two or more sections. There are some of her members whose attachment is now only weak, who have thought that there are now in our Prayer Book some remains of Romish error, and who would then probably leave us at once. Others, who are now thorough Churchmen, would have their loyalty shaken, and their fears aroused lest this step should prove the precursor of many more.

But what would be the effect on those who remained in the Church—assuming that the secession was not such as to break her up altogether?

Those who are now opposed to the Eastward Position would not cease to be so. Their opposition would be all the more resolute, because the evil would be aggravated.

As things are now, there are many who feel that the mischief is only a local or temporary one; that the expense of a legal prosecution is great, and the issue uncertain; that a new Incumbent or a new Bishop may restore the old custom, or that a new decision of the Privy Council or a new Act of Parliament may set things straight. And thus it is, that, though we are under an Act of most stringent Uniformity, local varieties have been tolerated.

And till lately this easing off of the hard and fast lines of Rubrical precision has been a great boon to the Church. But this toleration must be regulated by moderation on the one hand, and by forbearance on the other. *It cannot be prescribed.* If it is attempted to stretch it beyond the limits of moderation and forbearance, it must come to an end. And this, in the opinion of a large portion of the Church, has now been done. And if the license now proposed were actually given, either by judicial sentence or by legislation, we might bid farewell to all hopes of a restoration of peace in the Church.

There would be agitation through the country to procure a revocation of the license; and in this there would be great danger of a collision between Clergy and Laity, Convocation and Parliament.

There would be agitation in all, or almost all, parishes in which the Eastward Position was used or proposed to be used. There would be deputations to the Bishop, petitions to Convocation, petitions to Parliament, contested elections for the office of Churchwarden, party spirit discord and heart-burnings, all concentring round that Holy Feast which ought to bring all Christians into harmony together.

It is needless to say that the natural result of this continual controversy would, at least in many cases, be a growing deadness to all religious truth, if not absolute infidelity, as has often been the case in other controversies.

If, then, I am right in thinking that those who wish most for the Eastward Position have no such reason for it as absolutely to *prevent* their giving it up, while its opponents feel *bound* to continue their opposition, have we not ground for appealing to the former to be satisfied in this thing with the old custom of the Church of England, to be satisfied with that " position " which all can accept, and which alone can preserve in the Church that peace which we have, and restore that which we have lost ?

And have we not ground for appealing to that great body of Churchmen who have taken no part in this controversy, who by their position are best fitted to be mediators between the two extremes, entreating them not to give their countenance to a proposal, which will in the eyes of the world remove the old landmarks of the Church, and bring her nearer to Rome, which will destroy, or at least weaken, her parochial character, by sanctioning one use in one church and another use in another church, which will tolerate party symbols in the Administration of the Lord's Supper, and divide the Church into two hostile camps?

In the name of our common Master, let us preserve our unity as far as we can. At all events, let us not have our present diversity stereotyped and perpetuated.

If it is said to be a weakness in us to be offended at these things, let our stronger brethren bear with our infirmities.

These unhappy conflicts have been going on too long already. I trust that the spirit of wisdom and truth and righteousness and peace may guide the minds of our rulers, and of all who have any influence among us, that there may be such a settlement of the question at issue, as will allow the tempest of controversy, at least of angry controversy, to subside, and that we may henceforth be united in the bonds of peace, with one mind and one mouth glorifying our God and Father, and earnestly contending for the Faith once delivered to the Saints.

ROBERT W. KENNION.

THE RECTORY, ACLE, *March* 29, 1875.

BY THE SAME AUTHOR.

Preparing for Publication.

THE HISTORY AND MEANING

OF THE

REUNION CONFERENCES AT BONN.

ALSO

CHESTER CATHEDRAL SERMONS,

IN THREE PARTS.

(1) *EVENING SERIES.*

(2) *MORNING SERIES.*

(3) *AFTERNOON SERIES.*

May 1875.

A Catalogue of Theological Books, with a Short Account of their Character and Aim,

Published by

MACMILLAN AND CO.

Bedford Street, Strand, London, W.C.

Abbott (Rev. E. A.)—Works by the Rev. E. A. ABBOTT, D.D., Head Master of the City of London School.

BIBLE LESSONS. Second Edition. Crown 8vo. 4s. 6d.

"*Wise, suggestive, and really profound initiation into religious thought.*" —Guardian. *The Bishop of St. David's, in his speech at the Education Conference at Abergwilly, says he thinks* "*nobody could read them without being the better for them himself, and being also able to see how this difficult duty of imparting a sound religious education may be effected.*"

THE GOOD VOICES: A Child's Guide to the Bible. With upwards of 50 Illustrations. Crown 8vo. cloth gilt. 5s.

"*It would not be easy to combine simplicity with fulness and depth of meaning more successfully than Mr. Abbott has done.*"—Spectator. *The* Times *says—*"*Mr. Abbott writes with clearness, simplicity, and the deepest religious feeling.*"

PARABLES FOR CHILDREN. Crown 8vo. cloth gilt. 3s. 6d.

"*They are simple and direct in meaning and told in plain language, and are therefore well adapted to their purpose.*"—Guardian.

Abbott (Rev. E. A.)—*continued.*

CAMBRIDGE SERMONS PREACHED BEFORE THE UNIVERSITY. 8vo. 6s.

Ainger (Rev. Alfred).—SERMONS PREACHED IN THE TEMPLE CHURCH. By the Rev. ALFRED AINGER, M.A. of Trinity Hall, Cambridge, Reader at the Temple Church. Extra fcap. 8vo. 6s.

This volume contains twenty-four Sermons preached at various times during the last few years in the Temple Church. "*It is,*" *the* British Quarterly *says,* "*the fresh unconventional talk of a clear independent thinker, addressed to a congregation of thinkers . . . . Thoughtful men will be greatly charmed by this little volume.*"

Alexander.—THE LEADING IDEAS of the GOSPELS. Five Sermons preached before the University of Oxford in 1870–71. By WILLIAM ALEXANDER, D.D., Brasenose College; Lord Bishop of Derry and Raphoe; Select Preacher. Cr. 8vo. 4s. 6d.

"*Eloquence and force of language, clearness of statement, and a hearty appreciation of the grandeur and importance of the topics upon which he writes characterize his sermons.*"—Record.

Arnold.—A BIBLE READING BOOK FOR SCHOOLS. THE GREAT PROPHECY OF ISRAEL'S RESTORATION (Isaiah, Chapters 40–66). Arranged and Edited for Young Learners. By MATTHEW ARNOLD, D.C.L., formerly Professor of Poetry in the University of Oxford, and Fellow of Oriel. Third Edition. 18mo. cloth. 1s.

The Times *says*—"*Whatever may be the fate of this little book in Government Schools, there can be no doubt that it will be found excellently calculated to further instruction in Biblical literature in any school into which it may be introduced. . . . We can safely say that whatever school uses this book, it will enable its pupils to understand Isaiah, a great advantage compared with other establishments which do not avail themselves of it.*"

Baring-Gould.—LEGENDS OF OLD TESTAMENT CHARACTERS, from the Talmud and other sources. By the Rev. S. BARING-GOULD, M.A., Author of "Curious Myths of the Middle Ages," "The Origin and Development of Religious Belief," "In Exitu Israel," etc. In two vols. crown 8vo. 16s. Vol. I. Adam to Abraham. Vol. II. Melchizidek to Zechariah.

"*These volumes contain much that is strange, and to the ordinary English reader, very novel.*"—Daily News.

Barry, Alfred, D.D.—The ATONEMENT of CHRIST. Six Lectures delivered in Hereford Cathedral during Holy Week, 1871. By ALFRED BARRY, D.D., D.C.L., Canon of Worcester, Principal of King's College, London. Fcap. 8vo. 2s. 6d.

In writing these Sermons, it has been the object of Canon Barry to set forth the deep practical importance of the doctrinal truths of the Atonement. The Guardian *calls them "striking and eloquent lectures."*

Benham.—A COMPANION TO THE LECTIONARY, being a Commentary on the Proper Lessons for Sundays and Holydays. By the Rev. W. BENHAM, B.D., Vicar of Margate. Cheaper Edition. Crown 8vo. 6s.

The Author's object is to give the reader a clear understanding of the Lessons of the Church, which he does by means of general and special introductions, and critical and explanatory notes on all words and passages presenting the least difficulty. "A very useful book. Mr. Benham has produced a good and welcome companion to our revised Lectionary. Its contents will, if not very original or profound, prove to be sensible and practical, and often suggestive to the preacher and the Sunday School teacher. They will also furnish some excellent Sunday reading for private hours."—Guardian.

Benson.—BOY-LIFE; ITS TRIAL, ITS STRENGTH, ITS FULNESS. Sundays in Wellington College 1859—73. By E. W. BENSON, Master. Crown 8vo. 7s. 6d.

Bernard.—THE PROGRESS OF DOCTRINE IN THE NEW TESTAMENT, considered in Eight Lectures before the University of Oxford in 1864. By THOMAS D. BERNARD, M.A., Rector of Walcot and Canon of Wells. Third and Cheaper Edition. Crown 8vo. 5s. (Bampton Lectures for 1864.)

"We lay down these lectures with a sense not only of being edified by sound teaching and careful thought, but also of being gratified by conciseness and clearness of expression and elegance of style."—Churchman.

Binney.—SERMONS PREACHED IN THE KING'S WEIGH HOUSE CHAPEL, 1829—69. By THOMAS BINNEY, D.D. New and Cheaper Edition. Extra fcap. 8vo. 4s. 6d.

"Full of robust intelligence, of reverent but independent thinking on the most profound and holy themes, and of earnest practical purpose."—London Quarterly Review.

A SECOND SERIES OF SERMONS. Edited by the Rev. HENRY ALLON, D.D. With Portrait of Dr. Binney engraved by JEENS. 8vo. [*Shortly.*

Bradby.—SERMONS PREACHED AT HAILEYBURY. By E. H. BRADBY, M.A., Master. 8vo. 10s. 6d.

"He who claims a public hearing now, speaks to an audience accustomed to Cotton, Temple, Vaughan, Bradley, Butler, Farrar, and others...... Each has given us good work, several work of rare beauty, force, or originality; but we doubt whether any one of them has touched deeper chords, or brought more freshness and strength into his sermons, than the last of their number, the present Head Master of Haileybury."—Spectator.

Burgon.—A TREATISE on the PASTORAL OFFICE. Addressed chiefly to Candidates for Holy Orders, or to those who have recently undertaken the cure of souls. By the Rev. JOHN W. BURGON, M.A., Oxford. 8vo. 12s.

The object of this work is to expound the great ends to be accomplished by the Pastoral office, and to investigate the various means by which these ends may best be gained. Full directions are given as to preaching and sermon-writing, pastoral visitation, village education and catechising, and confirmation.—Spectator.

Butler (G.)—Works by the Rev. GEORGE BUTLER, M.A., Principal of Liverpool College:

FAMILY PRAYERS. Crown 8vo. 5s.

The prayers in this volume are all based on passages of Scripture—the morning prayers on Select Psalms, those for the evening on portions of the New Testament.

SERMONS PREACHED in CHELTENHAM COLLEGE CHAPEL. Crown 8vo. 7s. 6d.

Butler (Rev. H. M.)—SERMONS PREACHED in the CHAPEL OF HARROW SCHOOL. By H. MONTAGU BUTLER, Head Master. Crown 8vo. 7s. 6d.

"These sermons are adapted for every household. There is nothing more striking than the excellent good sense with which they are imbued."—Spectator.

A SECOND SERIES. Crown 8vo. 7s. 6d.

"Excellent specimens of what sermons should be,—plain, direct, practical, pervaded by the true spirit of the Gospel, and holding up lofty aims before the minds of the young."—Athenæum.

Butler (Rev. W. Archer).—Works by the Rev. WILLIAM ARCHER BUTLER, M.A., late Professor of Moral Philosophy in the University of Dublin:—

SERMONS, DOCTRINAL AND PRACTICAL. Edited, with a Memoir of the Author's Life, by THOMAS WOODWARD, Dean of Down. With Portrait. Ninth Edition. 8vo. 8s.

The Introductory Memoir narrates in considerable detail and with much interest, the events of Butler's brief life; and contains a few specimens of his poetry, and a few extracts from his addresses and essays, including a long and eloquent passage on the Province and Duty of the Preacher.

A SECOND SERIES OF SERMONS. Edited by J. A. JEREMIE, D.D., Dean of Lincoln. Seventh Edition. 8vo. 7s.

The North British Review *says, "Few sermons in our language exhibit the same rare combination of excellencies: imagery almost as rich as Taylor's; oratory as vigorous often as South's; judgment as sound as*

Butler (Rev. W. Archer.)—*continued.*

Barrow's; a style as attractive but more copious, original, and forcible than Atterbury's; piety as elevated as Howe's, and a fervour as intense at times as Baxter's. Mr. Butler's are the sermons of a true poet."

LETTERS ON ROMANISM, in reply to Dr. Newman's Essay on Development. Edited by the Dean of Down. Second Edition, revised by Archdeacon HARDWICK. 8vo. 10s. 6d.

These Letters contain an exhaustive criticism of Dr. Newman's famous "Essay on the Development of Christian Doctrine." "A work which ought to be in the Library of every student of Divinity."—BP. ST. DAVID'S.

Cambridge Lent Sermons.—SERMONS preached during Lent, 1864, in Great St. Mary's Church, Cambridge. By the BISHOP OF OXFORD, Revs. H. P. LIDDON, T. L. CLAUGHTON, J. R. WOODFORD, Dr. GOULBURN, J. W. BURGON, T. T. CARTER, Dr. PUSEY, Dean HOOK, W. J. BUTLER, Dean GOODWIN. Crown 8vo. 7s. 6d.

Campbell.—Works by JOHN M'LEOD CAMPBELL :—

THE NATURE OF THE ATONEMENT AND ITS RELATION TO REMISSION OF SINS AND ETERNAL LIFE. Fourth and Cheaper Edition, crown 8vo. 6s.

"Among the first theological treatises of this generation."—Guardian. *"One of the most remarkable theological books ever written."*—Times.

CHRIST THE BREAD OF LIFE. An Attempt to give a profitable direction to the present occupation of Thought with Romanism. Second Edition, greatly enlarged. Crown 8vo. 4s. 6d.

"Deserves the most attentive study by all who interest themselves in the predominant religious controversy of the day."—Spectator.

RESPONSIBILITY FOR THE GIFT OF ETERNAL LIFE. Compiled by permission of the late J. M'LEOD CAMPBELL, D.D., from Sermons preached chiefly at Row in 1829—31. Crown 8vo. 5s.

"There is a healthy tone as well as a deep pathos not often seen in sermons. His words are weighty and the ideas they express tend to perfection of life."—Westminster Review.

REMINISCENCES AND REFLECTIONS, referring to his Early Ministry in the Parish of Row, 1825—31. Edited with an Introductory Narrative by his Son, DONALD CAMPBELL, M.A., Chaplain of King's College, London. Crown 8vo. 7s. 6d.

These 'Reminiscences and Reflections,' written during the last year of his life, were mainly intended to place on record thoughts which might prove helpful to others. "We recommend this book cordially to all who are interested in the great cause of religious reformation."—Times.

Campbell (J. M'Leod)—*continued.*

"There is a thoroughness and depth, as well as a practical earnestness, in his grasp of each truth on which he dilates, which make his reflections very valuable."—Literary Churchman.

THOUGHTS ON REVELATION, with Special Reference to the Present Time. Second Edition. Crown 8vo. 5s.

Canterbury.—THE PRESENT POSITION OF THE CHURCH OF ENGLAND.
Seven Addresses delivered to the Clergy and Churchwardens of his Diocese, as his Charge, at his Primary Visitation, 1872. By ARCHIBALD CAMPBELL, Archbishop of Canterbury. Third Edition. 8vo. cloth. 3s. 6d.

The subjects of these Addresses are, I. Lay Co-operation. II. Cathedral Reform. III. and IV. Ecclesiastical Judicature. V. Ecclesiastical Legislation. VI. Missionary Work of the Church. VII. The Church of England in its relation to the Rest of Christendom. There are besides, a number of statistical and illustrative appendices.

Cheyne.—Works by T. K. CHEYNE, M.A., Fellow of Balliol College, Oxford:—

THE BOOK OF ISAIAH CHRONOLOGICALLY ARRANGED. An Amended Version, with Historical and Critical Introductions and Explanatory Notes. Crown 8vo. 7s. 6d.

The object of this edition is to restore the probable meaning of Isaiah, so far as can be expressed in appropriate English. The basis of the version is the revised translation of 1611, *but alterations have been introduced wherever the true sense of the prophecies appeared to require it. The* Westminster Review *speaks of it as "a piece of scholarly work, very carefully and considerately done."* The Academy *calls it "a successful attempt to extend a right understanding of this important Old Testament writing."*

NOTES AND CRITICISMS on the HEBREW TEXT OF ISAIAH. Crown 8vo. 2s. 6d.

This work is offered as a slight contribution to a more scientific study of the Old Testament Scriptures. The author aims at completeness, independence, and originality, and constantly endeavours to keep philology distinct from exegesis, to explain the form without pronouncing on the matter.

Choice Notes on the Four Gospels, drawn from Old and New Sources. Crown 8vo. 4s. 6d. each Vol. (St. Matthew and St. Mark in one Vol. price 9s.).

These Notes are selected from the Rev. Prebendary Ford's Illustrations of the Four Gospels, the choice being chiefly confined to those of a more simple and practical character.

Church.—Works by the Very Rev. R. W. CHURCH, M.A., Dean of St. Paul's.

SERMONS PREACHED BEFORE the UNIVERSITY OF OXFORD. By the Very Rev. R. W. CHURCH, M.A., Dean of St. Paul's. Second Edition. Crown 8vo. 4s. 6d.

Sermons on the relations between Christianity and the ideas and facts of modern civilized society. The subjects of the various discourses are:—" The Gifts of Civilization," " Christ's Words and Christian Society," " Christ's Example," and " Civilization and Religion." " Thoughtful and masterly... We regard these sermons as a landmark in religious thought. They help us to understand the latent strength of a Christianity that is assailed on all sides."—Spectator.

ON SOME INFLUENCES OF CHRISTIANITY UPON NATIONAL CHARACTER. Three Lectures delivered in St. Paul's Cathedral, Feb. 1873. Crown 8vo. 4s. 6d.

"Few books that we have met with have given us keener pleasure than this....... It would be a real pleasure to quote extensively, so wise and so true, so tender and so discriminating are Dean Church's judgments, but the limits of our space are inexorable. We hope the book will be bought." —Literary Churchman.

THE SACRED POETRY OF EARLY RELIGIONS. Two Lectures in St. Paul's Cathedral. 18mo. 1s. I. The Vedas. II. The Psalms.

Clay.—THE POWER OF THE KEYS. Sermons preached in Coventry. By the Rev. W. L. CLAY, M.A. Fcap. 8vo. 3s. 6d.

Clergyman's Self-Examination concerning the APOSTLES' CREED. Extra fcap. 8vo. 1s. 6d.

Colenso.—THE COMMUNION SERVICE FROM THE BOOK OF COMMON PRAYER; with Select Readings from the Writings of the Rev. F. D. MAURICE, M.A. Edited by the Right Rev. J. W. COLENSO, D.D., Lord Bishop of Natal. New Edition. 16mo. 2s. 6d.

Collects of the Church of England. With a beautifully Coloured Floral Design to each Collect, and Illuminated Cover. Crown 8vo. 12s. Also kept in various styles of morocco.

The distinctive characteristic of this edition is the coloured floral design which accompanies each Collect, and which is generally emblematical of the character of the day or saint to which it is assigned; the flowers which have been selected are such as are likely to be in bloom on the day to which the Collect belongs. The Guardian *thinks it "a successful attempt to associate in a natural and unforced manner the flowers of our fields and gardens with the course of the Christian year."*

Cotton.—Works by the late GEORGE EDWARD LYNCH COTTON, D.D., Bishop of Calcutta:—

SERMONS PREACHED TO ENGLISH CONGREGATIONS IN INDIA. Crown 8vo. 7s. 6d.

"*The sermons are models of what sermons should be, not only on account of their practical teachings, but also with regard to the singular felicity with which they are adapted to times, places, and circumstances.*"—Spectator.

EXPOSITORY SERMONS ON THE EPISTLES FOR THE SUNDAYS OF THE CHRISTIAN YEAR. Two Vols. Crown 8vo. 15s.

These two volumes contain in all fifty-seven Sermons. They were all preached at various stations throughout India.

Cure.—THE SEVEN WORDS OF CHRIST ON THE CROSS. Sermons preached at St. George's, Bloomsbury. By the Rev. E. CAPEL CURE, M.A. Fcap. 8vo. 3s. 6d.

Of these Sermons the John Bull *says*, "*They are earnest and practical;*" *the* Nonconformist, "*The Sermons are beautiful, tender, and instructive;*" *and the* Spectator *calls them* "*A set of really good Sermons.*"

Curteis.—DISSENT in its RELATION to the CHURCH OF ENGLAND. Eight Lectures preached before the University of Oxford, in the year 1871, on the foundation of the late Rev. John Bampton, M.A., Canon of Salisbury. By GEORGE HERBERT CURTEIS, M.A., late Fellow and Sub-Rector of Exeter College; Principal of the Lichfield Theological College, and Prebendary of Lichfield Cathedral; Rector of Turweston, Bucks. Third and Cheaper Edition, crown 8vo. 7s. 6d.

"*Mr. Curteis has done good service by maintaining in an eloquent, temperate, and practical manner, that discussion among Christians is really an evil, and that an intelligent basis can be found for at least a proximate union.*"—Saturday Review "*A well timed, learned, and thoughtful book.*"

Davies.—Works by the Rev. J. LLEWELYN DAVIES, M.A., Rector of Christ Church, St. Marylebone, etc. :—

THE WORK OF CHRIST; or, the World Reconciled to God. With a Preface on the Atonement Controversy. Fcap. 8vo. 6s.

SERMONS on the MANIFESTATION OF THE SON OF GOD. With a Preface addressed to Laymen on the present Position of the Clergy of the Church of England; and an Ap-

Davies (Rev. J. Llewelyn)—*continued.*
pendix on the Testimony of Scripture and the Church as to the possibility of Pardon in the Future State. Fcap. 8vo. 6s. 6d.

"*This volume, both in its substance, prefix, and suffix, represents the noblest type of theology now preached in the English Church.*"—Spectator.

BAPTISM, CONFIRMATION, AND THE LORD'S SUPPER, as Interpreted by their Outward Signs. Three Expository Addresses for Parochial use. Fcap. 8vo., limp cloth. 1s. 6d.

The method adopted in these addresses is to set forth the natural and historical meaning of the signs of the two Sacraments and of Confirmation, and thus to arrive at the spiritual realities which they symbolize. The work touches on all the principal elements of a Christian man's faith.

THE EPISTLES of ST. PAUL TO THE EPHESIANS, THE COLOSSIANS, and PHILEMON. With Introductions and Notes, and an Essay on the Traces of Foreign Elements in the Theology of these Epistles. 8vo. 7s. 6d.

THE GOSPEL AND MODERN LIFE; with a Preface on a Recent Phase of Deism. Second Edition. To which is added Morality according to the Sacrament of the Lord's Supper, or Three Discourses on the Names Eucharist, Sacrifice, and Communion. Extra fcap. 8vo. 6s.

WARNINGS AGAINST SUPERSTITION IN FOUR SERMONS FOR THE DAY. Extra fcap. 8vo. 2s. 6d

"*We have seldom read a wiser little book. The Sermons are short, terse, and full of true spiritual wisdom, expressed with a lucidity and a moderation that must give them weight even with those who agree least with their author....... Of the volume as a whole it is hardly possible to speak with too cordial an appreciation.*"—Spectator.

THE CHRISTIAN CALLING. Sermons. Extra fcap. 8vo. 6s.

De Teissier.—Works by G. F. DE TEISSIER, B.D.:—

VILLAGE SERMONS, FIRST SERIES. Crown 8vo. 9s.

This volume contains fifty-four short Sermons, embracing many subjects of practical importance to all Christians. - *The* Guardian *says they are* "*a little too scholarlike in style for a country village, but sound and practical.*"

VILLAGE SERMONS, SECOND SERIES. Crown 8vo. 8s. 6d.

"*This second volume of Parochial Sermons is given to the public in the humble hope that it may afford many seasonable thoughts for such as are Mourners in Zion.*" *There are in all fifty-two Sermons embracing a wide variety of subjects connected with Christian faith and practice.*

Donaldson.—THE APOSTOLICAL FATHERS: a Critical Account of their Genuine Writings and of their Doctrines. By JAMES DONALDSON, LL.D. Crown 8vo. 7s. 6d.

This book was published in 1864 as the first volume of a 'Critical History of Christian Literature and Doctrine from the death of the Apostles to the Nicene Council.' The intention was to carry down the history continuously to the time of Eusebius, and this intention has not been abandoned. But as the writers can be sometimes grouped more easily according to subject or locality than according to time, it is deemed advisable to publish the history of each group separately. The Introduction to the present volume serves as an introduction to the whole period.

Drake.—THE TEACHING OF THE CHURCH DURING THE FIRST THREE CENTURIES ON THE DOCTRINES OF THE CHRISTIAN PRIESTHOOD AND SACRIFICE. By the Rev. C. B. DRAKE, M.A., Warden of the Church of England Hall, Manchester. Crown 8vo. 4s. 6d.

Ecce Homo. A SURVEY OF THE LIFE AND WORK OF JESUS CHRIST. Eleventh Edition. Crown 8vo. 6s.

"A very original and remarkable book, full of striking thought and delicate perception; a book which has realised with wonderful vigour and freshness the historical magnitude of Christ's work, and which here and there gives us readings of the finest kind of the probable motive of His individual words and actions."—Spectator. *"The best and most established believer will find it adding some fresh buttresses to his faith."*—Literary Churchman. *"If we have not misunderstood him, we have before us a writer who has a right to claim deference from those who think deepest and know most."*—Guardian.

Faber.—SERMONS AT A NEW SCHOOL. By the Rev. ARTHUR FABER, M.A., Head Master of Malvern College. Cr. 8vo. 6s.

"These are high-toned, earnest Sermons, orthodox and scholarlike, and laden with encouragement and warning, wisely adapted to the needs of school-life."—Literary Churchman. *"Admirably realizing that combination of fresh vigorous thought and simple expression of wise parental counsel, with brotherly sympathy and respect, which are essential to the success of such sermons, and to which so few attain."*—British Quarterly Review.

Farrar.—Works by the Rev. F. W. FARRAR, M.A., F.R.S., Head Master of Marlborough College, and Hon. Chaplain to the Queen:—

THE FALL OF MAN, AND OTHER SERMONS. Third Edition. Extra fcap. 8vo. 4s. 6d.

This volume contains twenty Sermons. No attempt is made in these

Farrar (Rev. F. W.)—*continued.*

Sermons to develope a system of doctrine. In each discourse some one aspect of truth is taken up, the chief object being to point out its bearings on practical religious life. The Nonconformist *says of these Sermons,—"Mr. Farrar's Sermons are almost perfect specimens of one type of Sermons, which we may concisely call beautiful. The style of expression is beautiful—there is beauty in the thoughts, the illustrations, the allusions—they are expressive of genuinely beautiful perceptions and feelings." The* British Quarterly *says,—"Ability, eloquence, scholarship, and practical usefulness, are in these Sermons combined in a very unusual degree."*

THE WITNESS OF HISTORY TO CHRIST. Being the Hulsean Lectures for 1870. New Edition. Crown 8vo. 5s.

The following are the subjects of the Five Lectures:—I. "The Antecedent Credibility of the Miraculous." II. "The Adequacy of the Gospel Records." III. "The Victories of Christianity." IV. "Christianity and the Individual." V. "Christianity and the Race." The subjects of the four Appendices are:—A. "The Diversity of Christian Evidences." B. "Confucius." C. "Buddha." D. "Comte."

SEEKERS AFTER GOD. The Lives of Seneca, Epictetus, and Marcus Aurelius. *See* SUNDAY LIBRARY at end of Catalogue.

THE SILENCE AND VOICES OF GOD: University and other Sermons. Second Edition. Crown 8vo. 6s.

"We can most cordially recommend Dr. Farrar's singularly beautiful volume of Sermons...... For beauty of diction, felicity of style, aptness of illustration and earnest loving exhortation, the volume is without its parallel."—John Bull. *"They are marked by great ability, by an honesty which does not hesitate to acknowledge difficulties and by an earnestness which commands respect."*—Pall Mall Gazette.

Fellowship: LETTERS ADDRESSED TO MY SISTER MOURNERS. Fcap. 8vo. cloth gilt. 3s. 6d.

"A beautiful little volume, written with genuine feeling, good taste, and a right appreciation of the teaching of Scripture relative to sorrow and suffering."—Nonconformist. *"A very touching, and at the same time a very sensible book. It breathes throughout the truest Christian spirit."*—Contemporary Review.

Forbes.—THE VOICE OF GOD IN THE PSALMS. By GRANVILLE FORBES, Rector of Broughton. Cr. 8vo. 6s. 6d.

Gifford.—THE GLORY OF GOD IN MAN. By E. H. GIFFORD, D.D. Fcap. 8vo., cloth. 3s. 6d.

Golden Treasury Psalter. *See* p. 27.

Hardwick.—Works by the Ven. ARCHDEACON HARDWICK:
CHRIST AND OTHER MASTERS. A Historical Inquiry into some of the Chief Parallelisms and Contrasts between Christianity and the Religious Systems of the Ancient World. New Edition, revised, and a Prefatory Memoir by the Rev. FRANCIS PROCTER, M.A. Third and Cheaper Edition. Cr. 8vo. 10s. 6d.

The plan of the work is boldly and almost nobly conceived. . . . We commend it to the perusal of all those who take interest in the study of ancient mythology, without losing their reverence for the supreme authority of the oracles of the living God."—Christian Observer.

A HISTORY OF THE CHRISTIAN CHURCH. Middle Age. From Gregory the Great to the Excommunication of Luther, Edited by WILLIAM STUBBS, M.A., Regius Professor of Modern History in the University of Oxford. With Four Maps constructed for this work by A. KEITH JOHNSTON. New Edition. Crown 8vo. 10s. 6d.

For this edition Professor Stubbs has carefully revised both text and notes, making such corrections of facts, dates, and the like as the results of recent research warrant. The doctrinal, historical, and generally speculative views of the late author have been preserved intact. "As a Manual for the student of ecclesiastical history in the Middle Ages, we know no English work which can be compared to Mr. Hardwick's book."—Guardian.

A HISTORY of the CHRISTIAN CHURCH DURING THE REFORMATION. New Edition, revised by Professor STUBBS. Crown 8vo. 10s. 6d.

This volume is intended as a sequel and companion to the "History of the Christian Church during the Middle Age."

Hare.—THE VICTORY OF FAITH. By JULIUS CHARLES HARE, M.A., Archdeacon of Lewes. Edited by Prof. PLUMPTRE. With Introductory Notices by the late Prof. MAURICE and Dean STANLEY. Third Edition. Crown 8vo. 6s. 6d.

Harris.—SERMONS. By the late GEORGE COLLYER HARRIS, Prebendary of Exeter, and Vicar of St. Luke's, Torquay. With Memoir by CHARLOTTE M. YONGE, and Portrait. Extra fcap. 8vo. 6s.

Hervey.—THE GENEALOGIES OF OUR LORD AND SAVIOUR JESUS CHRIST, as contained in the Gospels of St. Matthew and St. Luke, reconciled with each other, and shown to be in harmony with the true Chronology of the Times. By Lord ARTHUR HERVEY, Bishop of Bath and Wells. 8vo. 10s. 6d.

Hymni Ecclesiæ.—Fcap. 8vo. 7s. 6d.
This collection was edited by Dr. Newman while he lived at Oxford.

Hyacinthe.—CATHOLIC REFORM. By FATHER HYACINTHE. Letters, Fragments, Discourses. Translated by Madame HYACINTHE-LOYSON. With a Preface by the Very Rev. A. P. STANLEY, D.D., Dean of Westminster. Cr. 8vo. 7s. 6d.

"A valuable contribution to the religious literature of the day, and is especially opportune at a time when a controversy of no ordinary importance upon the very subject it deals with is engaged in all over Europe."—Daily Telegraph.

Imitation of Christ.—FOUR BOOKS. 'Translated from the Latin. With Preface by the Rev. W. BENHAM, B.D., Vicar of Margate. Printed with Borders in the Ancient Style after Holbein, Dürer, and other Old Masters. Containing Dances of Death, Acts of Mercy, Emblems, and a variety of curious ornamentation. Cr. 8vo. gilt edges. 7s. 6d.

Jennings and Lowe.—THE PSALMS, with Introductions and Critical Notes. By A. C. JENNINGS, B.A., Jesus College, Cambridge, Tyrwhitt Scholar, Crosse Scholar, Hebrew University Scholar, and Fry Scholar of St. John's College; and W. H. LOWE, M.A., Hebrew Lecturer and late Scholar of Christ's College, Cambridge, and Tyrwhitt Scholar. Books III. and IV. (Psalm lxxiii. to cvi.) Crown 8vo. 6s.

Kempis, Thos. A.—DE IMITATIONE CHRISTI. LIBRI IV. Borders in the Ancient Style, after Holbein, Durer, and other Old Masters, containing Dances of Death, Acts of Mercy, Emblems, and a variety of curious ornamentation. In white cloth, extra gilt. 7s. 6d.

Kingsley.—Works by the late Rev. CHARLES KINGSLEY, M.A., Rector of Eversley, and Canon of Westminster.

THE WATER OF LIFE, AND OTHER SERMONS. Second Edition. Fcap. 8vo. 3s. 6d.

VILLAGE SERMONS. Seventh Edition. Fcap. 8vo. 3s. 6d.

THE GOSPEL OF THE PENTATEUCH. Second Edition. Fcap. 8vo. 3s. 6d.

GOOD NEWS OF GOD. Fourth Edition. Fcap. 8vo. 3s. 6d.

This volume contains thirty-nine short Sermons, preached in the ordinary course of the author's parochial ministrations.

Kingsley (Rev. C.)—*continued.*

SERMONS FOR THE TIMES. Third Edition. Fcap. 8vo. 3s. 6d.

Here are twenty-two Sermons, all bearing more or less on the every-day life of the present day, including such subjects as these:—"*Fathers and Children;*" "*A Good Conscience;*" "*Names;*" "*Sponsorship;*" "*Duty and Superstition;*" "*England's Strength;*" "*The Lord's Prayer;*" "*Shame;*" "*Forgiveness;*" "*The True Gentleman;*" "*Public Spirit.*"

TOWN AND COUNTRY SERMONS. Second Edition. Extra fcap. 8vo. 3s. 6d.

Some of these Sermons were preached before the Queen, and some in the performance of the writer's ordinary parochial duty. Of these Sermons the Nonconformist *says, "They are warm with the fervour of the preacher's own heart, and strong from the force of his own convictions. There is nowhere an attempt at display, and the clearness and simplicity of the style make them suitable for the youngest or most unintelligent of his hearers."*

SERMONS on NATIONAL SUBJECTS. Second Edition. Fcap. 8vo. 3s. 6d.

THE KING OF THE EARTH, and other Sermons, a Second Series of Sermons on National Subjects. Second Edition. Fcap. 8vo. 3s. 6d.

The following extract from the Preface to the 2nd Series will explain the preacher's aim in these Sermons:—"*I have tried......to proclaim the Lord Jesus Christ, as the Scriptures, both in their strictest letter and in their general method, from Genesis to Revelation, seem to me to proclaim Him; not merely as the Saviour of a few elect souls, but as the light and life of every human being who enters into the world; as the source of all reason, strength, and virtue in heathen or in Christian; as the King and Ruler of the whole universe, and of every nation, family, and man on earth; as the Redeemer of the whole earth and the whole human race... His death, as a full, perfect, and sufficient sacrifice, oblation, and satisfaction for the sins of the whole world, by which God is reconciled to the whole human race."*

DISCIPLINE, AND OTHER SERMONS. Fcp. 8vo. 3s. 6d.

The Guardian *says,—"There is much thought, tenderness, and devoutness of spirit in these Sermons, and some of them are models both in matter and expression."*

DAVID. FIVE SERMONS. Second Edition, enlarged. Fcap. 8vo. 2s. 6d.

These Sermons were preached before the University of Cambridge, and are specially addressed to young men. Their titles are,—"*David's Weakness;*" "*David's Strength;*" "*David's Anger;*" "*David's Deserts.*"

Kingsley (Rev. C.)—*continued.*

WESTMINSTER SERMONS. 8vo. 10s. 6d.

These Sermons were preached at Westminster Abbey or at one of the Chapels Royal. Their subjects are:—The Mystery of the Cross: The Perfect Love: The Spirit of Whitsuntide: Prayer: The Deaf and Dumb: The Fruits of the Spirit: Confusion: The Shaking of the Heavens and the Earth: The Kingdom of God: The Law of the Lord: God the Teacher: The Reasonable Prayer: The One Escape: The Word of God: I: The Cedars of Lebanon: Life: Death: Signs and Wonders: The Judgments of God: The War in Heaven: Noble Company: De Profundis: The Blessing and the Curse: The Silence of Faith: God and Mammon: The Beatific Vision.

Lightfoot.—Works by J. B. LIGHTFOOT, D.D., Hulsean Professor of Divinity in the University of Cambridge; Canon of St. Paul's.

ST. PAUL'S EPISTLE TO THE GALATIANS. A Revised Text, with Introduction, Notes, and Dissertations. Fourth Edition, revised. 8vo. cloth. 12s.

While the Author's object has been to make this commentary generally complete, he has paid special attention to everything relating to St. Paul's personal history and his intercourse with the Apostles and Church of the Circumcision, as it is this feature in the Epistle to the Galatians which has given it an overwhelming interest in recent theological controversy The Spectator *says "there is no commentator at once of sounder judgment and more liberal than Dr. Lightfoot."*

ST. PAUL'S EPISTLE TO THE PHILIPPIANS. A Revised Text, with Introduction, Notes, and Dissertations. Third Edition. 8vo. 12s.

"No commentary in the English language can be compared with it in regard to fulness of information, exact scholarship, and laboured attempt to settle everything about the epistle on a solid foundation."—Athenæum.

ST. PAUL'S EPISTLES TO THE COLOSSIANS AND PHILEMON. A Revised Text with Introduction, Notes, etc 8vo. 12s.

ST. CLEMENT OF ROME, THE TWO EPISTLES TO THE CORINTHIANS. A Revised Text, with Introduction and Notes. 8vo. 8s. 6d.

This volume is the first part of a complete edition of the Apostolic Fathers. The Introductions deal with the questions of the genuineness and authenticity of the Epistles, discuss their date and character, and analyse their contents. An account is also given of all the different epistles which bear the name of Clement of Rome. "By far the most copiously annotated

Lightfoot (Dr. J. B.)—*continued*:

edition of St. Clement which we yet possess, and the most convenient in every way for the English reader."—Guardian.

ON A FRESH REVISION OF THE ENGLISH NEW TESTAMENT. Second Edition. Crown 8vo. 6s.

The Author shews in detail the necessity for a fresh revision of the authorized version on the following grounds:—1. False Readings. 2. Artificial distinctions created. 3. Real distinctions obliterated. 4. Faults of Grammar. 5. Faults of Lexicography. 6. Treatment of Proper Names, official titles, etc. 7. Archaisms, defects in the English, errors of the press, etc. "The book is marked by careful scholarship, familiarity with the subject, sobriety, and circumspection."—Athenæum.

Luckock.—THE TABLES OF STONE. A Course of Sermons preached in All Saints' Church, Cambridge, by H. M. LUCKOCK, M.A., Vicar, Canon of Ely. Fcap. 8vo. 3s. 6d.

Maclaren.—SERMONS PREACHED at MANCHESTER. By ALEXANDER MACLAREN. Fifth Edition. Fcap. 8vo. 4s. 6d.

These Sermons represent no special school, but deal with the broad principles of Christian truth, especially in their bearing on practical, every day life. A few of the titles are:—"The Stone of Stumbling," "Love and Forgiveness," "The Living Dead," "Memory in Another World," "Faith in Christ," "Love and Fear," "The Choice of Wisdom," "The Food of the World."

A SECOND SERIES OF SERMONS. Third Edition. Fcap. 8vo. 4s. 6d.

The Spectator characterises them as "vigorous in style, full of thought, rich in illustration, and in an unusual degree interesting."

A THIRD SERIES OF SERMONS. Second Edition. Fcap. 8vo. 4s. 6d.

Sermons more sober and yet more forcible, and with a certain wise and practical spirituality about them it would not be easy to find."—Spectator.

Maclear.—Works by the Rev. G. F. MACLEAR, D.D., Head Master of King's College School :—

A CLASS-BOOK OF OLD TESTAMENT HISTORY. With Four Maps. Eighth Edition. 18mo. 4s. 6d.

"The present volume," says the Preface, "forms a Class-Book of Old Testament History from the Earliest Times to those of Ezra and Nehemiah. In its preparation the most recent authorities have been consulted, and wherever it has appeared useful, Notes have been subjoined illustrative of the Text, and, for the sake of more advanced students, references added to larger works. The Index has been so arranged as to form a concise Dictionary of the Persons and Places mentioned in the course of the

Maclear (G. F.)—*continued.*

Narrative." *The Maps, prepared by Stanford, materially add to the value and usefulness of the book. The* British Quarterly Review *calls it "A careful and elaborate, though brief compendium of all that modern research has done for the illustration of the Old Testament. We know of no work which contains so much important information in so small a compass."*

A CLASS-BOOK OF NEW TESTAMENT HISTORY. Including the Connexion of the Old and New Testament. Sixth Edition. 18mo. 5s. 6d.

The present volume forms a sequel to the Author's Class-Book of Old Testament History, and continues the narrative to the close of St. Paul's second imprisonment at Rome. The work is divided into three Books—I. The Connection between the Old and New Testaments. II. The Gospel History. III. The Apostolic History. In the Appendix are given Chronological Tables The Clerical Journal *says, "It is not often that such an amount of useful and interesting matter on biblical subjects, is found in so convenient and small a compass, as in this well-arranged volume."*

A CLASS-BOOK OF THE CATECHISM OF THE CHURCH OF ENGLAND. Third and Cheaper Edition. 18mo. 1s. 6d.

The present work is intended as a sequel to the two preceding books. "Like them, it is furnished with notes and references to larger works, and it is hoped that it may be found, especially in the higher forms of our Public Schools, to supply a suitable manual of instruction in the chief doctrines of our Church, and a useful help in the preparation of Candidates for Confirmation." The Literary Churchman *says, "It is indeed the work of a scholar and divine, and as such, though extremely simple, it is also extremely instructive. There are few clergy who would not find it useful in preparing candidates for Confirmation; and there are not a few who would find it useful to themselves as well."*

A FIRST CLASS-BOOK OF THE CATECHISM OF THE CHURCH OF ENGLAND, with Scripture Proofs for Junior Classes and Schools. New Edition. 18mo. 6d.

This is an epitome of the larger Class-book, meant for junior students and elementary classes. The book has been carefully condensed, so as to contain clearly and fully, the most important part of the contents of the larger book.

A SHILLING-BOOK of OLD TESTAMENT HISTORY. New Edition. 18mo. cloth limp. 1s.

This Manual bears the same relation to the larger Old Testament History, that the book just mentioned does to the larger work on the Catechism. It consists of Ten Books, divided into short chapters, and subdivided into

Maclear (G. F.)—*continued.*

sections, each section treating of a single episode in the history, the title of which is given in bold type.

A SHILLING-BOOK of NEW TESTAMENT HISTORY. New Edition. 18mo. cloth limp. 1s.

This bears the same relation to the larger *New Testament History* that the work just mentioned has to the large *Old Testament History*, and is marked by similar characteristics.

A MANUAL OF INSTRUCTION FOR CONFIRMATION AND FIRST COMMUNION, with Prayers and Devotions. 32mo. cloth extra, red edges. 2s.

This is an enlarged and improved edition of '*The Order of Confirmation.*' To it have been added the Communion Office, with Notes and Explanations, together with a brief form of Self Examination and Devotions selected from the works of Cosin, Ken, Wilson, and others.

Macmillan.—Works by the Rev. HUGH MACMILLAN, LL.D., F.R.S.E. (For other Works by the same Author, see CATALOGUE OF TRAVELS and SCIENTIFIC CATALOGUE).

THE TRUE VINE; or, the Analogies of our Lord's Allegory. Second Edition. Globe 8vo. 6s.

This work is not merely an exposition of the fifteenth chapter of St. John's Gospel, but also a general parable of spiritual truth from the world of plants. It describes a few of the points in which the varied realm of vegetable life comes into contact with the higher spiritual realm, and shews how rich a field of promise lies before the analogical mind in this direction. The Nonconformist says, "*It abounds in exquisite bits of description, and in striking facts clearly stated.*" The British Quarterly says, "*Readers and preachers who are unscientific will find many of his illustrations as valuable as they are beautiful.*"

BIBLE TEACHINGS IN NATURE. Eighth Edition. Globe 8vo. 6s.

In this volume the author has endeavoured to shew that the teaching of nature and the teaching of the Bible are directed to the same great end; that the Bible contains the spiritual truths which are necessary to make us wise unto salvation, and the objects and scenes of nature are the pictures by which these truths are illustrated. "*He has made the world more beautiful to us, and unsealed our ears to voices of praise and messages of love that might otherwise have been unheard.*"—British Quarterly Review. "*Mr. Macmillan has produced a book which may be fitly described as one of the happiest efforts for enlisting physical science in the direct service of religion.*"—Guardian.

Macmillan (H.)—*continued.*

THE MINISTRY OF NATURE. Second Edition. Globe 8vo. 6s.

In this volume the Author attempts to interpret Nature on her religious side in accordance with the most recent discoveries of physical science, and to shew how much greater significance is imparted to many passages of Scripture and many doctrines of Christianity when looked at in the light of these discoveries. Instead of regarding Physical Science as antagonistic to Christianity, the Author believes and seeks to shew that every new discovery tends more strongly to prove that Nature and the Bible have One Author. "Whether the reader agree or not with his conclusions, he will acknowledge he is in the presence of an original and thoughtful writer."—Pall Mall Gazette. *"There is no class of educated men and women that will not profit by these essays."*—Standard.

M'Cosh.—For Works by JAMES MCCOSH, LL.D., President of Princeton College, New Jersey, U.S., see PHILOSOPHICAL CATALOGUE.

Maurice.—Works by the late Rev. F. DENISON MAURICE, M.A., Professor of Moral Philosophy in the University of Cambridge.

Professor Maurice's Works are recognized as having made a deep impression on modern theology. With whatever subject he dealt he tried to look at it in its bearing on living men and their every-day surroundings, and faced unshrinkingly the difficulties which occur to ordinary earnest thinkers in a manner that showed he had intense sympathy with all that concerns humanity. By all who wish to understand the various drifts of thought during the present century, Mr. Maurice's works must be studied. An intimate friend of Mr. Maurice's, one who has carefully studied all his works, and had besides many opportunities of knowing the Author's opinions, in speaking of his so-called "obscurity," ascribes it to "the never-failing assumption that God is really moving, teaching and acting: and that the writer's business is not so much to state something for the reader's benefit, as to apprehend what God is saying or doing." The Spectator says—"Few of those of our own generation whose names will live in English history or literature have exerted so profound and so permanent an influence as Mr. Maurice."

THE PATRIARCHS AND LAWGIVERS OF THE OLD TESTAMENT. Third and Cheaper Edition. Crown 8vo. 5s.

The Nineteen Discourses contained in this volume were preached in the chapel of Lincoln's Inn during the year 1851. *The texts are taken from the books of Genesis, Exodus, Numbers, Deuteronomy, Joshua, Judges, and Samuel, and involve some of the most interesting biblical topics discussed in recent times.*

Maurice (F. D.)—continued.

THE PROPHETS AND KINGS OF THE OLD TESTAMENT. Third Edition, with new Preface. Crown 8vo. 10s. 6d.

Mr. Maurice, in the spirit which animated the compilers of the Church Lessons, has in these Sermons regarded the Prophets more as preachers of righteousness than as mere predictors—an aspect of their lives which, he thinks, has been greatly overlooked in our day, and than which, there is none we have more need to contemplate. He has found that the Old Testament Prophets, taken in their simple natural sense, clear up many of the difficulties which beset us in the daily work of life; make the past intelligible, the present endurable, and the future real and hopeful.

THE GOSPEL OF THE KINGDOM OF HEAVEN. A Series of Lectures on the Gospel of St. Luke. Crown 8vo. 9s.

Mr. Maurice, in his Preface to these Twenty-eight Lectures, says,—"In these Lectures I have endeavoured to ascertain what is told us respecting the life of Jesus by one of those Evangelists who proclaim Him to be the Christ, who says that He did come from a Father, that He did baptize with the Holy Spirit, that He did rise from the dead. I have chosen the one who is most directly connected with the later history of the Church, who was not an Apostle, who professedly wrote for the use of a man already instructed in the faith of the Apostles. I have followed the course of the writer's narrative, not changing it under any pretext. I have adhered to his phraseology, striving to avoid the substitution of any other for his."

THE GOSPEL OF ST. JOHN. A Series of Discourses. Third and Cheaper Edition. Crown 8vo. 6s.

These Discourses, twenty-eight in number, are of a nature similar to those on the Gospel of St. Luke, and will be found to render valuable assistance to any one anxious to understand the Gospel of the beloved disciple, so different in many respects from those of the other three Evangelists. Appended are eleven notes illustrating various points which occur throughout the discourses. The Literary Churchman *thus speaks of this volume:—"Thorough honesty, reverence, and deep thought pervade the work, which is every way solid and philosophical, as well as theological, and abounding with suggestions which the patient student may draw out more at length for himself."*

THE EPISTLES OF ST. JOHN. A Series of Lectures on Christian Ethics. Second and Cheaper Edition. Cr. 8vo. 6s.

These Lectures on Christian Ethics were delivered to the students of the Working Men's College, Great Ormond Street, London, on a series of Sunday mornings. Mr. Maurice believes that the question in which we are most interested, the question which most affects our studies and our daily lives, is the question, whether there is a foundation for human morality,

Maurice (F. D.)—*continued.*

or whether it is dependent upon the opinions and fashions of different ages and countries. This important question will be found amply and fairly discussed in this volume, which the National Review calls "*Mr. Maurice's most effective and instructive work. He is peculiarly fitted by the constitution of his mind, to throw light on St. John's writings.*" Appended is a note on "*Positivism and its Teacher.*"

EXPOSITORY SERMONS ON THE PRAYER-BOOK. The Prayer-book considered especially in reference to the Romish System. Second Edition. Fcap. 8vo. 5s. 6d.

After an Introductory Sermon, Mr. Maurice goes over the various parts of the Church Service, expounds in eighteen Sermons, their intention and significance, and shews how appropriate they are as expressions of the deepest longings and wants of all classes of men.

LECTURES ON THE APOCALYPSE, or Book of the Revelation of St. John the Divine. Crown 8vo. 10s. 6d.

Mr. Maurice, instead of trying to find far-fetched allusions to great historical events in the distant future, endeavours to discover the plain, literal, obvious meaning of the words of the writer, and shews that as a rule these refer to events contemporaneous with or immediately succeeding the time when the book was written. At the same time he shews the applicability of the contents of the book to the circumstances of the present day and of all times. "Never," says the Nonconformist, "has Mr. Maurice been more reverent, more careful for the letter of the Scripture, more discerning of the purpose of the Spirit, or more sober and practical in his teaching, than in this volume on the Apocalypse."

WHAT IS REVELATION? A Series of Sermons on the Epiphany; to which are added, Letters to a Theological Student on the Bampton Lectures of Mr. Mansel. Crown 8vo. 10s. 6d.

Both Sermons and Letters were called forth by the doctrine maintained by Mr. Mansel in his Bampton Lectures, that Revelation cannot be a direct Manifestation of the Infinite Nature of God. Mr. Maurice maintains the opposite doctrine, and in his Sermons explains why, in spite of the high authorities on the other side, he must still assert the principle which he discovers in the Services of the Church and throughout the Bible.

SEQUEL TO THE INQUIRY, "WHAT IS REVELATION?" Letters in Reply to Mr. Mansel's Examination of "Strictures on the Bampton Lectures." Crown 8vo. 6s.

This, as the title indicates, was called forth by Mr. Mansel's Examination of Mr. Maurice's Strictures on his doctrine of the Infinite.

THEOLOGICAL ESSAYS. Third Edition. Crown 8vo. 10s. 6d.

"*The book,*" says Mr. Maurice, "*expresses thoughts which have been*

Maurice (F. D.)—*continued.*

working in my mind for years: the method of it has not been adopted carelessly: even the composition has undergone frequent revision." There are seventeen Essays in all, and although meant primarily for Unitarians, to quote the words of the Clerical Journal, *" it leaves untouched scarcely any topic which is in agitation in the religious world; scarcely a moot point between our various sects; scarcely a plot of debateable ground between Christians and Infidels, between Romanists and Protestants, between Socinians and other Christians, between English Churchmen and Dissenters on both sides. Scarce is there a misgiving, a difficulty, an aspiration stirring amongst us now,—now, when men seem in earnest as hardly ever before about religion, and ask and demand satisfaction with a fearlessness which seems almost awful when one thinks what is at stake—which is not recognised and grappled with by Mr. Maurice."*

THE DOCTRINE OF SACRIFICE DEDUCED FROM THE SCRIPTURES. Crown 8vo. 7s. 6d.

Throughout the Nineteen Sermons contained in this volume, Mr. Maurice expounds the ideas which he has formed of the Doctrine of Sacrifice, as it is set forth in various parts of the Bible.

THE RELIGIONS OF THE WORLD, AND THEIR RELATIONS TO CHRISTIANITY. Fourth Edition. Fcap. 8vo. 5s.

These Eight Boyle Lectures are divided into two parts, of four Lectures each. In the first part Mr. Maurice examines the great Religious systems which present themselves in the history of the world, with the purpose of inquiring what is their main characteristic principle. The second four Lectures are occupied with a discussion of the questions, " In what relation does Christianity stand to these different faiths? If there be a faith which is meant for mankind, is this the one, or must we look for another?"

ON THE LORD'S PRAYER. Fourth Edition. Fcap. 8vo. 2s. 6d.

In these Nine Sermons the successive petitions of the Lord's Prayer are taken up by Mr. Maurice, their significance expounded, and, as was usual with him, connected with the every-day lives, feelings, and aspirations of the men of the present time.

ON THE SABBATH DAY; the Character of the Warrior, and on the Interpretation of History. Fcap. 8vo. 2s. 6d.

THE GROUND AND OBJECT OF HOPE FOR MANKIND. Four Sermons preached before the University of Cambridge. Crown 8vo. 3s. 6d.

In these Four Sermons Mr. Maurice views the subject in four aspects: —I. The Hope of the Missionary. II. The Hope of the Patriot. III. The Hope of the Churchman. IV. The Hope of Man. The Spectator

Maurice (F. D.)—*continued.*

says, "*It is impossible to find anywhere deeper teaching than this;*" and the Nonconformist, "*We thank him for the manly, noble, stirring words in these Sermons—words fitted to quicken thoughts, to awaken high aspiration, to stimulate to lives of goodness.*"

THE LORD'S PRAYER, THE CREED, AND THE COMMANDMENTS. A Manual for Parents and Schoolmasters. To which is added the Order of the Scriptures. 18mo. cloth limp. 1s.

This book is not written for clergymen, as such, but for parents and teachers, who are often either prejudiced against the contents of the Catechism, or regard it peculiarly as the clergyman's book, but, at the same time, have a general notion that a habit of prayer ought to be cultivated, that there are some things which ought to be believed, and some things which ought to be done. It will be found to be peculiarly valuable at the present time, when the question of religious education is occupying so much attention.

THE CLAIMS OF THE BIBLE AND OF SCIENCE. A Correspondence on some Questions respecting the Pentateuch. Crown 8vo. 4s. 6d.

This volume consists of a series of Fifteen Letters, the first and last addressed by a 'Layman' to Mr. Maurice, the intervening thirteen written by Mr. Maurice himself.

DIALOGUES ON FAMILY WORSHIP. Crown 8vo. 6s.

"*The parties in these Dialogues,*" says the Preface, "*are a Clergyman who accepts the doctrines of the Church, and a Layman whose faith in them is nearly gone. The object of the Dialogues is not confutation, but the discovery of a ground on which two Englishmen and two fathers may stand, and on which their country and their children may stand when their places know them no more.*"

THE COMMANDMENTS CONSIDERED AS INSTRUMENTS OF NATIONAL REFORMATION. Crown 8vo. 4s. 6d.

The author endeavours to shew that the Commandments are now, and ever have been, the great protesters against Presbyteral and Prelatical assumptions, and that if we do not receive them as Commandments of the Lord God spoken to Israel, and spoken to every people under heaven now, we lose the greatest witnesses we possess for national morality and civil freedom.

MORAL AND METAPHYSICAL PHILOSOPHY. Vol. I. Ancient Philosophy from the First to the Thirteenth Centuries. Vol. II. Fourteenth Century and the French Revolution, with a Glimpse into the Nineteenth Century. Two Vols. 8vo. 25s.

This is an edition in two volumes of Professor Maurice's History of

Maurice (F. D.)—*continued.*

Philosophy from the earliest period to the present time. It was formerly issued in a number of separate volumes, and it is believed that all admirers of the author and all students of philosophy will welcome this compact edition. In a long introduction to this edition, in the form of a dialogue, Professor Maurice justifies his own views, and touches upon some of the most important topics of the time.

SOCIAL MORALITY. Twenty-one Lectures delivered in the University of Cambridge. New and Cheaper Edition. Cr. 8vo. 10s. 6d.

"*Whilst reading it we are charmed by the freedom from exclusiveness and prejudice, the large charity, the loftiness of thought, the eagerness to recognise and appreciate whatever there is of real worth extant in the world, which animates it from one end to the other. We gain new thoughts and new ways of viewing things, even more, perhaps, from being brought for a time under the influence of so noble and spiritual a mind.*"—Athenæum.

THE CONSCIENCE: Lectures on Casuistry, delivered in the University of Cambridge. Second and Cheaper Edition. Crown 8vo. 5s.

In this series of nine Lectures, Professor Maurice, endeavours to settle what is meant by the word "Conscience," and discusses the most important questions immediately connected with the subject. Taking "Casuistry" in its old sense as being the "study of cases of Conscience," he endeavours to show in what way it may be brought to bear at the present day upon the acts and thoughts of our ordinary existence. He shows that Conscience asks for laws, not rules; for freedom, not chains; for education, not suppression. He has abstained from the use of philosophical terms, and has touched on philosophical systems only when he fancied "they were interfering with the rights and duties of wayfarers." The Saturday Review *says: "We rise from the perusal of these lectures with a detestation of all that is selfish and mean, and with a living impression that there is such a thing as goodness after all."*

LECTURES ON THE ECCLESIASTICAL HISTORY OF THE FIRST AND SECOND CENTURIES. 8vo. 10s. 6d.

In the first chapter on "The Jewish Calling," besides expounding his idea of the true nature of a "Church," the author gives a brief sketch of the position and economy of the Jews; while in the second he points out their relation to "the other Nations." Chapter Third contains a succint account of the various Jewish Sects, while in Chapter Fourth are briefly set forth Mr. Maurice's ideas of the character of Christ and the nature of His mission, and a sketch of events is given up to the Day of Pentecost. The remaining Chapters, extending from the Apostles' personal Ministry to the end of the Second Century, contain sketches of the character and

Maurice (F. D.)—*continued.*
work of all the prominent men in any way connected with the Early Church, accounts of the origin and nature of the various doctrines orthodox and heretical which had their birth during the period, as well as of the planting and early history of the Chief Churches in Asia, Africa and Europe.

    LEARNING AND WORKING. Six Lectures delivered in Willis's Rooms, London, in June and July, 1854.—THE RELIGION OF ROME, and its Influence on Modern Civilisation. Four Lectures delivered in the Philosophical Institution of Edinburgh, in December, 1854. Crown 8vo. 5s.

    SERMONS PREACHED IN COUNTRY CHURCHES. Crown 8vo. 10s. 6d.

"*Earnest, practical, and extremely simple.*"—Literary Churchman. "*Good specimens of his simple and earnest eloquence. The Gospel incidents are realized with a vividness which we can well believe made the common people hear him gladly. Moreover they are sermons which must have done the hearers good.*"—John Bull.

Moorhouse.—Works by JAMES MOORHOUSE, M.A., Vicar of Paddington:—

    SOME MODERN DIFFICULTIES RESPECTING the FACTS OF NATURE AND REVELATION. Fcap. 8vo. 2s. 6d.

The first of these Four Discourses is a systematic reply to the Essay of the Rev. Baden Powell on Christian Evidences in "Essays and Reviews." The fourth Sermon, on "The Resurrection," is in some measure complementary to this, and the two together are intended to furnish a tolerably complete view of modern objections to Revelation. In the second and third Sermons, on the "Temptation" and "Passion," the author has endeavoured "to exhibit the power and wonder of those great facts within the spiritual sphere, which modern theorists have especially sought to discredit."

    JACOB. Three Sermons preached before the University of Cambridge in Lent 1870. Extra fcap. 8vo. 3s. 6d.

    THE HULSEAN LECTURES FOR 1865. Cr. 8vo. 5s.

"*Few more valuable works have come into our hands for many years... a most fruitful and welcome volume.*"—Church Review.

O'Brien.—AN ATTEMPT TO EXPLAIN and ESTABLISH THE DOCTRINE OF JUSTIFICATION by FAITH ONLY. By JAMES THOMAS O'BRIEN, D.D., Bishop of Ossory. Third Edition. 8vo. 12s.

This work consists of Ten Sermons. The first four treat of the nature and mutual relations of Faith and Justification; the fifth and sixth examine the corruptions of the doctrine of Justification by Faith only, and the objections which have been urged against it. The four concluding sermons deal with the moral effects of Faith. Various Notes are added explanatory of the Author's reasoning.

Palgrave.—HYMNS. By FRANCIS TURNER PALGRAVE. Third Edition, enlarged. 18mo. 1s. 6d.

This is a collection of twenty original Hymns, which the Literary Churchman *speaks of as "so choice, so perfect, and so refined,—so tender in feeling, and so scholarly in expression."*

Paul of Tarsus. An Inquiry into the Times and the Gospel of the Apostle of the Gentiles. By a GRADUATE. 8vo. 10s. 6d.

The Author of this work has attempted, out of the materials which were at his disposal, to construct for himself a sketch of the time in which St. Paul lived, of the religious systems with which he was brought in contact, of the doctrine which he taught, and of the work which he ultimately achieved. "Turn where we will throughout the volume, we find the best fruit of patient inquiry, sound scholarship, logical argument, and fairness of conclusion. No thoughtful reader will rise from its perusal without a real and lasting profit to himself, and a sense of permanent addition to the cause of truth."—Standard.

Picton.—THE MYSTERY OF MATTER; and other Essays. By J. ALLANSON PICTON, Author of "New Theories and the Old Faith." Crown 8vo. 10s. 6d.

Contents—The Mystery of Matter: The Philosophy of Ignorance: The Antithesis of Faith and Sight: The Essential Nature of Religion: Christian Pantheism.

Prescott.—THE THREEFOLD CORD. Sermons preached before the University of Cambridge. By J. E. PRESCOTT, B.D. Fcap. 8vo. 3s. 6d.

Procter.—A HISTORY OF THE BOOK OF COMMON PRAYER: With a Rationale of its Offices. By FRANCIS PROCTER, M.A. Eleventh Edition, revised and enlarged. Crown 8vo. 10s. 6d.

The Athenæum *says:—"The origin of every part of the Prayer-book has been diligently investigated,—and there are few questions or facts connected with it which are not either sufficiently explained, or so referred to, that persons interested may work out the truth for themselves."*

Procter and Maclear.—AN ELEMENTARY INTRODUCTION TO THE BOOK OF COMMON PRAYER. Re-arranged and Supplemented by an Explanation of the Morning and Evening Prayer and the Litany. By F. PROCTER, M.A. and G. F. MACLEAR, D.D. New Edition. 18mo. 2s. 6d.

This book has the same object and follows the same plan as the Manuals already noticed under Mr. Maclear's name. Each book is subdivided into chapters and sections. In Book I. is given a detailed History of the Book of Common Prayer down to the Attempted Revision in the Reign of William III. Book II., consisting of four Parts, treats in order the various parts of the Prayer Book. Notes, etymological, historical, and critical, are given throughout the book, while the Appendix contains several articles of much interest and importance. Appended is a General Index and an Index of Words explained in the Notes. The Literary Churchman *characterizes it as* "*by far the completest and most satisfactory book of its kind we know. We wish it were in the hands of every schoolboy and every schoolmaster in the kingdom.*"

Psalms of David CHRONOLOGICALLY ARRANGED.
An Amended Version, with Historical Introductions and Explanatory Notes. By FOUR FRIENDS. Second and Cheaper Edition, much enlarged. Crown 8vo. 8s. 6d.

One of the chief designs of the Editors, in preparing this volume, was to restore the Psalter as far as possible to the order in which the Psalms were written. They give the division of each Psalm into strophes, and of each strophe into the lines which composed it, and amend the errors of translation. The Spectator *calls it* "*One of the most instructive and valuable books that have been published for many years.*"

Golden Treasury Psalter.—THE STUDENT'S EDITION.
Being an Edition with briefer Notes of the above. 18mo. 3s. 6d.

This volume will be found to meet the requirements of those who wish for a smaller edition of the larger work, at a lower price for family use, and for the use of younger pupils in Public Schools. The short notes which are appended to the volume will, it is hoped, suffice to make the meaning intelligible throughout. The aim of this edition is simply to put the reader as far as possible in possession of the plain meaning of the writer. "*It is a gem,*" *the* Nonconformist *says.*

Ramsay.—THE CATECHISER'S MANUAL; or, the
Church Catechism Illustrated and Explained, for the Use of Clergymen, Schoolmasters, and Teachers. By ARTHUR RAMSAY, M.A. Second Edition. 18mo. 1s. 6d.

Rays of Sunlight for Dark Days. A Book of Selections for the Suffering. With a Preface by C. J. VAUGHAN, D.D. 18mo New Edition. 3s. 6d. Also in morocco, old style.

Dr. Vaughan says in the Preface, after speaking of the general run of Books of Comfort for Mourners, "*It is because I think that the little volume now offered to the Christian sufferer is one of greater wisdom and of deeper experience, that I have readily consented to the request that I* would introduce it by a few words of Preface." The book consists of a series of very brief extracts from a great variety of authors, in prose and poetry, suited to the many moods of a mourning or suffering mind. "Mostly gems of the first water."—Clerical Journal.

Reynolds.—NOTES OF THE CHRISTIAN LIFE. A Selection of Sermons by HENRY ROBERT REYNOLDS, B.A., President of Cheshunt College, and Fellow of University College, London. Crown 8vo. 7s. 6d.

This work may be taken as representative of the mode of thought and feeling which is most popular amongst the freer and more cultivated Nonconformists. "It is long," says the Nonconformist, "since we have met with any published sermons better calculated than these to stimulate devout thought, and to bring home to the soul the reality of a spiritual life."

Roberts.—DISCUSSIONS ON THE GOSPELS. By the Rev. ALEXANDER ROBERTS, D.D. Second Edition, revised and enlarged. 8vo. 16s.

This volume is divided into two parts. Part I. "On the Language employed by our Lord and His Disciples," in which the author endeavours to prove that Greek was the language usually employed by Christ Himself, in opposition to the common belief that Our Lord spoke Aramæan. Part II. is occupied with a discussion "On the Original Language of St. Matthew's Gospel," and on "The Origin and Authenticity of the Gospels." "The author brings the valuable qualifications of learning, temper, and an independent judgment."—Daily News.

Robertson.—PASTORAL COUNSELS. Being Chapters on Practical and Devotional Subjects. By the late JOHN ROBERTSON, D.D. Third Edition, with a Preface by the Author of "The Recreations of a Country Parson." Extra fcap. 8vo. 6s.

These Sermons are the free utterances of a strong and independent thinker. He does not depart from the essential doctrines of his Church, but he expounds them in a spirit of the widest charity, and always having most prominently in view the requirements of practical life. "The sermons are admirable specimens of a practical, earnest, and instructive style of pulpit teaching."—Nonconformist.

Rowsell.—MAN'S LABOUR AND GOD'S HARVEST. Sermons preached before the University of Cambridge in Lent, 1861. Fcap. 8vo. 3s.

"We strongly recommend this little volume to young men, and especially to those who are contemplating working for Christ in Holy Orders."—Literary Churchman.

Salmon.—THE REIGN OF LAW, and other Sermons, preached in the Chapel of Trinity College, Dublin. By the Rev. GEORGE SALMON, D.D., Regius Professor of Divinity in the University of Dublin. Crown 8vo. 6s.

"Well considered, learned, and powerful discourses."—Spectator.

Sanday.—THE AUTHORSHIP AND HISTORICAL CHARACTER OF THE FOURTH GOSPEL, considered in reference to the Contents of the Gospel itself. A Critical Essay. By WILLIAM SANDAY, M.A., Fellow of Trinity College, Oxford. Crown 8vo. 8s. 6d.

The object of this Essay is critical and nothing more. The Author attempts to apply faithfully and persistently to the contents of the much disputed fourth Gospel that scientific method which has been so successful in other directions. "The facts of religion," the Author believes, "(i. e. the documents, the history of religious bodies, &c.) are as much facts as the lie of a coal-bed or the formation of a coral-reef." "The Essay is not only most valuable in itself, but full of promise for the future."—Canon Westcott in the *Academy*.

Selborne.—THE BOOK OF PRAISE: From the Best English Hymn Writers. Selected and arranged by Lord SELBORNE. With Vignette by WOOLNER. 18mo. 4s. 6d.

The present is an attempt to present, under a convenient arrangement, a collection of such examples of a copious and interesting branch of popular literature, as, after several years' study of the subject, have seemed to the Editor most worthy of being separated from the mass to which they belong. It has been the Editor's desire and aim to adhere strictly, in all cases in which it could be ascertained, to the genuine uncorrupted text of the authors themselves. The names of the authors and date of composition of the hymns, when known, are affixed, while notes are added to the volume, giving further details. The Hymns are arranged according to subjects. "*There is not room for two opinions as to the value of the 'Book of Praise.'*" —Guardian. "*Approaches as nearly as one can conceive to perfection.*" —Nonconformist.

BOOK OF PRAISE HYMNAL. *See* end of this Catalogue.

Sergeant.—SERMONS. By the Rev. E. W. SERGEANT, M.A., Balliol College, Oxford; Assistant Master at Westminster College. Fcap. 8vo. 2s. 6d.

Smith.—PROPHECY A PREPARATION FOR CHRIST. Eight Lectures preached before the University of Oxford, being the Bampton Lectures for 1869. By R. PAYNE SMITH, D.D., Dean of Canterbury. Second and Cheaper Edition. Crown 8vo. 6s.

The author's object in these Lectures is to shew that there exists in the Old Testament an element, which no criticism on naturalistic principles can either account for or explain away: that element is Prophecy. The author endeavours to prove that its force does not consist merely in its predictions. "*These Lectures overflow with solid learning.*"—Record.

Smith.—CHRISTIAN FAITH. Sermons preached before the University of Cambridge. By W. SAUMAREZ SMITH, M.A., Principal of St. Aidan's College, Birkenhead. Fcap. 8vo. 3s. 6d.

"*Appropriate and earnest sermons, suited to the practical exhortation of an educated congregation.*"—Guardian.

Stanley.—Works by the Very Rev. A. P. STANLEY, D.D., Dean of Westminster.

THE ATHANASIAN CREED, with a Preface on the General Recommendations of the RITUAL COMMISSION. Cr. 8vo. 2s.

The object of the work is not so much to urge the omission or change of the Athanasian Creed, as to shew that such a relaxation ought to give offence to no reasonable or religious mind. With this view, the Dean of Westminster discusses in succession—(1) the Authorship of the Creed, (2) its Internal Characteristics, (3) the Peculiarities of its Use in the Church of England, (4) its Advantages and Disadvantages, (5) its various Interpretations, and (6) the Judgment passed upon it by the Ritual Commission. In conclusion, Dr. Stanley maintains that the use of the Athanasian Creed should no longer be made compulsory. "*Dr. Stanley puts with admirable force the objections which may be made to the Creed; equally admirable, we think, in his statement of its advantages.*"—Spectator.

THE NATIONAL THANKSGIVING. Sermons preached in Westminster Abbey. Second Edition. Crown 8vo. 2s. 6d.

These Sermons are (1) "*Death and Life,*" *preached December* 10, 1871; (2) "*The Trumpet of Patmos,*" *December* 17, 1871; (3) "*The Day of Thanksgiving,*" *March* 3, 1872. "*In point of fervour and polish by far the best specimens in print of Dean Stanley's eloquent style.*"—Standard.

Sunday Library. See end of this Catalogue.

Swainson.—Works by C. A. SWAINSON, D.D., Canon of Chichester :—

THE CREEDS OF THE CHURCH IN THEIR RELATIONS TO HOLY SCRIPTURE and the CONSCIENCE OF THE CHRISTIAN. 8vo. cloth. 9s.

The Lectures which compose this volume discuss, amongst others, the following subjects: "*Faith in God,*" "*Exercise of our Reason,*" "*Origin and Authority of Creeds,*" *and* "*Private Judgment, its use and exercise.*" "*Treating of abstruse points of Scripture, he applies them so forcibly to Christian duty and practice as to prove eminently serviceable to the Church.*"—John Bull.

Swainson (C. A.)—*continued.*
THE AUTHORITY OF THE NEW TESTAMENT,
and other LECTURES, delivered before the University of Cambridge. 8vo. cloth. 12s.

The first series of Lectures in this work is on "The Words spoken by the Apostles of Jesus," "The Inspiration of God's Servants," "The Human Character of the Inspired Writers," and "The Divine Character of the Word written." The second embraces Lectures on "Sin as Imperfection," "Sin as Self-will," "Whatsoever is not of Faith is Sin," "Christ the Saviour," and "The Blood of the New Covenant." The third is on "Christians One Body in Christ," "The One Body the Spouse of Christ," "Christ's Prayer for Unity," "Our Reconciliation should be manifested in common Worship," and "Ambassadors for Christ."

Taylor.—THE RESTORATION OF BELIEF. New and Revised Edition. By ISAAC TAYLOR, Esq. Crown 8vo. 8s. 6d.

The earlier chapters are occupied with an examination of the primitive history of the Christian Religion, and its relation to the Roman government; and here, as well as in the remainder of the work, the author shews the bearing of that history on some of the difficult and interesting questions which have recently been claiming the attention of all earnest men. The last chapter of this New Edition treats of "The Present Position of the Argument concerning Christianity," with special reference to M. Renan's Vie de Jésus.

Temple.—SERMONS PREACHED IN THE CHAPEL of RUGBY SCHOOL. By F. TEMPLE, D.D., Bishop of Exeter. New and Cheaper Edition. Extra fcap. 8vo. 4s. 6d.

This volume contains Thirty-five Sermons on topics more or less intimately connected with every-day life. The following are a few of the subjects discoursed upon:—"Love and Duty;" "Coming to Christ;" "Great Men;" "Faith;" "Doubts;" "Scruples;" "Original Sin;" "Friendship;" "Helping Others;" "The Discipline of Temptation;" "Strength a Duty;" "Worldliness;" "Ill Temper;" "The Burial of the Past."

A SECOND SERIES OF SERMONS PREACHED IN THE CHAPEL OF RUGBY SCHOOL. Second Edition. Extra fcap. 8vo. 6s.

This Second Series of Forty-two brief, pointed, practical Sermons, on topics intimately connected with the every-day life of young and old, will be acceptable to all who are acquainted with the First Series. The following are a few of the subjects treated of:—"Disobedience," "Almsgiving," "The Unknown Guidance of God," "Apathy one of our Trials," "High Aims in Leaders," "Doing our Best," "The Use of Knowledge," "Use of Observances," "Martha and Mary," "John the Baptist," "Severity

Temple (F., D.D.)—*continued.*
before Mercy," "Even Mistakes Punished," " Morality and Religion," "Children," "Action the Test of Spiritual Life," "Self-Respect," "Too Late," " The Tercentenary."
A THIRD SERIES OF SERMONS PREACHED IN RUGBY SCHOOL CHAPEL IN 1867—1869. Extra fcap. 8vo. 6s.
This third series of Bishop Temple's Rugby Sermons, contains thirty-six brief discourses, including the " Good-bye" sermon preached on his leaving Rugby to enter on the office he now holds.

Thring.—Works by Rev. EDWARD THRING, M.A.
SERMONS DELIVERED AT UPPINGHAM SCHOOL. Crown 8vo. 5s.
In this volume are contained Forty-seven brief Sermons, all on subjects more or less intimately connected with Public-school life. " We desire very highly to commend these capital Sermons which treat of a boy's life and trials in a thoroughly practical way and with great simplicity and impressiveness. They deserve to be classed with the best of their kind."—Literary Churchman.
THOUGHTS ON LIFE-SCIENCE. New Edition, enlarged and revised. Crown 8vo. 7s. 6d.
In this volume are discussed in a familiar manner some of the most interesting problems between Science and Religion, Reason and Feeling.

Tracts for Priests and People. By VARIOUS WRITERS.
THE FIRST SERIES. Crown 8vo. 8s.
THE SECOND SERIES. Crown 8vo. 8s.
The whole Series of Fifteen Tracts may be had separately, price One Shilling each.

Trench.—Works by R. CHENEVIX TRENCH, D.D., Archbishop of Dublin. (For other Works by the same author, *see* BIOGRAPHICAL, BELLES LETTRES, and LINGUISTIC CATALOGUES).
NOTES ON THE PARABLES OF OUR LORD. Twelfth Edition. 8vo. 12s.
This work has taken its place as a standard exposition and interpretation of Christ's Parables. The book is prefaced by an Introductory Essay in four chapters:—I. On the definition of the Parable. II. On Teaching by Parables. III. On the Interpretation of the Parables. IV. On other Parables besides those in the Scriptures. The author then proceeds to take up the Parables one by one, and by the aid of philology, history,

Trench—*continued.*

antiquities, and the researches of travellers, shews forth the significance, beauty, and applicability of each, concluding with what he deems its true moral interpretation. In the numerous Notes are many valuable references, illustrative quotations, critical and philological annotations, etc., and appended to the volume is a classified list of fifty-six works on the Parables.

NOTES ON THE MIRACLES OF OUR LORD.
Ninth Edition. 8vo. 12s.

*In the 'Preliminary Essay' to this work, all the momentous and interesting questions that have been raised in connection with Miracles, are discussed with considerable fulness. The Essay consists of six chapters:— I. On the Names of Miracles, i. e. the Greek words by which they are designated in the New Testament. II. The Miracles and Nature—What is the difference between a Miracle and any event in the ordinary course of Nature? III. The Authority of Miracles—Is the Miracle to command absolute obedience? IV. The Evangelical, compared with the other cycles of Miracles. V. The Assaults on the Miracles—*1. *The Jewish.* 2. *The Heathen (Celsus etc.).* 3. *The Pantheistic (Spinosa etc.).* 4. *The Sceptical (Hume).* 5. *The Miracles only relatively miraculous (Schleiermacher).* 6. *The Rationalistic (Paulus).* 7. *The Historico-Critical (Woolston, Strauss).* VI. *The Apologetic Worth of the Miracles. The author then treats the separate Miracles as he does the Parables.*

SYNONYMS OF THE NEW TESTAMENT. New Edition, enlarged. 8vo. cloth. 12s.

The study of synonyms in any language is valuable as a discipline for training the mind to close and accurate habits of thought; more especially is this the case in Greek—" a language spoken by a people of the finest and subtlest intellect; who saw distinctions where others saw none; who divided out to different words what others often were content to huddle confusedly under a common term. . . . Where is it so desirable that we should miss nothing, that we should lose no finer intention of the writer, as in those words which are the vehicles of the very mind of God Himself?" This Edition has been carefully revised, and a considerable number of new synonyms added. Appended is an Index to the Synonyms, and an Index to many other words alluded to or explained throughout the work. "He is," the Athenæum *says, "a guide in this department of knowledge to whom his readers may intrust themselves with confidence. His sober judgment and sound sense are barriers against the misleading influence of arbitrary hypotheses."*

ON THE AUTHORIZED VERSION OF THE NEW TESTAMENT. Second Edition. 8vo. 7s.

After some Introductory Remarks, in which the propriety of a revision is briefly discussed, the whole question of the merits of the present version is gone into in detail, in eleven chapters. Appended is a chronological list

Trench—*continued.*

of works bearing on the subject, an Index of the principal Texts considered, an Index of Greek Words, and an Index of other Words referred to throughout the book.

STUDIES IN THE GOSPELS. Third Edition. 8vo. 10s. 6d.

This book is published under the conviction that the assertion often made is untrue,—viz. that the Gospels are in the main plain and easy, and that all the chief difficulties of the New Testament are to be found in the Epistles. These "Studies," sixteen in number, are the fruit of a much larger scheme, and each Study deals with some important episode mentioned in the Gospels, in a critical, philosophical, and practical manner. Many references and quotations are added to the Notes. Among the subjects treated are:—The Temptation; Christ and the Samaritan Woman; The Three Aspirants; The Transfiguration; Zacchæus; The True Vine; The Penitent Malefactor; Christ and the Two Disciples on the way to Emmaus.

COMMENTARY ON THE EPISTLES to the SEVEN CHURCHES IN ASIA. Third Edition, revised. 8vo. 8s. 6d.

The present work consists of an Introduction, being a commentary on Rev. i. 4—20, a detailed examination of each of the Seven Epistles, in all its bearings, and an Excursus on the Historico-Prophetical Interpretation of the Epistles.

THE SERMON ON THE MOUNT. An Exposition drawn from the writings of St. Augustine, with an Essay on his merits as an Interpreter of Holy Scripture. Third Edition, enlarged. 8vo. 10s. 6d.

The first half of the present work consists of a dissertation in eight chapters on "Augustine as an Interpreter of Scripture," the titles of the several chapters being as follow:—I. Augustine's General Views of Scripture and its Interpretation. II. The External Helps for the Interpretation of Scripture possessed by Augustine. III. Augustine's Principles and Canons of Interpretation. IV. Augustine's Allegorical Interpretation of Scripture. V. Illustrations of Augustine's Skill as an Interpreter of Scripture. VI. Augustine on John the Baptist and on St. Stephen. VII. Augustine on the Epistle to the Romans. VIII. Miscellaneous Examples of Augustine's Interpretation of Scripture. The latter half of the work consists of Augustine's Exposition of the Sermon on the Mount, not however a mere series of quotations from Augustine, but a connected account of his sentiments on the various passages of that Sermon, interspersed with criticisms by Archbishop Trench.

SERMONS PREACHED in WESTMINSTER ABBEY. Second Edition. 8vo. 10s. 6d.

These Sermons embrace a wide variety of topics, and are thoroughly

Trench—*continued.*

practical, earnest, and evangelical, and simple in style. The following are a few of the subjects:—"*Tercentenary Celebration of Queen Elizabeth's Accession;*" "*Conviction and Conversion;*" "*The Incredulity of Thomas;*" "*The Angels' Hymn;*" "*Counting the Cost;*" "*The Holy Trinity in Relation to our Prayers;*" "*On the Death of General Havelock;*" "*Christ Weeping over Jerusalem;*" "*Walking with Christ in White.*"

SHIPWRECKS OF FAITH. Three Sermons preached before the University of Cambridge in May, 1867. Fcap. 8vo. 2s. 6d.

These Sermons are especially addressed to young men. The subjects are "Balaam," "Saul," and "Judas Iscariot." These lives are set forth as beacon-lights, "to warn us off from perilous reefs and quicksands, which have been the destruction of many, and which might only too easily be ours." The John Bull *says, "they are, like all he writes, affectionate and earnest discourses."*

SERMONS Preached for the most part in Ireland. 8vo. 10s. 6d.

This volume consists of Thirty-two Sermons, the greater part of which were preached in Ireland; the subjects are as follows:—*Jacob, a Prince with God and with Men—Agrippa—The Woman that was a Sinner—Secret Faults—The Seven Worse Spirits—Freedom in the Truth—Joseph and his Brethren—Bearing one another's Burdens—Christ's Challenge to the World—The Love of Money—The Salt of the Earth—The Armour of God—Light in the Lord—The Jailer of Philippi—The Thorn in the Flesh—Isaiah's Vision—Selfishness—Abraham interceding for Sodom—Vain Thoughts—Pontius Pilate—The Brazen Serpent—The Death and Burial of Moses—A Word from the Cross—The Church's Worship in the Beauty of Holiness—Every Good Gift from Above—On the Hearing of Prayer—The Kingdom which cometh not with Observation—Pressing towards the Mark—Saul—The Good Shepherd—The Valley of Dry Bones—All Saints.*

Tudor.—The DECALOGUE VIEWED as the CHRISTIAN'S LAW. With Special Reference to the Questions and Wants of the Times. By the Rev. RICH. TUDOR, B.A. Crown 8vo. 10s. 6d.

The author's aim is to bring out the Christian sense of the Decalogue in its application to existing needs and questions. The work will be found to occupy ground which no other single work has hitherto filled. It is divided into Two Parts, the First Part consisting of three lectures on "Duty," and the Second Part of twelve lectures on the Ten Commandments. The Guardian *says of it, "His volume throughout is an outspoken and sound exposition of Christian morality, based deeply upon true foundations, set forth systematically, and forcibly and plainly expressed—as good a specimen of what pulpit lectures ought to be as is often to be found."*

Tulloch.—THE CHRIST OF THE GOSPELS AND THE CHRIST OF MODERN CRITICISM. Lectures on M. RENAN's "Vie de Jésus." By JOHN TULLOCH, D.D., Principal of the College of St. Mary, in the University of St. Andrew's. Extra fcap. 8vo. 4s. 6d.

Vaughan.—Works by CHARLES J. VAUGHAN, D.D., Master of the Temple:—

CHRIST SATISFYING THE INSTINCTS OF HUMANITY. Eight Lectures delivered in the Temple Church. New Edition. Extra fcp. 8vo. 3s. 6d.

The object of these Sermons is to exhibit the spiritual wants of human nature, and to prove that all of them receive full satisfaction in Christ. The various instincts which He is shewn to meet are those of Truth, Reverence, Perfection, Liberty, Courage, Sympathy, Sacrifice, and Unity. "We are convinced that there are congregations, in number unmistakeably increasing, to whom such Essays as these, full of thought and learning, are infinitely more beneficial, for they are more acceptable, than the recognised type of sermons."—John Bull.

MEMORIALS OF HARROW SUNDAYS. A Selection of Sermons preached in Harrow School Chapel. With a View of the Chapel. Fourth Edition. Crown 8vo. 10s. 6d.

"Discussing," says *the* John Bull, *"those forms of evil and impediments to duty which peculiarly beset the young, Dr. Vaughan has, with singular tact, blended deep thought and analytical investigation of principles with interesting earnestness and eloquent simplicity."* The Nonconformist says *"the volume is a precious one for family reading, and for the hand of the thoughtful boy or young man entering life."*

THE BOOK AND THE LIFE, and other Sermons, preached before the University of Cambridge. New Edition. Fcap. 8vo. 4s. 6d.

These Sermons are all of a thoroughly practical nature, and some of them are especially adapted to those who are in a state of anxious doubt.

TWELVE DISCOURSES on SUBJECTS CONNECTED WITH THE LITURGY and WORSHIP of the CHURCH OF ENGLAND. Fcap. 8vo. 6s.

Four of these discourses were published in 1860, *in a work entitled* Revision of the Liturgy; *four others have appeared in the form of separate sermons, delivered on various occasions, and published at the time by request; and four are new. The Appendix contains two articles,—one on "Subscription and Scruples," the other on the "Rubric and the Burial Service." The* Press *characterises the volume as "eminently wise and temperate."*

Vaughan (Dr. C. J.)—*continued.*

LESSONS OF LIFE AND GODLINESS. A Selection of Sermons preached in the Parish Church of Doncaster. Fourth and Cheaper Edition. Fcap. 8vo. 3*s*. 6*d*.

This volume consists of Nineteen Sermons, mostly on subjects connected with the every-day walk and conversation of Christians. They bear such titles as "The Talebearer," "Features of Charity," "The Danger of Relapse," "The Secret Life and the Outward," "Family Prayer," "Zeal without Consistency," "The Gospel an Incentive to Industry in Business," "Use and Abuse of the World." The Spectator *styles them "earnest and human. They are adapted to every class and order in the social system, and will be read with wakeful interest by all who seek to amend whatever may be amiss in their natural disposition or in their acquired habits."*

WORDS FROM THE GOSPELS. A Second Selection of Sermons preached in the Parish Church of Doncaster. Second Edition. Fcap. 8vo. 4*s*. 6*d*.

The Nonconformist *characterises these Sermons as "of practical earnestness, of a thoughtfulness that penetrates the common conditions and experiences of life, and brings the truths and examples of Scripture to bear on them with singular force, and of a style that owes its real elegance to the simplicity and directness which have fine culture for their roots."*

LESSONS OF THE CROSS AND PASSION. Six Lectures delivered in Hereford Cathedral during the Week before Easter, 1869. Fcap. 8vo. 2*s*. 6*d*.

The titles of the Sermons are:—I. "Too Late" (Matt. xxvi. 45). II. "The Divine Sacrifice and the Human Priesthood." III. "Love not the World." IV. "The Moral Glory of Christ." V. "Christ made perfect through Suffering." VI. "Death the Remedy of Christ's Loneliness." "This little volume," the Nonconformist *says, "exhibits all his best characteristics. Elevated, calm, and clear, the Sermons owe much to their force, and yet they seem literally to owe nothing to it. They are studied, but their grace is the grace of perfect simplicity."*

LIFE'S WORK AND GOD'S DISCIPLINE. Three Sermons. New Edition. Fcap. 8vo. 2*s*. 6*d*.

The Three Sermons are on the following subjects:—I. "The Work burned and the Workmen saved." II. "The Individual Hiring." III. "The Remedial Discipline of Disease and Death."

THE WHOLESOME WORDS OF JESUS CHRIST. Four Sermons preached before the University of Cambridge in November 1866. Second Edition. Fcap. 8vo. cloth. 3*s*. 6*d*.

Dr. Vaughan uses the word "Wholesome" here in its literal and original sense, the sense in which St. Paul uses it, as meaning healthy,

Vaughan (Dr. C. J.)—*continued.*

sound, conducing to right living; *and in these Sermons he points out and illustrates several of the "wholesome" characteristics of the Gospel, —the Words of Christ. The* John Bull *says this volume is "replete with all the author's well-known vigour of thought and richness of expression."*

FOES OF FAITH. Sermons preached before the University of Cambridge in November 1868. Fcap. 8vo. 3s. 6d.

The "Foes of Faith" preached against in these Four Sermons are:— I. "Unreality." II. "Indolence." III. "Irreverence." IV. "Inconsistency." "They are written," the London Review *says, "with culture and elegance, and exhibit the thoughtful earnestness, piety, and good sense of their author."*

LECTURES ON THE EPISTLE to the PHILIPPIANS. Third and Cheaper Edition. Extra fcap. 8vo. 5s.

Each Lecture is prefaced by a literal translation from the Greek of the paragraph which forms its subject, contains first a minute explanation of the passage on which it is based, and then a practical application of the verse or clause selected as its text.

LECTURES ON THE REVELATION OF ST. JOHN. Third and Cheaper Edition. Two Vols. Extra fcap. 8vo. 9s.

In this Edition of these Lectures, the literal translations of the passages expounded will be found interwoven in the body of the Lectures themselves. In attempting to expound this most-hard-to-understand Book, Dr. Vaughan, while taking from others what assistance he required, has not adhered to any particular school of interpretation, but has endeavoured to shew forth the significance of this Revelation by the help of his strong common sense, critical acumen, scholarship, and reverent spirit. "Dr. Vaughan's Sermons," the Spectator *says, "are the most practical discourses on the Apocalypse with which we are acquainted." Prefixed is a Synopsis of the Book of Revelation, and appended is an Index of passages illustrating the language of the Book.*

EPIPHANY, LENT, AND EASTER. A Selection of Expository Sermons. Third Edition. Crown 8vo. 10s. 6d.

The first eighteen of these Sermons were preached during the seasons of 1860, *indicated in the title, and are practical expositions of passages taken from the lessons of the days on which they were delivered. Each Lecture is prefaced with a careful and literal rendering of the original of the passage of which the Lecture is an exposition. The* Nonconformist *says that "in simplicity, dignity, close adherence to the words of Scripture, insight into 'the mind of the Spirit,' and practical thoughtfulness, they are models of that species of pulpit instruction to which they belong."*

THE EPISTLES OF ST. PAUL. For English Readers. PART I., containing the FIRST EPISTLE TO THE THESSALONIANS. Second Edition. 8vo. 1s. 6d.

Vaughan (Dr. C. J.)—*continued.*

It is the object of this work to enable English readers, unacquainted with Greek, to enter with intelligence into the meaning, connection, and phraseology of the writings of the great Apostle.

ST. PAUL'S EPISTLE TO THE ROMANS. The Greek Text, with English Notes. Fourth Edition. Crown 8vo. 7s. 6d.

This volume contains the Greek Text of the Epistle to the Romans as settled by the Rev. B. F. Westcott, D.D., for his complete recension of the Text of the New Testament. Appended to the text are copious critical and exegetical Notes, the result of almost eighteen years' study on the part of the author. The "Index of Words illustrated or explained in the Notes" will be found, in some considerable degree, an Index to the Epistles as a whole. Prefixed to the volume is a discourse on "St. Paul's Conversion and Doctrine," suggested by some recent publications on St. Paul's theological standing. The Guardian *says of the work,—"For educated young men his commentary seems to fill a gap hitherto unfilled. ... As a whole, Dr. Vaughan appears to us to have given to the world a valuable book of original and careful and earnest thought bestowed on the accomplishment of a work which will be of much service and which is much needed."*

THE CHURCH OF THE FIRST DAYS.
    Series I. The Church of Jerusalem. Third Edition.
    " II. The Church of the Gentiles. Second Edition.
    " III. The Church of the World. Second Edition.
Fcap. 8vo. cloth. 4s. 6d. each.

Where necessary, the Authorized Version has been departed from, and a new literal translation taken as the basis of exposition. All possible topographical and historical light has been brought to bear on the subject; and while thoroughly practical in their aim, these Lectures will be found to afford a fair notion of the history and condition of the Primitive Church. The British Quarterly *says,—"These Sermons are worthy of all praise, and are models of pulpit teaching."*

COUNSELS for YOUNG STUDENTS. Three Sermons preached before the University of Cambridge at the Opening of the Academical Year 1870-71. Fcap. 8vo. 2s. 6d.

. The titles of the Three Sermons contained in this volume are:—I. "The Great Decision." II. "The House and the Builder." III. "The Prayer and the Counter-Prayer." They all bear pointedly, earnestly, and sympathisingly upon the conduct and pursuits of young students and young men generally.

NOTES FOR LECTURES ON CONFIRMATION, with suitable Prayers. Eighth Edition. Fcap. 8vo. 1s. 6d.

In preparation for the Confirmation held in Harrow School Chapel, Dr. Vaughan was in the habit of printing week by week, and distributing among the Candidates, somewhat full notes of the Lecture he purposed to

Vaughan (Dr. C. J.)—*continued.*

deliver to them, together with a form of Prayer adapted to the particular subject. He has collected these weekly Notes and Prayers into this little volume, in the hope that it may assist the labours of those who are engaged in preparing Candidates for Confirmation, and who find it difficult to lay their hand upon any one book of suitable instruction.

THE TWO GREAT TEMPTATIONS. The Temptation of Man, and the Temptation of Christ. Lectures delivered in the Temple Church, Lent 1872. Extra fcap. 8vo. 3s. 6d.

Vaughan.—Works by DAVID J. VAUGHAN, M.A., Vicar of St. Martin's, Leicester:—

SERMONS PREACHED IN ST. JOHN'S CHURCH, LEICESTER, during the Years 1855 and 1856. Cr. 8vo. 5s. 6d.

CHRISTIAN EVIDENCES AND THE BIBLE. New Edition, revised and enlarged. Fcap. 8vo. cloth. 5s. 6d.

"*This little volume,*" *the* Spectator *says,* "*is a model of that honest and reverent criticism of the Bible which is not only right, but the duty of English clergymen in such times as these to put forth from the pulpit.*"

Venn.—ON SOME OF THE CHARACTERISTICS OF BELIEF, Scientific and Religious. Being the Hulsean Lectures for 1869. By the Rev. J. VENN, M.A. 8vo. 6s. 6d.

These discourses are intended to illustrate, explain, and work out into some of their consequences, certain characteristics by which the attainment of religious belief is prominently distinguished from the attainment of belief upon most other subjects.

Warington.—THE WEEK OF CREATION; OR, THE COSMOGONY OF GENESIS CONSIDERED IN ITS RELATION TO MODERN SCIENCE. By GEORGE WARINGTON, Author of "The Historic Character of the Pentateuch Vindicated." Crown 8vo. 4s. 6d.

The greater part of this work is taken up with the teaching of the Cosmogony. Its purpose is also investigated, and a chapter is devoted to the consideration of the passage in which the difficulties occur. "*A very able vindication of the Mosaic Cosmogony by a writer who unites the advantages of a critical knowledge of the Hebrew text and of distinguished scientific attainments.*"—Spectator.

Westcott.—Works by BROOKE FOSS WESTCOTT, D.D., Regius Professor of Divinity in the University of Cambridge; Canon of Peterborough :—

The London Quarterly, *speaking of Mr. Westcott, says,*—"*To a learning and accuracy which command respect and confidence, he unites what are not always to be found in union with these qualities, the no less valuable faculties of lucid arrangement and graceful and facile expression.*"

Westcott (Dr. B. F.)—*continued.*

AN INTRODUCTION TO THE STUDY OF THE GOSPELS. Fourth Edition. Crown 8vo. 10s. 6d.

The author's chief object in this work has been to shew that there is a true mean between the idea of a formal harmonization of the Gospels and the abandonment of their absolute truth. After an Introduction on the General Effects of the course of Modern Philosophy on the popular views of Christianity, he proceeds to determine in what way the principles therein indicated may be applied to the study of the Gospels. The treatise is divided into eight Chapters:—I. The Preparation for the Gospel. II. The Jewish Doctrine of the Messiah. III. The Origin of the Gospels. IV. The Characteristics of the Gospels. V. The Gospel of St. John. VI. and VII. The Differences in detail and of arrangement in the Synoptic Evangelists. VIII. The Difficulties of the Gospels. The Appendices contain much valuable subsidiary matter.

A GENERAL SURVEY OF THE HISTORY OF THE CANON OF THE NEW TESTAMENT DURING THE FIRST FOUR CENTURIES. Third Edition, revised. Crown 8vo. 10s. 6d.

The object of this treatise is to deal with the New Testament as a whole, and that on purely historical grounds. The separate books of which it is composed are considered not individually, but as claiming to be parts of the apostolic heritage of Christians. The Author has thus endeavoured to connect the history of the New Testament Canon with the growth and consolidation of the Catholic Church, and to point out the relation existing between the amount of evidence for the authenticity of its component parts and the whole mass of Christian literature. "The treatise," says the British Quarterly, *"is a scholarly performance, learned, dispassionate, discriminating, worthy of his subject and of the present state of Christian literature in relation to it."*

THE BIBLE IN THE CHURCH. A Popular Account of the Collection and Reception of the Holy Scriptures in the Christian Churches. New Edition. 18mo. 4s. 6d.

The present volume has been written under the impression that a History of the whole Bible, and not of the New Testament only, would be required, if those unfamiliar with the subject were to be enabled to learn in what manner and with what consent the collection of Holy Scriptures was first made and then enlarged and finally closed by the Church. Though the work is intended to be simple and popular in its method, the author, for this very reason, has aimed at the strictest accuracy.

A GENERAL VIEW OF THE HISTORY OF THE ENGLISH BIBLE. Second Edition. Crown 8vo. 10s. 6d.

In the Introduction the author notices briefly the earliest vernacular versions of the Bible, especially those in Anglo-Saxon. Chapter I. is oc-

Westcott (Dr. B. F.)—*continued.*

cupied with an account of the Manuscript English Bible from the 14th century downwards; and in Chapter II. is narrated, with many interesting personal and other details, the External History of the Printed Bible. In Chapter III. is set forth the Internal History of the English Bible, shewing to what extent the various English Translations were independent, and to what extent the translators were indebted to earlier English and foreign versions. In the Appendices, among other interesting and valuable matter, will be found "Specimens of the Earlier and Later Wycliffite Versions;" "Chronological List of Bibles;" "An Examination of Mr. Froude's History of the English Bible." The Pall Mall Gazette calls the work "A brief, scholarly, and, to a great extent, an original contribution to theological literature."

THE CHRISTIAN LIFE, MANIFOLD AND ONE.
Six Sermons preached in Peterborough Cathedral. Crown 8vo. 2s. 6d.

The Six Sermons contained in this volume are the first preached by the author as a Canon of Peterborough Cathedral. The subjects are:— I. "Life consecrated by the Ascension." II. "Many Gifts, One Spirit." III. "The Gospel of the Resurrection." IV. "Sufficiency of God." V. "Action the Test of Faith." VI. "Progress from the Confession of God." The Nonconformist calls them "Beautiful discourses, singularly devout and tender."

THE GOSPEL OF THE RESURRECTION.
Thoughts on its Relation to Reason and History. Third Edition. Fcap. 8vo. 4s. 6d.

The present Essay is an endeavour to consider some of the elementary truths of Christianity, as a miraculous Revelation, from the side of History and Reason. The author endeavours to shew that a devout belief in the Life of Christ is quite compatible with a broad view of the course of human progress and a frank trust in the laws of our own minds. In the third edition the author has carefully reconsidered the whole argument, and by the help of several kind critics has been enabled to correct some faults and to remove some ambiguities, which had been overlooked before. He has not however made any attempt to alter the general character of the book.

ON THE RELIGIOUS OFFICE OF THE UNIVERSITIES.
Crown 8vo. 4s. 6d.

"There is certainly, no man of our time—no man at least who has obtained the command of the public ear—whose utterances can compare with those of Professor Westcott for largeness of views and comprehensiveness of grasp...... There is wisdom, and truth, and thought enough, and a harmony and mutual connection running through them all, which makes the collection of more real value than many an ambitious treatise."— Literary Churchman.

Wilkins.—THE LIGHT OF THE WORLD. An Essay, by A. S. WILKINS, M.A., Professor of Latin in Owens College, Manchester. Second Edition. Crown 8vo. 3s. 6d.

This is the Hulsean Prize Essay for 1869. *The subject proposed by the Trustees was,* "*The Distinctive Features of Christian as compared with Pagan Ethics.*" *The author has tried to show that the Christian ethics so far transcend the ethics of any or all of the Pagan systems in method, in purity and in power, as to compel us to assume for them an origin, differing in kind from the origin of any purely human system.* "*It would be difficult to praise too highly the spirit, the burden, the conclusions, or the scholarly finish of this beautiful Essay.*"—British Quarterly Review.

Wilson.—RELIGIO CHEMICI. With a Vignette beautifully engraved after a Design by Sir NOEL PATON. By GEORGE WILSON, M.D. Crown 8vo. 8s. 6d.

"*George Wilson,*" *says the Preface to this volume,* "*had it in his heart for many years to write a book corresponding to the* Religio Medici *of Sir Thomas Browne, with the title* Religio Chemici. *Several of the Essays in this volume were intended to form chapters of it, but the health and leisure necessary to carry out his plans were never attainable, and thus fragments only of the designed work exist. These fragments, however, being in most cases like finished gems waiting to be set, some of them are now given in a collected form to his friends and the public.*"—"*A more fascinating volume,*" *the* Spectator *says,* "*has seldom fallen into our hands.*"

Wilson.—THE BIBLE STUDENT'S GUIDE TO THE MORE CORRECT UNDERSTANDING of the ENGLISH TRANSLATION OF THE OLD TESTAMENT, BY REFERENCE TO THE ORIGINAL HEBREW. By WILLIAM WILSON, D.D., Canon of Winchester. Second Edition, carefully revised. 4to. 25s.

"*The author believes that the present work is the nearest approach to a complete Concordance of every word in the original that has yet been made: and as a Concordance, it may be found of great use to the Bible student, while at the same time it serves the important object of furnishing the means of comparing synonymous words, and of eliciting their precise and distinctive meaning. The knowledge of the Hebrew language is not absolutely necessary to the profitable use of the work. The plan of the work is simple: every word occurring in the English Version is arranged alphabetically, and under it is given the Hebrew word or words, with a full explanation of their meaning, of which it is meant to be a translation, and a complete list of the passages where it occurs. Following the general work is a complete Hebrew and English Index, which is, in effect, a Hebrew-English Dictionary.*"

Worship (The) of God and Fellowship among Men. Sermons on Public Worship. By Professor MAURICE, and others. Fcap. 8vo. 3s. 6d.

This volume consists of Six Sermons preached by various clergymen, and although not addressed specially to any class, were suggested by recent efforts to bring the members of the Working Class to our Churches. The preachers were—Professor Maurice, Rev. T. J. Rowsell, Rev. J. Ll. Davies, Rev. D. J. Vaughan.

Yonge (Charlotte M.)—SCRIPTURE READINGS for SCHOOLS AND FAMILIES. By CHARLOTTE M. YONGE, Author of "The Heir of Redclyffe." Globe 8vo. 1s. 6d. With Comments. 3s. 6d.

SECOND SERIES. From Joshua to Solomon. Extra fcap. 8vo. 1s. 6d. With Comments. 3s. 6d.

THIRD SERIES. The Kings and Prophets. Extra fcap. 8vo., 1s. 6d., with Comments, 3s. 6d.

Actual need has led the author to endeavour to prepare a reading book convenient for study with children, containing the very words of the Bible, with only a few expedient omissions, and arranged in Lessons of such length as by experience she has found to suit with children's ordinary power of accurate attentive interest. The verse form has been retained because of its convenience for children reading in class, and as more resembling their Bibles; but the poetical portions have been given in their lines. Professor Huxley at a meeting of the London School-board, particularly mentioned the Selection made by Miss Yonge, as an example of how selections might be made for School reading. "Her Comments are models of their kind."—Literary Churchman.

In crown 8vo. cloth extra, Illustrated, price 4s. 6d. each Volume; also kept in morocco and calf bindings at moderate prices, and in Ornamental Boxes containing Four Vols., 21s. each.

MACMILLAN'S SUNDAY LIBRARY.

A SERIES OF ORIGINAL WORKS BY EMINENT AUTHORS.

The Guardian *says—"All Christian households owe a debt of gratitude to Mr. Macmillan for that useful 'Sunday Library.'"*

THE FOLLOWING VOLUMES ARE NOW READY:—

The Pupils of St. John the Divine.—By CHARLOTTE M. YONGE, Author of "The Heir of Redclyffe."

The author first gives a full sketch of the life and work of the Apostle himself, drawing the material from all the most trustworthy authorities, sacred and profane; then follow the lives of his immediate disciples, Ignatius,

Quadratus, Polycarp, and others; which are succeeded by the lives of many of their pupils. She then proceeds to sketch from their foundation the history of the many churches planted or superintended by St. John and his pupils, both in the East and West. In the last chapter is given an account of the present aspect of the Churches of St. John,—the Seven Churches of Asia mentioned in Revelations; also those of Athens, of Nîmes, of Lyons, and others in the West. "Young and old will be equally refreshed and taught by these pages, in which nothing is dull, and nothing is far-fetched."—Churchman.

The Hermits.—By CANON KINGSLEY.

The volume contains the lives of some of the most remarkable early Egyptian, Syrian, Persian, and Western hermits. The lives are mostly translations from the original biographies. "It is from first to last a production full of interest, written with a liberal appreciation of what is memorable for good in the lives of the Hermits, and with a wise forbearance towards legends which may be due to the ignorance, and, no doubt, also to the strong faith of the early chroniclers."—London Review.

Seekers after God.—LIVES OF SENECA, EPICTETUS, AND MARCUS AURELIUS. By the Rev. F. W. FARRAR, M.A., F.R.S., Head Master of Marlborough College.

In this volume the author seeks to record the lives, and gives copious samples of the almost Christ-like utterances of, with perhaps the exception of Socrates, "the best and holiest characters presented to us in the records of antiquity." The volume contains portraits of Aurelius, Seneca, and Antoninus Pius. "We can heartily recommend it as healthy in tone, instructive, interesting, mentally and spiritually stimulating and nutritious."—Nonconformist.

England's Antiphon.—By GEORGE MACDONALD.

This volume deals chiefly with the lyric or song-form of English religious poetry, other kinds, however, being not infrequently introduced. The author has sought to trace the course of our religious poetry from the 13th to the 19th centuries, from before Chaucer to Tennyson. He endeavours to accomplish his object by selecting the men who have produced the finest religious poetry, setting forth the circumstances in which they were placed, characterising the men themselves, critically estimating their productions, and giving ample specimens of their best religious lyrics, and quotations from larger poems, illustrating the religious feeling of the poets or their times. "Dr. Macdonald has very successfully endeavoured to bring together in his little book a whole series of the sweet singers of England, and makes them raise, one after the other, their voices in praise of God."—Guardian.

Great Christians of France: ST. LOUIS and CALVIN. By M. GUIZOT.

From among French Catholics, M. Guizot has, in this volume, selected

Louis, King of France in the 13th century, and among Protestants, Calvin the Reformer in the 16th century, "as two earnest and illustrious representatives of the Christian faith and life, as well as of the loftiest thought and purest morality of their country and generation." In setting forth with considerable fulness the lives of these prominent and representative Christian men, M. Guizot necessarily introduces much of the political and religious history of the periods during which they lived. "A very interesting book," says the Guardian.

Christian Singers of Germany. — By CATHERINE WINKWORTH.

In this volume the authoress gives an account of the principal hymn-writers of Germany from the 9th to the 19th century, introducing ample specimens from their best productions. In the translations, while the English is perfectly idiomatic and harmonious, the characteristic differences of the poems have been carefully imitated, and the general style and metre retained. "Miss Winkworth's volume of this series is, according to our view, the choicest production of her pen."—British Quarterly Review.

Apostles of Mediæval Europe.—By the Rev. G. F. MACLEAR, D.D., Head Master of King's College School, London.

In two Introductory Chapters the author notices some of the chief characteristics of the mediæval period itself; gives a graphic sketch of the devastated state of Europe at the beginning of that period, and an interesting account of the religions of the three great groups of vigorous barbarians—the Celts, the Teutons, and the Sclaves—who had, wave after wave, overflowed its surface. He then proceeds to sketch the lives and work of the chief of the courageous men who devoted themselves to the stupendous task of their conversion and civilization, during a period extending from the 5th to the 13th century; such as St. Patrick, St. Columba, St. Columbanus, St. Augustine of Canterbury, St. Boniface, St. Olaf, St. Cyril, Raymond Sull, and others. "Mr. Maclear will have done a great work if his admirable little volume shall help to break up the dense ignorance which is still prevailing among people at large."—Literary Churchman.

Alfred the Great.—By THOMAS HUGHES, Author of "Tom Brown's School Days." Third Edition.

"The time is come when we English can no longer stand by as interested spectators only, but in which every one of our institutions will be sifted with rigour, and will have to shew cause for its existence.... As a help in this search, this life of the typical English King is here offered." Besides other illustrations in the volume, a Map of England is prefixed, shewing its divisions about 1000 A.D., as well as at the present time. "Mr. Hughes has indeed written a good book, bright and readable we need hardly say, and of a very considerable historical value."—Spectator.

Nations Around.—By Miss A. KEARY.

This volume contains many details concerning the social and political life, the religion, the superstitions, the literature, the architecture, the commerce, the industry, of the Nations around Palestine, an acquaintance with which is necessary in order to a clear and full understanding of the history of the Hebrew people. The authoress has brought to her aid all the most recent investigations into the early history of these nations, referring frequently to the fruitful excavations which have brought to light the ruins and hieroglyphic writings of many of their buried cities. "Miss Keary has skilfully availed herself of the opportunity to write a pleasing and instructive book."—Guardian. "A valuable and interesting volume."—Illustrated Times.

St. Anselm.—By the Very Rev. R. W. CHURCH, M.A., Dean of St. Paul's. Second Edition.

In this biography of St. Anselm, while the story of his life as a man, a Christian, a clergyman, and a politician, is told impartially and fully, much light is shed on the ecclesiastical and political history of the time during which he lived, and on the internal economy of the monastic establishments of the period. The author has drawn his materials from contemporary biographers and chroniclers, while at the same time he has consulted the best recent authors who have treated of the man and his time. "It is a sketch by the hand of a master, with every line marked by taste, learning, and real apprehension of the subject."—Pall Mall Gazette.

Francis of Assisi.—By Mrs. OLIPHANT.

The life of this saint, the founder of the Franciscan order, and one of the most remarkable men of his time, illustrates some of the chief characteristics of the religious life of the Middle Ages. Much information is given concerning the missionary labours of the saint and his companions, as well as concerning the religious and monastic life of the time. Many graphic details are introduced from the saint's contemporary biographers, which shew forth the prevalent beliefs of the period; and abundant samples are given of St. Francis's own sayings, as well as a few specimens of his simple tender hymns. "We are grateful to Mrs. Oliphant for a book of much interest and pathetic beauty, a book which none can read without being the better for it."—John Bull.

Pioneers and Founders; or, Recent Workers in the Mission Field. By CHARLOTTE M. YONGE, Author of "The Heir of Redclyffe." With Frontispiece, and Vignette Portrait of BISHOP HEBER.

The missionaries whose biographies are here given, are—John Eliot, the Apostle of the Red Indians; David Brainerd, the Enthusiast; Christian F. Schwartz, the Councillor of Tanjore; Henry Martyn, the Scholar-Missionary; William Carey and Joshua Marshman, the Serampore Missionaries; the Judson Family; the Bishops of Calcutta,—Thomas Middleton, Reginald Heber, Daniel Wilson; Samuel Marsden, the Australian Chaplain and Friend of the Maori; John Williams, the Martyr of *Erromango; Allen Gardener, the Sailor Martyr; Charles Frederick Mackenzie, the Martyr of Zambesi.* "*Likely to be one of the most popular of the 'Sunday Library' volumes.*"—Literary Churchman.

Angelique Arnauld, Abbess of Port Royal. By FRANCES MARTIN. Crown 8vo. 4s. 6d.

This new volume of the 'Sunday Library' contains the life of a very remarkable woman founded on the best authorities. She was a Roman Catholic Abbess who lived more than 200 years ago, whose life contained much struggle and suffering. But if we look beneath the surface, we find that sublime virtues are associated with her errors, there is something admirable in everything she does, and the study of her history leads to a continual enlargement of our own range of thought and sympathy.

THE "BOOK OF PRAISE" HYMNAL,
COMPILED AND ARRANGED BY
LORD SELBORNE.

In the following four forms:—

A. Beautifully printed in Royal 32mo., limp cloth, price 6d.
B. ,, ,, Small 18mo., larger type, cloth limp, 1s.
C. Same edition on fine paper, cloth, 1s. 6d.
Also an edition with Music, selected, harmonized, and composed by JOHN HULLAH, in square 18mo., cloth, 3s. 6d.

The large acceptance which has been given to "The Book of Praise" by all classes of Christian people encourages the Publishers in entertaining the hope that this Hymnal, which is mainly selected from it, may be extensively used in Congregations, and in some degree at least meet the desires of those who seek uniformity in common worship as a means towards that unity which pious souls yearn after, and which our Lord prayed for in behalf of his Church. "The office of a hymn is not to teach controversial Theology, but to give the voice of song to practical religion. No doubt, to do this, it must embody sound doctrine; but it ought to do so, not after the manner of the schools, but with the breadth, freedom, and simplicity of the Fountain-head." On this principle has Sir R. Palmer proceeded in the preparation of this book.

The arrangement adopted is the following:—

PART I. *consists of Hymns arranged according to the subjects of the Creed*—"God the Creator," "Christ Incarnate," "Christ Crucified," "Christ Risen," "Christ Ascended," "Christ's Kingdom and Judgment," *etc.*

PART II. *comprises Hymns arranged according to the subjects of the Lord's Prayer.*

PART III. *Hymns for natural and sacred seasons.*

There are 320 Hymns in all.

CAMBRIDGE:—PRINTED BY J. PALMER.

www.ingramcontent.com/pod-product-compliance
Lightning Source LLC
Chambersburg PA
CBHW032133230426
43672CB00011B/2321